Published in 1975 By

R AND E RESEARCH ASSOCIATES
4843 Mission Street, San Francisco 94112
18581 McFarland Avenue, Saratoga, CA 95070

Publishers and Distributors of Ethnic Studies
Editor: Adam S. Eterovich
Publisher: Robert D. Reed

Library of Congress Card Catalog Number
75-18122

ISBN 0-88247-348-4

THE ANTI-LYNCHING MOVEMENT: 1883-1932

by

Donald L. Grant

The Fort Valley State College

San Francisco

1975

The Anti-Lynching Movement: 1883-1932

Donald L. Grant

ACKNOWLEDGEMENTS

It gives me great pleasure to acknowledge my indebtedness to Professor Arvarh E. Strickland for his encouragement and direction all through graduate school, and in particular for his great patience and understanding in guiding this study. I am also indebted to Professors Herbert Aptheker, Donnie D. Bellamy, and Richard S. Kirkendall who read the manuscript and offered valuable suggestions.

Acknowledgement is due the Ford Foundation for a grant which financed much of the research. I wish to express my appreciation for their help to the staffs of the National Archives, the Library of Congress, the Hoover Presidential Library, the Missouri State Historical Society the Western Historical Manuscripts Collection and above all to the dedicated librarians of the University of Missouri-Columbia.

My wife, Mildred Bricker Grant, was doubly helpful. Not only was she supportive, deeply interested and informed on the subject, but she found time to exercise her skills as a librarian in the writer's behalf.

CONTENTS

	PAGE
Introduction	iii

CHAPTER

I.	The Function and Mythology of Lynching	1
II.	The Organization of the Attack on Lynching	20
III.	Politics and Lynching	48
IV.	National and State Anti-Lynching Legislation	65
V.	The Role of the Press, Education, and the Church	76
VI.	Militancy and Migration	104
VII.	After World War I	131
VIII.	The Anti-Lynching Reform Movement, 1922-1932	156

Conclusions	173
Bibliography	176
Index	201

INTRODUCTION

Many previous studies of lynching have emphasized the history of the development of the custom and its practice on the frontier or have dealt with specific lynchings or single aspects of the reform movement. The earliest broad scholarly work was written in 1905 by a Yale professor, James Elbert Butler. His study reflected the public interest in lynching that increased with the recognition that the practice had become more frequent after the country was settled and was, therefore, not a frontier phenomenon after all. Cutler attempted to determine the social conditions giving rise to lynching and to assess the validity of the arguments for and against the practice. The best early popular treatment of race relations by a white interested in lynching was by Ray Stannard Baker who believed that lynching resulted from prejudice and competition and that the application of the Golden Rule would end it.[1]

Thousands of articles on lynching have appeared in the popular and scholarly press. These sources are important to the study of anti-lynching movements because they were a significant influence on the formation of, and later changes in, the public's concensus about lynching. Many of the writers had no ties to any organization concerned with the problem. Daniel T. Williams has compiled a bibliography of over 400 of the more important of these articles and books.[2] The author has an unpublished bibliography of over 3,000 periodical articles on lynching.

Of the many organizations that grew as a result of their participation in the anti-lynching reform, only two, the NAACP and the Commission on Interracial Cooperation, have been the subject of published studies which adequately emphasize the importance of anti-lynching activities to their development. The most valuable overall study of the early history of the most important anti-lynching organization is Charles Flint Kellogg's study of the NAACP. This work clearly indicates that the NAACP was a product of the anti-lynching impulse and that it grew strong by opposing lynching. The best monograph on one aspect of the NAACP's activities is Robert Zangrando's dissertation on the NAACP's efforts to obtain federal anti-lynching legislation. His study is primarily concerned with the NAACP lobbying efforts which peaked in the early 1920's and again in the late 1930's. An excellent popular account of the Commission on Interracial Cooperation, the white liberal Southern wing of the anti-lynching reform movement, is contained in a biography of its prime mover, Will Alexander.[3]

Because of the increasingly racist nature of lynching and because Blacks perceived lynching to be the greatest obstacle to their progress as well as the most brutal and irrational manifestation of racism, the subject was an impelling one for Black writers. The Black press was an important source of material for this study. The newspapers listed in the bibliography did not necessarily feature the continuing lynching story more than others, as almost all of the Black newspapers gave it extended coverage.

The ministers in the Social Gospel wing of the Black church were not only the best educated and the most inclined to put their thoughts in writing, but they were also the ones most likely to discuss lynching. Francis J. Grimke and Reverdy C. Ransom were two of several whose correspondence, addresses, and articles have been of value to this study. The attitudes of Black attorneys, doctors, businessmen, artists, political leaders, and educators appear in biographies, autobiographies, in their contribution to both the Black and white press, and in separate studies.

Because the anti-lynching reformers always looked to the political process for positive action, the Congressional Record, Senate and House documents, reports, and hearings provided much valuable information. Another important source for this study was the material produced by and about the organizations that opposed or defended lynching.

Although there are several studies on the NAACP and its leaders, little recognition has been given to the long and arduous struggle led by Blacks, individually and through organizations, that involved anti-lynching activity on many fronts both before and after the birth of the NAACP. The role of lynching as the chief energizer of protest by Blacks has not received the attention it deserves. Most of the books on race relations underestimate the importance of lynching and the fact that Black organizations which did not engage in anti-lynching activities often failed to acquire followers. Since the founding of the NAACP, scholars have tended to concentrate on its work, the work of its guiding genius, W. E. B. Du Bois, and on the political aspects of the anti-lynching struggle. The political front was only one of many on which the battle against lynching was fought. The religious, educational, economic, and demographic changes in the United States were perhaps even more important than long run surface political changes. This study attempts to link the development of the anti-lynching reform to these types of social change.

Sufficient recognition has not been given to the fact that before 1908, Blacks had little help in forcing whites to face up to the fact that lynching was a denial of all the high-sounding principles on which the society was founded. After 1908, in the second half of the period covered, although more whites joined the reform movement, their number was small considering the nature of the problem. In the main, the white-dominated political parties; federal, state, and local governments; the judicial system and the legal establishment; business and industry; the press; the educational system; and the church all failed to support simple justice for Blacks. Whites joined the anti-lynching reform in greatest numbers when they believed that the practice was either increasing or spreading. Although some of the white recruits were idealistic, many perceived lynching to be a threat to their way of life and no longer necessary to maintain a basically racist society.

Lynching was used to maintain the new patterns of economic, psychological and sexual exploitation of Blacks that were initiated following the Civil War. Protest against any aspect of these relationships could result in the formation of a lynch mob. To obscure the basic function of lynching, the myths of racial inferiority that developed to support slavery were elaborated and new myths supporting lynching were invented and effectively propagated. Because lynching was the starkest symbol of the obstacles that slowed the progress of Blacks, opposition to lynching was the common denominator and chief energizer of the Black protest movement from the 1880's until the Great Depression.

The year 1883 marked a turning point in the struggle of Afro-Americans for equality. In that year the Supreme Court nullified the Civil Rights Act of 1875. Frederick Douglass and other Black leaders realized that the decision signaled the beginning of a new period in race relations that came to be characterized by all-Black or predominately Black efforts to effect reforms. White reformers were turning their attention to toher problems.

The anti-lynching reform began in the 1880's with efforts by Blacks to undermine the mythology of lynching and to establish the right of self-defense against mob actions. This was done by the editors of the Black newspapers and their correspondents, by the ministers in their sermons and their published works, and by educators and other articulate Blacks whose ideas were published in articles and books. These activities were encouraged and supported by the many Black cultural and historical societies and suffrage leagues that formed in the 1880's and 1890's. As the knowledge grew that lynching was increasingly the greatest obstacle to Black advancement, the reformers moved from this stage to one characterized by the creation of protest-oriented organizations. The Afro-American League, organized by T. Thomas Fortune in 1890, and the Equal Rights Council, organized by Bishop Henry McNeal Turner in 1893, were two of many Black organizations primarily created to oppose lynching. The Niagara Movement, organized by W. E. B. Du Bois in 1905, and the National Equal Rights League, rooted in the work of the England Suffrage Leagues and that of William Monroe Trotter in the 1900's, were also largely responses to the problems created by lynching.

Lynching was the issue which most clearly exposed the contradictions between the political, religious, and economic theories of the United States and the practice of race relations. Blacks used these contradictions to obtain white allies and the anti-lynching reform movement became one of the earliest and most important vehicles for interracial cooperation. During the twenty-five year period, 1883 to 1908, most whites viewed lynching as one path to law and order. There was always some white opposition to lynching, but after 1908 white support for the reform increased more rapidly. The launching of the NAACP in 1910 and the Commission on Interracial Cooperation in 1919 were important milestones in this development.

The great increase in the migration of Southern rural Blacks to the Northern urban centers which began in 1915, increased the force of the reform movement because the urban newcomers quickly acquired greater sophistication and militancy. As the ability of Blacks to protest was increased by their changing attitudes and increasingly effective organization and leadership, lynching became a disruptive factor threatening white supremacy more than supporting it. The Black retaliatory violence of the "Red Summer" of 1919 led many to recognize that the "New Negro" could not be returned to his pre-World War I status. The migration was also important because, as the Black vote increased in the North after 1915, elected officials became more responsive to Black demands. The increased political participation of women was also a positive force.

A major political goal of Blacks was to secure enactment of federal legislation to stop lynching but the desirability of a national law was not generally accepted by white citizens. The NAACP succeeded in lobbying the Dyer bill through the House of Representatives in 1922, but a short filibuster by Southern senators quickly killed it. Some whites supported the anti-lynching reform by working for state and private action in order to forestall federal legislation. Blacks continued to attempt to obtain federal action against lynching when Calvin Coolidge was president. By the time Herbert Hoover was in the White House, Blacks were already suffering from the economic effects of the depression and this had a decisive effect on the nature of the anti-lynching reform.

After 1932, the nature of the anti-lynching reform changed sufficiently to make the period ushered in by the New Deal a new era in the struggle against lynching. The changes involved the relative decline in the role of Blacks due to the decline in lynching, the increase in white support for the reform, the subordination of the fight against lynching to a broader campaign for civil and economic rights, and the selection of the Democratic party as the primary vehicle for social change. The ability of Blacks and whites to unite on issues that affected them similarly was stimulated by the economic crisis and the new political directions. This increased ability to work together for a common cause was one reason Blacks did not have to carry as large a share of the burden of the anti-lynching reform after 1932. Also contributing to the decline in the importance of Black leadership was the fact that the economic crisis greatly reduced the flow of funds coming from the Black rank and file to the Black leaders. This tended to place the leaders in a position of greater dependence on white support. The very success of the reform in reducing the number of lynchings from a high of 230 in 1892 to a low of eight in 1932 tended to reduce the relative importance of the anti-lynching cause. For the first time in fifty years its importance to Blacks was overshadowed by other problems, primarily economic, and lynching ceased to be the prime energizer of Black protest. As segments of the New Deal coalition joined the anti-lynching reform after 1932, this cause was subordinated to efforts to organize labor unions, to resist evictions and to obtain jobs or relief. As part of the general change in direction, Blacks increasingly looked to the Democratic party as the vehicle for social change.

FOOTNOTES

INTRODUCTION

[1] James Elbert Cutler, <u>Lynch Law: An Investigation Into the History of Lynching in the United States</u> (New York: Longmans, Green, and Co., 1905); Ray Stannard Baker, <u>Following the Color Line: An Account of Negro Citizenship in the American Democracy</u> (New York: Young Peoples Missionary Movement of the United States and Canada, 1908).

[2] Daniel T. Williams, "Lynching in America: A Bibliography," in Eight Negro Bibliographies, comp. by Daniel T. Williams (New York: Kraus Repring Co., 1970), pp. 16-39.

[3] Charles Flint Kellogg, <u>NAACP: A History of the National Association for the Advancement of Colored People: 1909-1920</u> (Baltimore: Johns Hopkins Press, 1967); Robert Lewis Zangrando, "The Efforts of the National Association for the Advancement of Colored People to Secure the Passage of a Federal Anti-Lynching Law, 1920-1940." James Stokely, <u>Seeds of Southern Change: The Life of Will Alexander</u> (Chicago: University of Chicago Press, 1962).

CHAPTER I

THE FUNCTION AND MYTHOLOGY OF LYNCHING

Lynching, a practice which first appeared in America during the colonial period, became the most effective method of maintaining the racial caste system which developed after Reconstruction. This caste system relegated Blacks to the position of a conquered people and made it possible for whites to receive the economic, psychological, and sexual tribute which they had been conditioned by slavery to expect as their due. Nevertheless, not all the gains of Reconstruction had been swept away, and Blacks were able to retain a larger portion of the fruits of their labor than had been possible under slavery. White society, unwilling to admit that it profited from the subordination of Blacks, developed a mythology to justify lynching. There was a great variety of these myths which were all based on the double falsehood that lynching was a new solution to a new problem, the increase in rape. Factual refutation did not receive credence; instead, the myths were accepted by most whites in all regions of the United States.

Lynching was not new in the United States when the Chicago Tribune began to publish statistics on the practice in 1882. Colonial records indicated that the custom had a pre-Revolutionary history. Lynching was associated with the frontier and was considered a proper precursor to the establishment of legally constituted courts. Historians and folklorists have fostered an interpretation of such lynchings as positive contributions to civilization which cleared away the anti-social elements and allowed the establishment of law and order. Actually, much of the lynching on the Western frontier in the nineteenth century was aimed at the Mexican-American, Oriental, and southern European ethnic minorities.[1]

In the more settled areas of the country, lynching declined after the Revolution until the abolitionists became targets for mob violence. The activity of the anti-abolitionist mobs in the North increased rapidly in the early 1830's, reached a peak in 1835, and then rapidly declined as the base of the abolitionist reform movement was broadened and abolition became a more respectable cause. In the South, however, lynching continued to increase down to the Civil War. The dominant class used it attempting to suppress slave rebellion and criticism of slavery. Niles Weekly Register observed in 1835, "In the South we almost daily hear of Judge Lynch, and of persons who are flogged and driven away or executed."[2]

The use of violence by whites, in order to limit or prevent Black progress, continued during the Civil War and increased afterward. The South continued to use force to repress efforts by slaves to weaken the Confederate war effort, while the worst race riot in the nation's history occurred in New York City in 1863. The fighting between the Northern and Southern armies may have ended at Appomattox, but the white South continued to use force against Blacks and their allies. Para-military units financed by the states, private vigilante groups such as the Ku Klux Klan, and lynch mobs all combined to resist any change in race relations. The white South had always used violence to control the slaves and continued to use it to control the freedmen.[3]

Reconstruction had opened the closed society of the South to new concepts and practices which Blacks used to their advantage. The new amendments to the Constitution said that slavery was ended, that Blacks were equally entitled to due process of law, and that they could vote. Blacks responded to the new freedoms by participating in the political process to promote education, to provide a wide range of social welfare programs, to abolish imprisonment for debt, to remove property qualifications for voting and officeholding, and to frame state constitutions that would be in harmony with the new federal amendments. One result of these changes was that Blacks were in a stronger position to challenge the old threefold pattern of economic, psychological, and sexual exploitation rooted so deeply in two centuries of slavery that it was viewed by most whites as the natural, the only desirable, and even the God-given, order of things. Whites succeeded in warding off this attack on their privileged position by overthrowing Reconstruction and by 1883, they had generally restored the exploitative patterns which had characterized slavery.[4]

A great majority of Blacks worked in agriculture and it was in this area that the pattern of oppression was most apparent and complete. The Black agricultural worker was robbed of the fruits of his labor by a variety of methods which included the furnish system, fradulent accounts, usurious interest rates, the crop-lien laws, and various pressures to insure the maximum production of the cash crop and minimum production of food for the tenant's family. All of these functioned to increase dependency on the landlord and the company store.[5]

The system so obviously worked against the interests of Blacks that a set of severe sanctions was required to maintain it. Among the sanctions were starvation resulting from the loss of livelihood, exile, the whipping post, prison, and the lynching tree. There were also less severe methods of insuring that Blacks would remain impoverished and victim of the exploitative nexus. For example, there was much simple cheating of Blacks in the settlement of accounts relating to the tenant's share of the crop and his bill at the company store. Blacks were aware of this cheating. In one survey of Blacks, 85.6 per cent of those questioned believed that the white man cheated the Black farmer.[6] Because most Blacks were without financial resources at the start of the agricultural season, their only recourse was to mortgage their share of the next crop to the same landlord or merchant who had cheated them earlier. This was usually the only way to obtain the credit for the food, clothing, and supplies that were necessary for survival. The crop-lien laws insured the workers, because they had no money or other assets except their labor and the already mortgaged crop. There was general agreement among whites not to hire any Black away from any employer to whom the Black was indebted. In addition, the full force of the law would descend upon those who tried to escape the system by running out on their debts. "False Pretense" laws were enacted to replace imprisonment for debt. Under these laws, anyone who did not pay his debts could be imprisoned for borrowing under "false pretenses."[7]

The planters and merchants who furnished credit charged from 30 to 300 per cent interest in addition to marking up the goods as much as 100 per cent. In 1886, an Arkansas store was reported to be selling meat at 12 1/2 cents per pound when it could be bought elsewhere for 6 1/2 cents; flour costing $4.00 a barrel elsewhere was $7.50; and forty-cents-a-gallon molasses sold for one dollar a gallon. At the same time, the plantation served by the store was paying seventy-five cents a day in scrip which was discounted 50 per cent at the store. If anything was purchased on credit, there was an additional charge

2

for interest. The use of scrip was widespread. In 1892 it was reported that Black agricultural laborers in South Carolina would bind themselves to contracts and "receive one dollar in money and the rest in scrip accepted at ruinous discount at the plantation store." At Palestine, Texas, twenty plantation workers were lynched in 1910 for protesting their wage of one dollar per day which was paid in scrip good only at the company store. The practice of usurious interest and unconscionable markups continued for decades.[8]

The contracts by which the Black agricultural workers were bound were interpreted and enforced by the officials and courts usually in full sympathy with landlords. Many of the contracts were verbal, and the officials would routinely take the landlord's word as to the terms of the contract. Consequently, the sheriff and the judge became key officials in enforcing peonage. The Black worker was required by law to work for his employer until he was out of debt, but the system operated to keep him constantly in debt. Bradstreet's, a Wall Street financial journal, in the 1880's defended the necessity of peonage laws by noting that a Georgia sharecropper could produce four bales of cotton in the season, worth $160, and that the cropper's one-half share would be largely "eaten up" at the company store by harvest time, thereby necessitating the full force of the law to keep him on the job and prevent his migration to other places. Benjamin Quarles observed that although the freedman was no longer a chattel, he was still bound to the soil as a serf or peon.[9]

The lynch mob was often considered a quasi-official dispenser of justice augmenting local enforcement of economic exploitation. One such mob left a note on its victim, "Negroes must pay their honest debts." It was signed "Friends of Governor Blease." There were many lynchings for "jumping" labor contracts and for objecting to the terms of the annual settlements.[10]

The Southern penal institutions, by virtue of the brutality associated with them, also helped to enforce the economic exploitation. The convict lease was the most brutal facet of this system. Under this arrangement, convicts were leased to private employers who proceeded literally to work the convicts to death while incurring the minimum expenses for food and shelter. William S. Scarborough, then scholarly head of the Classics Department and later President of Wilberforce University, said of the convict lease system, "There is no system of penal punishment . . . that is so degrading, so inhuman, so barbarous, so revolting in all its aspects." An investigation in Arkansas in 1898 uncovered the bodies of seventy prisoners who had been beaten and tortured to death. In the Texas wood-cutting camps, less than half the prisoners survived two years. The leasing of convicts provided a source of cheap labor for the entrepreneur and formed the basis for the fortunes of several Southern leaders. In addition, the state governments also profited greatly from convict leasing. Booker T. Washington noted that Alabama received over one million dollars from leasing convicts in 1911. He said:

> At least $900,000 of this came from Negro convicts, who were for the most part rented to the coal-mining companies in the northern part of the state. The result of this policy had been to get as many able-bodied convicts as possible into the mines so that the contractors might increase their profits. Alabama, of course, is not the only state that had yielded to the temptation to make money out of human misery.

The state penitentiary showing the largest profit was considered the best penitentiary.[11]

The administrators of the law not only upheld the economic exploitation by landlord and merchant, but also derived much of their personal incomes from the arrest and convictions of Blacks. The fee system which paid law enforcement officers and court officials according to the number of arrests, trials, and convictions, encouraged police harassment of the powerless. W. E. B. Du Bois's Atlanta study of 1904 on Negro crime showed that Blacks were often falsely accused in order that they might be robbed by the fee system which extended from arrest through sentencing. The Houston Chronicle reported in 1913, "There are communities in Texas where a Negro imperils his liberty if it gets out that he has as much as $50.00." That same year an Atlanta grand jury revealed the systematic robbery of Blacks by illegal arrests. Sometimes Blacks were arrested to swell the number of convicts available for leasing to private contractors or to increase the size of unpaid county work crews. One hundred Blacks were arrested at a church social in Savannah, Georgia, in 1907, to provide labor for county drainage projects.[12]

The harshness of white "justice" toward Blacks contributed to the number of lynchings as mobs retaliated for the murder of white law enforcement officers, killed by desperate Blacks resisting arrest. The desperation stemmed from the knowledge that the courts and penal institutions discriminated against Blacks and that any sentence to a convict camp could easily be a death sentence.

Any Black who became an independent farmer, businessman, or professional was a threat to white supremacy. Those who did move up not only disproved the stereotype that Blacks could not function without constant white supervision, but they also served as role models for other Blacks. The warning to Blacks to shun attempts to move up from the bottom rung of society, issued by Daniel L. Russell, Governor of North Carolina, was representative of many such statements. Governor Russell advised that Black aspirations for financial and industrial equality were as bad as those for "social equality;" for a Black "to get above his ordained station in life is to invite assassination." This was a continuing aspect of the Black experience. One study cited in the 1930's established that the Black who endeavored to improve his status could still be marked for death by the mob.[13]

Threats to the caste system were dealt with severely. Blacks were lynched for being successful farmers, owning their own land, and marketing their own crops. They were also lynched for acquiring education and rising into the middle class as merchants or professional men. In 1892, whites near Waverly, Tennessee, drove out twenty Black families who owned land worth about twenty dollars an acre. The Blacks were forced to sacrifice their property--one 108-acre place sold for forty dollars and one 90-acre farm sold for twenty dollars. This practice was widespread and continued into the twentieth century. The Chicago Defender in 1915 carried a picture of a Black farmer and his three sons hanging from the same tree in Texas. Their "crime" was harvesting the first cotton in the county that season. The lynching of Anthony Crawford in 1916 was one of the more publicized cases of mob murder to dispose of a successful and prosperous Black farmer. Crawford owned 427 acres near Abbeville, South Carolina, and had assets valued at $20,000.[14]

Whitecapping, the use of terrorism and lynching to control or drive away persons deemed harmful to the community, was used by some white farmers to eliminate Black competition. Sometimes merchants seeking to increase their profits would finance Black agricultural laborers so that they could move up the agricultural ladder from day laborer to tenant. Poorer white farmers who had profited from the cheap labor and who resented Black competition in renting land would attempt to prevent this upward movement. One Black farmer in Mississippi was driven from his place by whitecappers because one member of the mob owed him $1,200, and this was an easy way to avoid payment. Reports from Oklahoma in 1911 and 1912 stated that nightriders were attempting to drive out the Blacks who were buying land to grow cotton. Similar reports came from Georgia in 1913. There were several lynchings in Missouri growing out of attempts by the "poorer class of whites, fearing higher rents and lower wages," to drive Black workers out. Willis Duke Weatherford, in his study of race relations, concluded that "night riding" and "whitecapping" were means of discouraging the more successful Black farmers. "It will be noted," he pointed out, "that the highest figures for lynchings of Negroes corresponds closely with the period of most bitter struggly of this Southern white working class for economic status and social security."[15]

The white South was never united on the tactics of enforcing white supremacy. Whitecapping created tensions between the smaller farmers and the large landholders and merchants. The merchants and larger landowners found themselves arrayed against the lynchers and because of their greater political power were able to use the state militia against the whitecappers. Such tensions among whites were skillfully used by Blacks to augment the anti-lynching reform.

The economic factors in Southern agriculture that led to violence and lynching also had industrial counterparts which sometimes led to similar results. Employers made astute use of race prejudice to divide white and Black labor. Du Bois held that the support of Booker T. Washington by William H. Baldwin, vice-president of the Southern Railway, was motivated by the desire to create two interchangeable work forces in the South, one white and the other Black. Each then could be used to undermine the efforts of the other to improve wages or working conditions. Professor Graham Brooks, author and lecturer on economic subjects, asked one of the largest employers of labor in the South if he feared the development of trade unions and was told:

> No, it is one good result of race prejudice, that the Negro will enable us in the long run to weaken the trade union so that it cannot harm us. We can keep wages down with the Negro, and we can prevent too much organization.

Clarence Darrow reported a conversation with Philip Armour, Chicago meat packer, who said, "I like Negroes because they are loyal to me in time of strikes."[16]

The employers' use of Blacks to break strikes in the North contributed to the willingness of the Northern white workers to participate in lynch mobs and race riots. In the 1904 strike of stockyard workers in Chicago, the strikers threatened to lynch scabs. The following year, Blacks were again imported from the South to break a teamsters' strike, and twenty lives were lost. This practice of playing the white worker off against the Black worker in industry continued as it had in agriculture, and it was, in part, a cause of racial violence.[17]

Not only were Black workers attacked by white labor when employers used Blacks as "union-busting" pawns, but they were attacked by employers when they organized to improve their own economic status. The organization of Black workers in agriculture began immediately after the Civil War and was encouraged by the Knights of Labor in the 1880's. Unlike many labor organizations, the Knights welcomed Black membership and opposed drawing the color line between those who shared the same class interests. Among the Black leaders who endorsed the trade union concept for Black labor in the 1880's were John R. Lynch, the Mississippi Republican leader; New York editor T. Thomas Fortune; and Augustus Straker, Detroit attorney and civil rights leader.[18]

There were several violent clashes between organized Black workers and their employers in this period, some of them ending in lynchings. A sugar strike among Louisiana workers in 1880 to raise wages from seventy-five cents to one dollar a day was broken by the state militia. The South Carolina legislature strengthened the militia in 1886 and made interference with a labor contract punishable as conspiracy. Speeches in the legislature indicated that a strike at cottonpicking time would lead to widespread slaughter of the strikers. In 1887, Black workers, organized by the Knights of Labor, struck in Louisiana against a cut in the seventy-five cents a day they were earning and demanded a raise to $1.25 a day. Four Blacks were killed when the governor sent ten companies of militia to evict the strikers. Four whites were wounded in the fighting, and the militia was withdrawn. The local judge then declared martial law, and the order was enforced by white mobs. Thirty Blacks were killed and hundreds wounded in the massacre that ended the strike. The two Cox brothers, Black organizers who had been arrested early in the strike, were taken from the jail and lynched. In Arkansas, a strike in 1888 of Black workers on a plantation alarmed the planters, who asked the governor to send the militia. T. Thomas Fortune, in an editorial on this strike, noted that the militia was only used to protect white interests. In another Arkansas strike three years later, Black cotton pickers asked for an increase in their pay of 50 cents per one hundred pounds for picking cotton because this rate provided only subsistence income for even the most expert picker. Mobs organized by the landlords lynched ten of the strikers. Although white opposition caused these early organizational attempts to fail, these efforts laid the groundwork for the Colored Farmer's Alliance.[19]

It was not surprising that the Colored Farmer's Alliance came into conflict with the white Southern Alliance which attracted the yeoman and small capitalist farmers who often hired Black labor. The backbone of the Colored Alliance was the sharecropper and the agricultural wage worker. This difference in interests led the Southern Alliance to oppose strikes by Black workers for higher pay for picking cotton and contributed to later divisions. In the early 1890's, however, leaders such as Tom Watson were calling for Blacks and whites to submerge these smaller differences in order to attack their common enemy, the Southern Bourbon who was controlled by Northern capital. When the Colored Alliance at Durant, Mississippi, planned to demand more pay for cottonpicking in 1889 and were prepared to "guard the fields with shotguns to prevent others from gathering the crops," the Farmer's Alliance store at Durant sold them guns. In 1892, Tom Watson's followers came to the defense of a Black Populist organizer who was threatened with lynching. Unfortunately such incidents were more the exception than the rule. C. Vann Woodward's assessment of the Populist period as being one of great interracial cooperation among the poorer agricultural interests in which white farmers defended Blacks from lynching has been revised. Democrats were as likely to speak generally against lynching as the Populists, though neither were active in denouncing specific lynchings, let alone calling for punishment for lynchers.[20]

Even these small efforts at interracial cooperation with the Southern Alliance and the Populists were a threat to white supremacy and the caste system and were successfully countered by violence initiated by the Democrats. The 1892 election in Georgia demonstrated the pattern. There the Democrats used "violence, lynching, fraud, and murder" to prevent the Blacks from voting against them. Moreover, the common interests of the Southern agriculturalists were not strong enough to overcome the racism of the white Populists. The Democrats defrauded the Populists of election victories and blamed the Blacks, then the Populists joined in a cry for Black disfranchisement and blamed the Blacks for being the victims of election frauds. Both white groups united in a series of constitutional conventions which introduced the poll tax, the literacy clause, the grandfather clause, and other devices of franchise discrimination.

The new white supremacy governments organized under these constitutions enacted all manner of discriminatory "Jim Crow" laws that were enforced by lynch mobs. As Blacks lost political power, they also lost some of their ability to defend their remaining rights. T. Thomas Fortune discussed the connection between voting and the ability to resist lynching. He submitted that a voteless citizen was easier to lynch because he had no power to force out of office those who tolerated and encouraged mobs.[21]

The psychological benefits of slavery to the whites were among those that had been undermined during Reconstruction, and a part of the extreme brutality and violence of the attacks on Reconstruction stemmed from the desire of whites to limit their loss in this area, and if possible, restore Blacks to their former position as ego-enhancers for the whites. The new post-Reconstruction society demanded a complicated etiquette of race relations aimed at producing the frequent, open, and acknowledged evidences of Black servility, deference, and submission, very gratifying to the white ego. This etiquette was enforced by the same sanctions that made economic exploitation possible, and violation of the racial etiquette could lead to lynching.[22]

Any violation of the racial etiquette was viewed as the falling of the first domino in a line in which the last domino was labeled "inter-marriage." Many Blacks were lynched for actions which would seem normal in a rational society, but Southern society was not rational. It rested on the myth of Black racial inferiority. This meant that Blacks who rose above "their place" thereby refuting the myth ran the risk of being lynched. Enough examples were made of "uppity" Blacks to made violations of the code of racial etiquette a clear and constant danger.

The fate of Sewell Smith in 1903 was typical of hundreds of similar cases. Smith was a barber in Rayville, Louisiana, who had invested the profits from his barbershop in land. Later a railroad company purchased land from him, making him relatively rich. On a business trip to Shreveport, a white boy, wanting to earn a tip, asked to carry his satchel. They walked in front of a saloon where loitering whites attacked Smith for presuming to have a white as a servant. Smith defended himself and was killed. That was the end of it. No one was indicted or even arrested for killing an "insolent" Black who had not kept his place.[23]

The racial etiquette which demanded that Blacks always play the role of inferiors strengthened the whites' belief in their superiority and led to greater dislike for Blacks. Some thought the whites were caught up in a vicious circle of abusing Blacks because they feared them, and then fearing Blacks because they abused them. In any event, as Benjamin Mays, a former president of Morehouse College, remarked, "Hundreds of innocent Negroes were insulted, cheated, beaten, and even lynched, for the sole reason that they had incurred the displeasure of some white man." This psychological oppression reinforced the economic oppression and both increased the white male's opportunity to exploit Black women sexually.[24]

The sexual gain to whites from slavery permitted males of the master class to have access to the women of the slave class while it prohibited sexual contact between Black males and white females. This double standard, which worked to the advantage of the white male, was weakened during Reconstruction when the Black family acquired more stability and Blacks acquired a greater degree of psychological and economic independence. The other aspect of this double standard, that white women and Black men should have no sexual contact, was a vigorously enforced aspect of post-Reconstruction race relations. Black threats to the psychological and economic gains of whites were beaten off by allegations that the true Black motivation was a desire for white women. Black desires for higher living standards, security, upward mobility, education for their children, civil rights, and dignity, could not be denied on the grounds that they were undesirable goals for Blacks, but they could be denied on the grounds that they led to intermarriage. The domino theory explained why the least concession to Blacks would lead to "social equality." Whites defined "social equality" as intermarriage, but Blacks defined it as non-discrimination. After Reconstruction, any Black who moved against any aspect of the caste system could be lynched if it was believed by whites that the other sanctions were inadequate. George Tindall's statement about lynching in South Carolina was true in a larger context also. He wrote, "Lynching became, willy-nilly, a factor in the establishment of a white terror that transformed the fluid situation created by the Reconstruction back into a rigid caste system of white supremacy."[25]

The caste system provided a framework for a society which existed for the benefit of the superordinate group. In the United States, for one group to deny a fair share of such benefits to another ran counter to the professed philosophy, the stated law, and all the long-standing claims to democracy and brotherhood. There was nothing in the democratic creed which could be used to justify the robbing of the weak by the strong. Such robbery had to be obscured by a complex mythology which provided the armor of righteousness for the defenders of the caste system and disarmed its opponents by directing attention away from the real characteristics of the system.

The overarching myth of Black genetic inferiority that supported postwar white supremacy had been used to justify slavery. Whites commonly believed that "the Negro is a lower form of organism, biologically more primitive, mentally inferior, and emotionally underdeveloped. He is insensitive to pain, incapable of learning, and animal-like in his behavior." In the immediate postwar period, the Democrats made skillful use of this myth to limit the amount of social reform. After Reconstruction, racism became a mania, and the desire to prove the Negro a beast became an obsession to some. H. G. Wells, who toured the United States in 1906, said that racism was a cult in this country. According to Wells, "Hardly any Americans at all seem to be in possession of the elementary facts in relation to this question. . . . We English, a century or so ago, said all these things of the native

Irish." Wells noted the similarity in attitudes between whites he met in the United States and those in South Africa, where a man in Johannesburg

> Gave me clearly enough the attitude of the common white man out there; the dull prejudice; the readiness to take advantage of the "boy;" the utter disrespect for colored womenkind; the savage, intolerant resentment, dashed with fear, which the native arouses in him.[26]

This myth of racial inferiority was propagated in most of the white press, and it was the subject of a vast literature of "scientific racism" to which intellectuals from all fields contributed. It was extensively popularized and found expression in all aspects of the popular culture.[27] Grafted on to the myth of inferiority with its implications of bestiality was the myth of supervirility. The dual myths combined in the folklore to invent a Black sex-mad fiend who lusted after white women so intensely that not even the ever-present threat of a lynch mob would deter him. The final polish on this image owed much to the fervid imagination of the Reverend Thomas Dixon, Jr., author of The Clansman and The Leopard's Spots, who was assisted by a corps of editors such as W. C. Brann of Texas, editor of Brann's Iconoclast. Brann favored driving all Blacks out of the state, perhaps to the North, with an advance warning to the North that "she will have to put sheet-iron lingerie on her marble Goddess of Liberty or some morning she'll find the old girl with her head mashed in and bearing the marks of sexual violence."[28]

An important element in the lynching mythology was the idea that it was limited to punishment for rape. Therefore, as the number of lynchings increased in the 1880's and early 1890's, it was necessary to explain that rape had also increased. To establish this, the history of slavery had to be rewritten. The myth that there had been no rape by Blacks of white women during slavery was created after Reconstruction and capped off with the happy thought that even during the Civil War, when the white man was away at the front, the loyal slaves had protected the white women, even those on the isolated plantations. This was a cleverly insidious myth, because Blacks, and white friends of Blacks, as well as the most extreme racist, could subscribe to it. The myth appeared frequently in public addresses and in newspaper accounts by both supporters and opponents of lynching. Thomas Wentworth Higginson, an early abolitionist, told a Boston audience in the late 1890's:

> It was my fortune to lead for two years a regiment of colored troops. . . taken from the lowest and most ignorant portion of the cotton plantations of Carolina. . . . If they had those innate tendencies to a licentious self-indulgence which are constantly announced in some newspapers, it is absolutely impossible that I should not have found it out.

Senator Baird Z. Vance of North Carolina, no friend of Blacks, told a Grand Army of the Republic at about the same time:

> Permit me to call your attention to the conduct of the Southern slaves during the war. . . . Within hearing of the guns that were roaring to set them free, with the land stripped of its male population, and none around them except the aged, the women and children . . . they remained on our plantation, cultivated our fields, and cared for our mothers, wives,

and little ones, with faithful love and loyal kindness which, in the nature of things, could only be born of sincere good will.

Senator John J. Ingalls of Kansas, speaking on the floor of the Senate against the Butler bill which would have provided funds for African colonization, declared, "The slaves were guilty of no violence. . . . They lighted no midnight flame; they shed no innocent blood." Booker T. Washington said much the same thing in his Atlanta Exposition Address of 1895. When commending the desirable qualities of Blacks to the whites, he described Blacks as those "whose fidelity and love you have tested in days when to have proved treacherous meant the ruin of your firesides."[29]

The myth that Blacks were lynched mainly for rape was established by virtue of its constant repetition. Although it could be disproved by date from both Black and white sources, the myth was cultivated so assiduously that it flourished. Politicians constantly repeated the charge on the hustings and in the legislative chambers. The pulpit accepted the myth and thus further weakened its mild and only occasional deprecation of lynching by making it appear that at least half the blame lay in Black criminality. A typical religious voice was that of E. E. Hoss, editor of the Christian Advocate, Nashville, who attacked both lynching and rape but assumed that rape was the reason for lynching. Bishop Henry McNeal Turner charged Hoss in 1893 with joining those who wildly exaggerated the problem. The secular press was given to even more extreme statements and the examples of the propagation of this myth by newspapers are legion. As late as 1919 the Birmingham News advised its readers that "all of these race riots have been caused by the attempts of Negro men to override the race line and make white women the victims of their lustful passions."[30]

The mythology that characterized the Black man as docile, submissive, and Christlike before and during the Civil War and then converted him into a ravening lecher by the 1890's had no difficulty accounting for the change. According to the ruling whites of the "New South," the culprit was that source of all evils, Reconstruction. It had encouraged Black aspirations, had given Blacks a sense of political power, and had encouraged pretensions toward "social equality." The New South's creed held that these Black pretensions had fortunately been thwarted by the return of the Democrats to power and that disappointed Blacks then took their frustrations out on white women.

Like the myth about Black docility, this myth about Reconstruction was accepted by Southerners representing a wide variety of views on the race issue. Senator James K. Vardaman of Mississippi, an avowed racist, selected the subject, "The Crime of Rape," to write about on page one of the first issue of his newspaper, The Issue (later renamed Vardaman's Weekly). After blaming Reconstruction for encouraging Black aspirations, Vardaman wrote:

> I am unable to account for the frequency of this crime upon any other theory than the growing disposition and consuming aspiration among the negroes to break down the social barriers which debar them from equality with the white race and deny them the enjoyment of all the sacred privileges of social equality.

Emmet O'Neal, ex-governor of Alabama, conservative on the subject of race though not as virulent, at least in his rhetoric, as Vardaman, agreed with Vardaman on this point.[31]

The myth that lynching was punishment for rape was contradicted by the many press accounts of lynchings for other reasons. To ward off this intrusion of reality, the mythology was adjusted to justify the great majority of lynchings that even the mobs knew were not for rape. This rationalization held that mobs first became accustomed to lynching for rape and then gradually extended the practice to lynching Blacks accused of murder, arson, theft, and finally, "wrong behavior." The fact that rape was not even alleged in over 80 per cent of all lynchings did not weaken the belief of most whites that rarely were Blacks lynched for reasons other than rape. Some supporters of the caste system, such as Benjamin Tillman, Democratic leader in South Carolina, won undeserved reputations as opponents of lynching because they said they opposed these "rare" lynchings for other reasons. But, such Southern spokesmen continued to falsely claim most lynchings were for rape. Benjamin F. Riley, historian and retired president of Howard College, Alabama, was more sympathetic to Black aspirations, but he, also, argued that lynching had started as punishment for rape and then spread to include other charged offenses. Unlike Tillman, Riley opposed all lynchings and warned that the custom had gotten out of hand, even to the point that white men were sometimes victims of the mob.[32]

The apologists for lynching blamed all of the other lynchings on the rapists, by charging that they had been responsible for originally teaching society to resort to mob law. There were many letters, editorials, and articles in the newspapers pointing out that if rape would stop, then lynchings for other reasons would stop. These statements continued to be published through the 1930's. They attempted to absolve the white community of guilt by transferring the responsibility for all lynchings to the alleged rapist. An NAACP study for the 1889-1918 period stated that 148 Blacks were lynched for trivial offenses against Southern mores such as "testifying against whites," and "suing whites." The study also stated that fifty Black women were lynched in this period. According to the mythology of the apologists for lynching, the ultimate responsibility for even these lynchings rested on the shoulders of the Black rapist who had forced whites to learn to lynch.[33]

Another myth explained why the mobs got out of hand and attacked other than alleged rapists. Fundamental to this explanation was the contention that the mobs were composed of "rabble." The corollary to this was that the "best people" deplored lynching and sometimes acted to prevent it. This myth prevailed despite hundreds of newspapers' accounts of mobs which included in their ranks United States senators and congressmen, judges, state legislators, doctors, lawyers, teachers, planters, and merchants. Even reputable scholars helped give credence to the myth that middle- and upper-class people did not support lynching and that mobs were composed exclusively of lower-class whites.[34]

Lynching and mob rule were in such contradiction to the tenets of the legal profession and the Anglo-Saxon tradition of jurisprudence, that lawyers and judges might have been expected to be in the forefront of any anti-lynching reform, as some were, but they were exceptions. The judicial consensus was reflected in the Supreme Court rulings beginning in the 1870's. These denied that civil rights were a national concern and delivered Blacks into the hands of the white supremacist state governments. This encouraged disfranchisement, unequal education, and lynching. Following the lead of the highest court, many members of the legal profession accepted the fact of second-class citizenship for Blacks and joined in supporting the caste system and its mythology concerning lynching.

Lynching was explained by many jurists and attorneys on the grounds that the court system was defective. Justice Walter Clark of the North Carolina Supreme Court said in a decision, "Lynch law, evil that it is, is a protest of society against the utter inefficiency of the courts." United States Supreme Court Associate Justice David J. Brewer shared this opinion. In an address to the Yale Law School, he remarked, "It is not to be wondered at that some communities have arisen in their wrath and have inflicted summary punishment that the machinery of the law has delayed." Many whites came to believe that Blacks charged with heinous crimes were able to escape punishment in the court system by hiring clever attorneys who would prolong the jury selection process or cause the judge to make some trivial error which would result in a reversal or a new trial. Theodore Roosevelt added a presidential endorsement to the idea that leniency encouraged lynching when he said, "Every pardon of a murderer who should have been executed is to my mind just so much encouragement to lynching." William Howard Taft elaborated the myth two years later in 1905:

> Every man of affairs who has studied the subject at all knows that if men who commit crimes were promptly arrested and convicted, there would be no mob for the purpose of lynching. . . . A mob, after it has been organized, loses all conscience and cannot be controlled, but it is the delay of justice that leads to its organization.[35]

The idea that ineffective court procedures led to lynching also received clerical support. Robert Strange, Bishop of the Diocese of Eastern North Carolina, set forth his plan for court reform in "Some Thoughts on Lynching." He called for immediate and private trials for rape cases, for immediate action on appeals which could be made only if the evidence was insufficient, and for execution to follow the crime by no more than ten days. "Then," according to Strange, "there would be no excuse for lynching." When a mob of 10,000 lynched a Black and a white in Cairo, Illinois, in 1909, the mayor and the local clergy were pleased with the lynching, which they blamed on the failure of the courts to convict speedily. One lynch mob published a manifesto signed "Judge Lynch" which stated, "If you don't do something with your jury system, your lawyers, and your rules of evidence pretty soon, I shall assume jurisdiction in more cases." Some of the arguments were sheer fantasy. Justice Clark of North Carolina wrote that in 1892 there were twice as many lynchings as legal executions because defense attorneys had too many preemptory challenges and could pack the jury with the defendant's friends. In this era few Blacks served on juries, and the white juries did not convict the mob members who were occasionally tried.[36]

Another part of the "positive good" theory of lynching was that it spared the rape victim the embarrassment of having to appear in an open court to testify. What often actually happened had more potential for embarrassment than an appearance in court. The mob would frequently take the accused to the woman's home with great fanfare and publicity. In the prevailing atmosphere of mob hysteria, the alleged rape victim could be intimidated into making a false charge or an incorrect identification.

Many whites thought that lynching was a positive good because they believed it caused more terror among Blacks than a trial. An extreme white view was presented by Fanny M. Preston in her contribution to a symposium on lynching printed in 1894. She wrote that it was better to lynch a few innocent Blacks than to have white women terrorized. She believed lynching was to be preferred to a trial because the Black would be lionized by the attention of the court and then go free. Preston rejoiced "that the South is still 'in the saddle,' in its own domains: for while Southern white men rule, women will be respected." Even those who knew that Blacks were usually completely at the mercy of the courts and seldom escaped conviction if there was the slightest evidence, sometimes defended lynching. Judge Andrew N. Bradley of the District of Columbia Supreme Court said of a certain lynching, "Lynching probably would be better than putting the government to the expense of keeping and hanging the brute." The Galveston News commented in 1885 on the lynching of four Blacks--three men and a woman, "Judge Lynch's court up at Elkhard seems to dispose of business in a very prompt and energetic manner . . . saved the taxpayers of the County considerable expense."[37]

Lynching served to imbed the caste society in the South after the overthrow of Reconstruction. A new labor system was designed to insure that whites would expropriate the wealth produced by Black labor. The true function of lynching was to silence any protest against the exploitation. Because this true function could not be openly acknowledged by whites, an elaborate mythology was created to obscure the reasons for the intimidation to which Blacks were subjected.

FOOTNOTES--CHAPTER I

[1] For the view that lynching was civilizing see Popular Tribunals, vols. 36 and 37 of The Works of Hubert Howe Bancroft (San Francisco: The History Company, 1888); Thomas J. Dimsdale, The Vigilantes of Montana: Or Popular Justice in the Rocky Mountains (3d ed.; Helena, Montana: State Publishing Co., 1915). For the lynching of ethnic minorities see Richard Hofstadter and Michael Wallace, American Violence: A Documentary History, Vintage Books (New York: Random House, 1971), pp. 304-36; U. S. Congress, House, Indemnity for Chinese Killed at Rock Springs, Wyoming, September 2, 1885, H. Rept. 2044, 49th Cong., 1st sess., 1886; George Ticknow Curtis, "Law and the Lynchers," North American Review, 152 (June, 1891), 691-5; Henry Cabot Lodge, "Lynch Law and Unrestricted Immigration," North American Review, 152 (May, 1891), 602-12; U. S. Congress, House, The Lynching of Luis Moreno, H. Doc. 237, 55th Cong., 2d sess., 1898; U. S. Congress, Senate, Lynching of Two Seminoles, S. Doc. 44, 55th Cong., 2d sess., 1898.

[2] Leonard L. Richards, Gentlemen of Property and Standing: Anti-Abolition Mobs in Jacksonian America (New York: Oxford University Press, 1970), p. 30; Niles' Weekly Register, October 3, 1835, p. 65. See also Garrison's Liberator, December 19, 1856, p. 14, for statement that 300 abolitionists were lynched in the South since 1835. Lynching in this period was often defined as including punishments short of death by mobs. For the lynching of slaves see Herbert Aptheker, To Be Free: Studies in American Negro History (New York: International Publishers, 1948), p. 26; Winfield H. Collins, The Truth About Lynching and the Negro in the South, Ch. 1; Dwight Lowell Dumond, Antislavery Origins of the Civil War in the United States, Ann Arbor Paperbacks (Ann Arbor: The University of Michigan Press, 1959); Gustavus Myers, History of Bigotry in the United States (New York: Capricorn Books, 1960), p. 214; Russel B. Nye, Fettered Freedom (E. Lansing: Michigan State University Press, 1963); U. B. Phillips, American Negro Slavery (New York: Peter Smith, 1952), pp. 460-63; Kenneth M. Stampp, The Peculiar Institution: Slavery in the Ante-Bellum South, Vintage Books (New York: Random House, 1956), p. 190; James Truslow Adams, "Our Lawless Heritage," Atlantic Monthly, 142 (December, 1928), 732-40; Joseph Mathew Sullivan, "Lynching Statistics," Journal of Criminal Law, 9 (May, 1918), 144-46; "Recollections of a Retired Lawyer," Southern Literary Messenger, 5 (March, 1839), 218.

[3] Hofstadter, American Violence, pp. 211-17.

[4] John Hope Franklin, Reconstruction After the Civil War (Chicago: University of Chicago Press, 1961), pp. 219-20; Kenneth M. Stampp, The Era of Reconstruction: 1865-1877, Vintage Books (New York: Random House, 1967), p. 214.

[5] Gunnar Myrdal, An American Dilemma (Twentieth Anniversary ed.; New York: Harper & Row, 1972), pp. 245-50; C. Vann Woodward, Origins of the New South: 1877-1913 (Baton Rouge: Louisiana State University Press, 1951), pp. 205-16.

⁶Benjamin Mays, <u>Born to Rebel</u> (New York: Charles Scribner's Sons, 1971), p. 6.

⁷Pete Daniel, "Up From Slavery and Down to Peonage: The Alonzo Bailey Peonage Case," <u>Journal of American History</u>, 57 (December, 1970), 654-70.

⁸New York <u>Freeman</u>, August 7, 1886, p. 1; Indianapolis <u>Freeman</u>, January 23, 1892, p. 2; Mary Frances Berry, <u>Black Resistance/White Law</u> (New York: Meredith Corp., 1971), p. 134.

⁹New York <u>Freeman</u>, September 18, 1886, p. 4; Benjamin Quarles, <u>The Negro in the Making of America</u> (London: Collier-Macmillian Ltd., 1964), p. 150. For discussions of the sociology of agricultural poverty see Charles S. Johnson, <u>Growing up in the Black Belt: Negro Youth in the Rural South</u> (New York: American Council on Education, 1941); Katherine Lumpkin, The South in Progress (New York: International Publishers, 1940); Hortense Powdermaker, <u>After Freedom: A Cultural Study in the Deep South</u> (New York: Atheneum, 1968). Although the above three studies are of conditions in the 1930s, they all indicate that there had been little basic change from the 1880s.

¹⁰Chicago Broad Ax, December 28, 1912, p. 1; Carter G. Woodson, <u>A Century of Negro Migration</u> (Washington: Association for the Study of Negro Life and History, 1918), p. 155.

¹¹William S. Scarborough, "An Inside View of the Convict-Lease System." Indianapolis <u>Freeman</u>, December 7, 1891, p. 5; Indianapolis <u>Freeman</u>, October 15, 1898, p. 1; Lawrence D. Rice, <u>The Negro in Texas: 1874-1900</u> (Baton Rouge: Louisiana State University Press, 1971), p. 249; Woodward, <u>Origins of the New South</u>, pp. 4, 15-16, 212-15; Booker T. Washington, "Is the Negro Having a Fair Chance?" <u>Century, 75</u> (November, 1912), 46-55; A. C. Hutson, Jr., "The Coal Miners' Insurrection of 1891 in Anderson County," <u>East Tennessee Historical Society's Publications</u>, 7 (1935), 103-15. See also Fletcher Melvin Green, "Some Aspects of the Convict Lease System in the Southern States," in <u>Essays in Southern History</u>, ed. by F. M. Green (Chapel Hill: The University of North Carolina Press, 1951); Shelby M. Harrison, "A Cash-Nexus for Crime," <u>Survey</u>, 27 (January 6, 1915), 1541-56; Marc N. Goodnow, "Turpentine: Impressions of the Convict Camps in Florida," <u>International Social Review</u>, 15 (June, 1915), 274; Monroe N. Work, "Negro Criminality in the South," American Academy of Political and Social Science <u>Annals</u>, 49 (September, 1913), 74-80; Blake McKelvey, "Penal Slavery and Southern Reconstruction," <u>Journal of Negro History</u>, 20 (January, 1935), pp. 153-79; Jane Zimmerman, "The Penal Reform Movement in the South During the Progressive Era," <u>Journal of Southern History</u>, 27 (November, 1951), 462-92.

¹²<u>Some Notes on Negro Crime, Particularly in Georgia</u>, Atlanta University Publications, 9 (Atlanta: Atlanta University Press, 1904); <u>Crisis</u>, 5 (February, 1913), 177; Chicago <u>Broad Ax,</u> October 19, 1907, p. 1.

¹³Chicago <u>Broad Ax,</u> March 19, 1904, p. 1; John Dollard, <u>Caste and Class in a Southern Town</u> (New Haven: Yale University Press, 1937), p. 359, 361.

[14] Indianapolis Freeman, October 22, 1892, p. 1; For a similar incident see Royal Nash, "The Cherokee Fires," Crisis, 11 (March, 1916), 265-70. Chicago Defender, August 30, 1915; Anthony Crawford was beaten and jailed for "impudence" October 21, 1916 for arguing with a merchant about the price of cotton seed. A few hours later he was lynched; he had fought in self-defense. He is reported to have said, "The day a white man hits me is the day I die." Crisis, 13 (December, 1916), 67; 13 (January, 1917), 120, 135; Norfolk Journal and Guide, December 2, 1916, p. 1; Emmet J. Scott, Negro Migration During the War (New York: Oxford University Press, 1920), p. 47; Charles Flint Kellogg, NAACP: A History of the National Association for the Advancement of Colored People: 1909-1920 (Balitmore: The Johns Hopkins Press, 1967), p. 219.

[15] William F. Holmes, "Whitecapping: Agrarian Violence in Mississippi, 1902-1906," Journal of Southern History, 35 (May, 1969), 165-85; Chicago Broad Ax, December 24, 1904, p. 1; Crisis, 1 (March, 1911), 6; 3 (January, 1912), 8; 5 (March, 1913), 247; Irving G. Wyllie, "Race and Class Conflict on Missouri's Cotton Frontier," Journal of Southern History, 20 (May, 1954), 183-96; Willis Duke Weatherford and Charles S. Johnson, Race Relations: Adjustment of Whites and Negroes in the United States (Boston: D. C. Heath, 1934), p. 57.

[16] W. E. B. Du Bois to Merle Curti, December 9, 1932, cited in Robert L. Factor, The Black Response to America: Men, Ideals, and Organizations from Frederick Douglass to the NAACP (Reading, Mass.: Addison-Wesley Pub. Co., 1970), p. 199; James F. Morton, Jr., The Curse of Race Prejudice (New York: James F. Morton, 1906), p. 43; Broad Ax, December 29, 1906, p. 2.

[17] Allen F. Davis, Spearheads for Reform: The Social Settlements and the Progressive Movement, 1890-1914 (New York: Oxford University Press, 1967), p. 118; William M. Tuttle, Jr. Race Riot: Chicago in the Red Summer of 1919 (New York: Atheneum, 1970), p. 120. For use of Blacks as strikebreakers see Charles H. Wesley, Negro Labor in the United States: 1850-1925 (New York: Vanguard Press, 1927), 257; Henry Lee Moon, The Balance of Power: The Negro Vote (Garden City: Doubleday & Company, 1940), p. 132. Blacks had no monopoly on strikebreaking; in fact, their overall role in this was minor. Police, militia, federal troops and recent immigrants played a far larger role. For the thousands of strikes of white workers against Black employment see W. E. B. Du Bois, The Negro Artisan (Atlanta University Publications, 7; Atlanta: Atlanta University Press, 1902), p. 173.

[18] Martin E. Dann, The Black Press 1827-1890: The Quest for National Identity (New York: G. P. Putman's Sons, 1971), pp. 219-20, 226; New York Freeman, October 9, 16, 1886; T. Thomas Fortune, Black and White: Land, Labor, and Politics in the South (New York: Fords, Howard, & Hulbert, 1884); D. Augustus Straker, The New South Investigated (Detroit: Ferguson Printing Co., 1888).

[19] Dann, Black Press, pp. 203, 223-4, 228; Berry, Black Resistance, p. 111; Hofstadter, American Violence, pp. 139-41; New York Freeman, July 17, 1886, p. 2; New York Age, October 17, 1891, p. 2. The best general history of the labor movement in the United States which includes the role of the Black worker in this period is Philip S.

Foner, History of the Labor Movement in the United States, Vol. 1; From Colonial Times to the Founding of the American Federation of Labor (New York: International Publishers, 1947).

[20] Dann, Black Press, p. 229; Robert H. Brisbane, The Black Vanguard: Origins of the Negro Social Revolution: 1900-1960 (Valley Forge, Pa.: The Judson Press, 1970), p. 22; C. Vann Woodward, Tom Watson, Agrarian Rebel (New York: Macmillan Co., 1938), pp. 239-40; The Strange Career of Jim Crow (2d ed.; New York: Oxford University Press, 1966), p. 64. For the view that the Populists sought the Black vote without espousing the Black cause see Clarence A. Bacote, "Negro Proscriptions, Protests, and Proposed Solution in Georgia: 1880-1908," Journal of Southern History, 25 (November, 1959), 471-98; William B. Rogers, "The Negro Alliance in Alabama," Journal of Negro History, 45 (January, 1960), 38-48; William H. Chafe, "The Negro and Populism: A Kansas Case Study," Journal of Southern History, 34 (August, 1968), 402-419; Robert Saunders, "Southern Populists and the Negro, 1893-1905," Journal of Negro History, 54 (July, 1969), 240-61; Charles Crowe, "Tom Watson, Populists, and Blacks Reconsidered," Journal of Negro History, 55 (April, 1970), 99-116; Herbert Shapiro, "The Populists and the Negro: A Reconsideration," in The Making of Black America, Vol. 2: The Black Community in Modern America, ed. by August Meier and Elliott Rudwick (New York: Atheneum, 1969), pp. 27-36. For a more general view of the agricultural unrest of this period see Theodore Saloutos, Farmer Movements in the South: 1865-1933 (Berkeley: The University of California Press, 1960); Stuart N. Jamieson, Labor Unionism in American Agriculture (Washington: Bureau of Labor Statistics Bulletin 836, 1945); Richard Hofstadter, The Age of Reform, Vintage Books (New York, Random House, 1955), pp. 60-93.

[21] Hanes Walton, Jr., The Negro in Third Party Politics (Philadelphia: Dorrance & Col, 1968), p. 43; T. Thomas Fortune, "The Voteless Citizen." The Voice of the Negro, 1 (September, 1904), 397-402.

[22] John Hope Franklin, "The Great Confrontation: The South and the Problem of Change," Journal of Southern History, 38 (February, 1972), 14; Dollard, Caste and Class, p. 177.

[23] Wilford H. Smith, "The Negro and the Law," in The Negro Problem: A Series of Articles by Representative American Negroes of To-day (New York: James Pott & Co., 1903), pp. 157-59.

[24] Frank Tannenbaum, Darker Phases of the South (New York: G. P. Putnam's Sons, 1924), pp. 15, 175; Mays, Born to Rebel, p. 23.

[25] George B. Tindall, South Carolina Negroes: 1877-1900 (Columbia: University of South Carolina Press, 1952), p. 239.

[26] Allison Davis, Burleigh B. Gardner, and Mary R. Gardner, Deep South: A Social Anthropological Study of Caste and Class (Chicago: The University of Chicago Press, 1941), p. 16; Forrest G. Wood, Black Scare: The Racist Response to Emancipation and Reconstruction (Berkeley: The University of California Press, 1968); H. G. Wells, The Future in America: A Search After Realities (New York: Harper & Bros., 1906), pp. 187-90.

See also I. A. Newby, Jim Crow's Defense: Anti-Negro Thought in America 1900-1930 (Baton Rouge: Louisiana State University Press, 1965).

[27] W. H. Crogman found the minstrel shows particularly offensive; see his Talks for the Times (Cincinnati: Jennings & Pye, 1896), p. 105.

[28] Charles Carver, Brann and the Iconoclast (Austin: University of Texas Press, 1957), p. 122.

[29] For Higginson and Vance statements see Carter G. Woodson, ed., The Works of Francis J. Grimke, (Washington: The Associated Publishers, Inc., 1942), 1: 306; U. S., Congress, Senate, Congressional Record, 55th Cong., 1st sess., 1890, 30 pt. 1:803; Booker T. Washington, Up From Slavery (Garden City, N. Y.: Doubleday & Co., 1946), pp. 218-25. The loyalty of the slaves to the Confederacy is a historic myth, see Georgia Lee Tatum, Disloyalty in the Confederacy (Chapel Hill: University of North Carolina Press, 1934); Harvey Wish, "Slave Disloyalty under the Confederacy," Journal of Negro History, 23 (October, 1938), 426-34; Charles H. Wesley, "The Civil War and the Negro-American," Journal of Negro History, 47 (April, 1962), 77-96.

[30] E. E. Hoss, "Lynching, its Cause and Cure," Independent, February 1, 1894, p. 128; Edwin S. Redkey, ed., Respect Black: The Writings and Speeches of Henry McNeal Turner (New York: Arno Press and the New York Times, 1971), p. 149. Birmingham News cited in Herbert J. Seligmann, The Negro Faces America (New York: Harper & Bros., 1920), p. 259.

[31] The Issue, February 1, 1908, p. 1; William Henry Skaggs, The Southern Oligarchy: An Appeal of the Silent Masses of our Country against the Despotic Rule of the Few (New York: The Devin-Adair Co., 1924), pp. 317-18. Politicians also contributed to this process of mythmaking. For one of innumerable examples see Claude G. Bowers, The Tragic Era: The Revolution After Lincoln (Cambridge: Houghton Mifflin Co., 1929), p. 308.

[32] Indianapolis Freeman, August 21, 1897, p. 2; B. F. Riley, The White Man's Burden (Birmingham: B. F. Riley, 1910), p. 153.

[33] NAACP, Thirty Years of Lynching in the United States: 1889-1918 (New York: Arno Press and the New York Times, 1969).

[34] Dollard, Caste and Class, p. 77; Charles S. Johnson, Edwin R. Embree, and Will W. Alexander, The Collapse of Cotton Tenancy (Chapel Hill: The University of North Carolina Press, 1935), p. 10 are two examples of this view. For criticism of Robert Park's similar view see Oliver Cromwell Cox, Caste, Class, and Race (Garden City, N. Y.: Doubleday & Co., 1948), p. 473.

[35] "Lynching: How far the Courts are Responsible for its Prevalence," American Law Review, 33 (July-August, 1899), 596-98; Clarence Poe, "Lynching: A Southern View," Atlantic Monthly, 93 (February, 1904), 155-165; Hannis Taylor, "The True Remedy for Lynch-Law," American Law Review, 41 (March-April, 1907), 255-66; Letter

Theodore Roosevelt to Philander Knox, July 24, 1903, cited in Nathaniel Weyle and William Marina, American Statesmen on Slavery and the Negro (New Rochelle, N. Y.: Arlington House, 1971), p. 315; Christian Advocate, July 27, 1905, p. 1164.

[36] Robert Strange, "Some Thoughts on Lynching," South Atlantic Quarterly, 5 (October, 1905), 349-51; "Lynching," Outlook, November 27, 1909, pp. 637-38; Christian Advocate, May 5, 1887, p. 285; Walter Clark, "True Remedy for Lynch Law," American Law Review, 28 (November-December, 1894), 801-07.

[37] Independent, February 1, 1894, p. 130; Indianapolis Freeman, April 16, 1898, p. 4; July 4, 1885, p. 2.

CHAPTER II

THE ORGANIZATION OF THE ATTACK ON LYNCHING

During the fifty-year period 1883 to 1933, there was general agreement among Black people that lynching was the greatest obstacle to improving their status. Although this general agreement existed, there was no consensus on the tactics that would be most effective in putting an end to lynching. This diversity was expressed through a wide variety of religious, secular, and cultural organizations. Some of these organizations were formed specifically in response to lynchings; others were organized in response to more general political events and social currents which were thought to contribute to the climate in which lynching flourished. These organizations interacted, cooperated, and competed. Their many meetings, services, lectures, and conventions served to provide an ever enlarging platform for critics of the entire caste system as well as of its starkest symbol -- lynching. Parallel to this Black organizational activity, but lagging behind it, was the involvement of whites in separate and interracial organizations opposing lynching. This support was welcomed by most Blacks who developed tactics to encourage such white participation. Whites whose commitment to the defense of the caste system led them to defend lynching, attacked the organized manifestations of the anti-lynching reform.

After the 1870s, the nature of the problem of racial violence changed. The generalized "riots" initiated by armed Democrats against Black efforts for race advancement were replaced by community lynchings to prevent individual Blacks from advancing. The growing consciousness that lynching was a problem in the 1880s was reflected by the annual publication of lynching statistics by the Chicago Tribune, beginning with the year 1882 when 113 were recorded. This number had more than doubled by 1892, when the peak of 230 lynchings was recorded. Many authorities believed that many lynchings went unrecorded. As lynchings increased, they became the prime criterion used by Blacks to assess the state of race relations which they knew was determined by many social and political factors. In 1883, the endeavor of President Chester A. Arthur to develop the Republican party in the South at the expense of Blacks and the increase of lynching were factors which led to a revival of the Black convention movement.[1]

Frederick Douglass threw his influence behind a call for a national Colored Convention which was to meet September 24, 1883, in Louisville. This call led to an increase in organizing activities by Blacks in several states. Texas, South Carolina, and Arkansas held state conventions which recognized the importance of the lynching problems. The Arkansas group met in Little Rock on August 29 and passed a resolution calling for the punishment of lynchers.[2] At Louisville, 300 delegates from twenty-seven states heard Douglass denounce lynch law. The practice of placing lynching high on the agenda became routine for practically all Black civil rights meetings during the next fifty years. The convention failed in its main purpose of influencing the Republican party to defend the rights of Blacks.[3] This abandonment of Blacks was reflected by the Supreme Court when it voided the Civil Rights Act of 1875, thereby absolving the federal government of concern for the increasing racial segregation then under way and thus encouraging an increase in the frequency of lynching.[4]

The decision of the Supreme Court on the Civil Rights cases came a few weeks after the Louisville Convention and was the result of forces at work within the Republican party. The underlying racism of the North made the Republicans sympathetic to the white South's contention that the continued violence there was only occasioned by the "superior" civilization defending itself from the "barbarians." A defense of Black rights was politically inexpedient for the Republicans, as it would further increase the rising political strength of the Democrats in the North with no balancing increase in Republican strength in the South. The class identification of the Republican party with Northeastern business interests blunted its interest in social reform and diverted Republicans to the issues of developing capitalism--the tariff, monetary policies, and resource disposal.[5]

The Supreme Court decision of 1883 was immediately recognized as of transcendent importance by Blacks. It was a catalyst that brought some to the realization that they were almost totally without allies in the struggle against Southern Democrats. Bishop Henry McNeal Turner, A. M. E. church leader, said that it revived the Ku Klux Klan, and Frederick Douglass said that it placed Blacks into the hands of their enemies.[6]

Douglass's statement was made at a mass meeting in Washington one week after the Supreme Court decision. Consistent with the strategy of enlisting white allies, Douglass had also invited Robert Ingersoll to speak, Ingersoll had been an abolitionist in the Democratic party in 1860 when he earned his reputation as a great orator by denunciations of slavery and the Fugitive Slave Act while campaigning for Congress. Douglass introduced Ingersoll as "one who loves his fellowman," and later wrote that Ingersoll had "ably and eloquently" presented the Black cause. In order to obtain a wider distribution of Ingersoll's speech, T. Thomas Fortune printed it with Douglass's introduction in a ten-cent pamphlet.[7]

The mass meeting became a significant tactic of the anti-lynching reform. The meetings were usually called in response to specific outrages and the cumulative effect was to draw additional people into a more active anti-lynching stance. Such meetings were a continuing source of resolutions and memorials to public officials and they contributed a portion of the meager funds that were available for the early anti-lynching work.

More permanent organizations were formed to foster intellectual activities and race pride after the Civil War. These organizations provided platforms and training grounds for speakers and writers who sharpened their abilities as social critics while they worked to involve their audiences in greater political and social activism. The Bethel Literary and Historical Association of the Metropolitan African Methodist Episcopal Church of Washington was an outstanding example of these groups. In the decade following the civil rights decision such groups held many meetings which associated the 1883 decision voiding the 1875 Civil Rights Act with Southern violence and lynchings.[8]

The response to the Supreme Court decision which had the most far-reaching influence on the anti-lynching reform was the formation of groups with a wide geographic base whose primary motivation was the protection of civil rights. In the beginning these groups had a tendency to be politically partisan, but their consistent concern about lynching gradually led them away from partisan politics. They evolved into the more permanent nationally-based organizations of the twentieth century which functioned as critics of both major parties and of the overall society.

Within four months of the 1883 decision, state-wide Black organizations appeared in Ohio, Connecticut, Tennessee and Illinois. They all viewed the Court's action as encouraging lynching.[9] An even broader-based group met in Pittsburgh at the call of the Colored Men's Central Committee of Illinois. Illinois was a logical origin for such a call, as Chicago was already developing into a Black metropolis whose leaders were in the forefront of the protest against Southern violence. The call stated that they were "looking with alarm and disgust upon the rise and growth of political despotism in the South," that they were troubled by the 1883 decision and federal apathy which pointed up the "absolute importance of self-action." The call listed three areas of discussion: violence in the South, political activity, and the need to hearten the Negro in the South. Seventy-five delegates from twelve states came to Pittsburgh seeking better methods to deal with lynching and other problems. One of the founders of Wilberforce University, A. M. E. Bishop James Alexander Shorter of Ohio, and Frederick Douglass were the two most prominent delegates.[10]

This convention developed several themes that would recur in similar meetings over the next few decades. The Reverend C. S. Smith drew attention to the fact that the site was also the site of the 1853 Free Soil Convention to illustrate the continuity of the postwar civil rights struggle with the pre-war opposition to slavery. Smith also noted the apparent success of the Irish struggle which he thought was "slmost over" and credited the racial solidarity of the Irish as an important factor in their success. He made it clear that Blacks were interested in reform and not in revolution and opposed all "communistic and socialistic elements." Another theme, that of cooperation with white allies, was underlined by John P. Green of Cleveland, who made use of the work of George W. Cable to attack the convict lease system.[11]

T. Thomas Fortune noted in the summer of 1885 that perhaps the convention movement was being overdone as he commented on a new call issued by Frederick Douglass, Richard T. Greener, John Mercer Langston, and Blanche K. Bruce for a convention to be held in Frankfort, Kentucky. Fortune's criticism was based more on his belief that the callers were primarily interested in strengthening the Republican party than it was on his belief that conventions per se lacked value. This latest convention, to be held on November 26, was the product of considerable planning. Several county conventions were held as part of the advance preparation.[12]

At the Frankfort convention, 420 delegates representing the 271,000 Blacks of Kentucky met. This group protested that they wanted civil, not social, rights, and they especially wanted an end to lynching. Although there was a generalized acknowledgement that Blacks must help themselves, there was no specific organization developed from this convention. It did petition the state legislature to appoint an investigative committee, but this was promptly pigeonholed.[13]

Many of these Black efforts at organization were small, little known, and ephemeral. In 1888, an Arkansas minister reported the existence of a Negro Legal Aid Society of the

United States which hoped to unify the entire race so that the fight for justice could be strengthened. Also in 1888, a Georgia convention of 350 Blacks favored the Blair bill, temperance, industrial education, and opposed the chain gang, Jim Crow, lynching, disfranchisement, and jury discrimination. Though these groups had little success in achieving their goals, the cumulative effect of all these groupings and re-groupings was to keep alive and to strengthen the idea that the goals of liberty and equality for Blacks in the United States would only be achieved by Black initiatives. The most consistent single point these groups had in common was opposition to lynching. They wanted white allies and believed that it was up to Blacks to emphasize to whites the injustice and inherent barbarism of lynching. It was hoped that whites, who would not lend support for other Black goals, would at least join anti-lynching efforts.[14]

In the search for allies, Douglass gave one of his better known orations, "The Lessons of the Hour," to an audience in Wilmington which was 90 per cent white. There he was introduced by Delaware Supreme Court Justice Charles P. Lore.[15] George Washington Cable, one of the earliest white allies, was invited frequently to speak on conditions in the South. Later that year Boston celebrated the anniversary of Wendell Phillips's famous speech delivered at Faneuil Hall in 1837 which marked his entry into the ranks of the militant abolitionists. Speakers recalled that Phillips's decision was precipitated by the lynching of Elijah Lovejoy. This meeting was another example of the search for continuity by linking past and present struggles for justice.[16]

The failure in the 1880s to organize a strong anti-lynching reform movement did not result in the abandonment of attempts to form the one organization that would speak for, and be supported by, all Blacks. Two major efforts were made to this end in the early 1890s. The first of these was the formation of the Afro-American League. The second was the Equal Rights Council.

The founding of the Afro-American League represented a major attempt to deal with Southern violence and lynch mobs. Unfortunately, however, the League's activities shifted from its original raison d'etre, and it became exclusively involved in promoting the interests of the Black elite and never developed a mass base.

T. Thomas Fortune has been given credit for the formation of the League, but he was not alone in realizing that a more effective organization of Blacks was needed. Earlier in the 1880s he had advocated a new political party, "organized along class lines and based on the interests of working men and women." By 1887 he favored independent Black action because he had come to believe that whites had left the Blacks to struggle on their own. In May of 1887, Fortune published a proposal for the League which emphasized the need for an organization to deal with the lynching problem.[17]

Fortune's hope was to unite the many Black organizations so that they could speak with one voice. There were many who found this idea attractive. To demonstrate the need for the organization, Fortune filled the next few issues of the Freeman with more items on Southern outrages and lynchings than had been his custom. An enthusiastic response came from Ida B. Wells, the Black journalist and anti-lynching crusader, who described the League as "the grandest idea ever originated by colored men." She saw it as a means of protecting the life, citizenship, and property of "innocent men, and women . . . victims of mob law."[18]

Fortune's proposal elicited an extensive dialogue in the Black press. Although a great diversity of opinion on anti-lynching tactics was expressed, all agreed that lynching was of paramount importance. Black Southerners opposed the League because they believed that any militancy would be counterproductive. The Jacksonville Southern Leader said:

> The condition of the race is constantly improving and the reign of mob law was much more oppressive and grinding ten years ago than it is now. . . . The League would intensify rather than allay the race troubles in the South.

Some thought Blacks should not set themselves apart in separate organizations and others mentioned the danger of causing the Klan to revive. Z. T. Pearsall, editor of the Alabama Advocate, feared that whites would respond to the League by killing off all the Blacks in the South "while T. Thomas Fortune sits in New York and collects money for complaining about what is happening."[19]

Fortune's proposal was received more positively in the North. A few local branches were formed in 1887, with the strongest being in Boston, and plans were made for a national convention in Richmond on December 6. However, too many thought that it might be construed as criticism of the Republican party, thus weakening Republican chances for a victory in 1888, so the convention plans were set aside. Since lynchings continued to increase, the idea did not die, and more local branches were formed. With the election safely behind, Fortune issued a call for a national convention to meet January 15, 1890. This call led to the formation of more local branches.[20]

John Mercer Langston, urbane Black Congressman from Virginia, published a letter that was widely circulated in the Black press in October, 1889, which did much to stimulate interest in a strong organization for self-defense. The letter cited the Irish National League as an example of what an organization bound together by both economic and ethnic ties could accomplish. The Black press had for some time been pointing out what it believed Jewish solidarity had accomplished and had long drawn invidious comparisons between the lack of Black unity and the perceived great racial solidarity within the immigrant groups.[21]

To encourage racial solidarity, the League organizers proclaimed Friday, June 2, 1889, a day of fasting and prayer. Concerning the reason for such a day, the proclamation stated:

> Mobs are formed . . . at whose approach the keys of these jails and prisons are surrendered and the suspicioned party is ruthlessly forced from the custody of the law and tortured, hanged, shot, butchered, dismembered, and burned in the most fiendish manner. . . . Mobs no longer conceal themselves in the shadows of the night.[22]

Many meetings were held to discuss the League and anti-lynching activity in the following months. A statement by the Douglass League of Rochester was an example of how the League and the anti-lynching reform became linked together in the minds of many Blacks:

> We heartily approve the growing sentiment in favor of an Afro-American Alliance dedicated to the work of arousing public opinion against Southern outrages, whose fierceness and frequency are a living reproach to our liberty and laws.[23]

Fortune promoted the League the best way he knew, by publishing accounts of the violence. One account, "A Week of Blood," stated that the Mississippi Democratic party had denounced Negro political activity, and a riot in Leflore County resulted in the killing of twenty Blacks by the militia; in Louisiana, a Negro excursion train was shot up, a church was burned, and several lynchings occurred; and a Black was burned at the stake in Somerset, Kentucky.[24]

Although some Southern editors opposed the League in 1887, by 1889 all Black editors had joined Fortune in publicizing and supporting the League. J. William Menard, editor of the <u>Southern Leader</u> and former member of the Florida legislature, had opposed the League in 1887 because he thought the race question was resolving itself, but in 1889, he stated that the South was the same as in 1865, which meant to him that a battle of two to three generations was shaping up. Southern support also came from A. N. Johnson, Republican leader in Selma, Alabama. He noted that organized anti-lynching activities were already underway in the South in 1889 which would be made more effective by the League. Johnson wrote:

> In nearly all Southern states, there have been committees appointed to lay before Congress the grievances of the Negro race in the South. I think if all these committees would attend the convention which you have called, we can get a suitable committee to represent the "whole" and could then demand something.

Emanuel Fortune, Jr., T. Thomas Fortune's older brother, expressed what was a growing consensus, "Let us organize for protection." He stated that this would be obeying the first law of nature.[25]

The Afro-American League met in Chicago January 15 to 17, 1890. The delegates heard much oratory against lynching and resolved "to resist by all legal and reasonable means, mob and lynch law whereof we are made the victims and to insist upon the arrest and punishment of all such offenders." The convention submitted a petition to Congress, "Address of the Convention of Colored Americans of the United States, Praying for Equal Rights," which was referred to the Judiciary Committee of the House without being read on the floor or otherwise noted.[26]

Although the formation of the Afro-American League was primarily motivated by the need to oppose lynching, it did not devote itself to anti-lynching activities after the convention. By 1891, Fortune was deploring the League's failure to secure a mass base. Such a base might have resulted if the League had devoted itself to the common-denominator issue of lynching. Instead it became more concerned with public accommodation and transportation discriminations. These issues were primarily the concern of the Black elite.[27]

The League also failed to develop lines of communication with any of the three most important fields of Black activity. The most important was the church, but the Black church, in the South especially, had not yet developed to the point of defying the white society by openly organizing to agitate for social justice. The Republican party was another institution that had great appeal for the Black masses, but the party's white leadership was not interested in attacking lynching or any other aspect of the caste system, nor were Black Republican leaders enthusiastic about pressuring the white leadership because of the Black's dependency on patronage. In a perceptive editorial, Fortune said that Black leaders were depandent on white support which they would have to give up if they supported the all-Black Afro-American League. The leaders of the Afro-American League had little or no contact with the third mass movement of Blacks, the Colored Alliance. The League was primarily the creation of Black editors. The Black press did not circulate much among the masses, and the League failed to develop the oral lines of communication represented by the pulpit and the hustings.[28]

The second annual convention of the League attempted to develop a mass base by appealing to the Black Republican leaders. It praised President Harrison for supporting the Blair bill, but it did not criticize him for his failure to enforce the Constitutional guarantees of the franchise and due process. Thus it failed to offer a focus for political insurgency as it failed originally to offer a focus for religious or economic rebels.[29]

Although the League was clearly conceived as primarily an anti-lynching organization, it was unable to alter the course of events. There were more lynchings in the United States in the two years following the League's formation than in any other two-year period during which records were kept. The anti-lynching agitation which led to the organization of the League continued after the first national convention, and new local Leagues were formed in 1890 and in 1891. Some of these locals were successful in winning civil rights suits against discrimination in public transportation and accomodations, but by 1893, although a few local Leagues still functioned, the national organization was dormant.[30]

The Afro-American League attracted some church support. Although two bishops signed the call for the convention of 1890 which was also supported by the A. M. E. Church Review, the Black church's most outspoken advocate of civil rights and anti-lynching activities, Bishop Turner, did not attend the convention or become active in the League. The Afro-American League did not have his support because he believed that Black salvation lay in the redemption of Africa, and he resented the disparagement of his proposals for emigration to Africa by the leaders of the League. Nevertheless, Turner's interest in Africa did not blind him to the need to fight for civil rights and against lynching in the United States.[31]

Apart from his belief in emigration as the only real solution, Turner realized that some organization was needed to protect Blacks in the United States. He had contemplated calling a convention in the mid-1880s but did not do so. Perhaps the movement which culminated in the Afro-American League influenced him to wait and see. With the failure of the League obvious by the summer of 1893, he issued a call on September 30 for a convention to meet in Cincinnati November 28 through December 1, 1893. From the first sentence of the call to the last sentence of Turner's keynote address, the problem of lynching was uppermost. The call began:

> For four consecutive years I have been prompted by the impulse of an honest conviction, that the way we as a race are being decimated in this country by mobs, lynchers, and fire fiends, necessitates a national convention for the purpose of crystalizing our sentiments and unifying our endeavours.

Turner's keynote address ended with the point, "Until we are free from menace by lynchers... we are destined to be a dwarfed people." The desire to oppose lynching was the common bond that brought together the delegates to the Turner convention, as surely as it was the motivation of the Afro-American League delegated three years earlier.[32]

George L. Knox, editor of the Indianapolis _Freeman_, played the role of chief spokesman for the Turner convention which T. Thomas Fortune had performed for the Afro-American League. Knox approved Turner's call and stated that the delegates' would have to decide between submission, emigration, and the struggle for manhood.[33]

The call had more than 300 prominent and distinguished endorsers, and to stimulate interest, Knox invited many Black leaders to state their thoughts on the upcoming convention. These were published in a special Thanksgiving Day issue on November 25, 1893, in which several dozen Black leaders stated their ideas. The opinions as to how Blacks could defend themselves from lynching varied from enthusiastic endorsement of militant self-defense to conservative reliance on education and property accumulation.[34]

In view of the diverse opinions expressed by the prominent Blacks, it is not surprising that the Turner convention went the way of the Afro-American League. However, the delegates addressed themselves to the lynching problem in a much more systematic manner than had those of the League, and the convention did create an organization with the primary function of opposing lynching. One of the first acts of the convention was to appoint committees. Charles Bundy of Ohio was chairman of the "Mobs and Lynching Committee." A. J. Warner of Montgomery, Alabama, was made chairman of a committee to investigate the charge that Blacks were naturally rapists and all lynch victims were guilty. The Warner Committee's conclusions, arrived at by interviewing every member of the convention, were very conservative. They stated that the lynch mobs comprised only a small percentage of any community. They accepted the current figures of the white press that rape was alleged in one-third of all lynching, and that while some of the rape charges were true, 20 per cent were doubtful, and 10 per cent of the Blacks lynched for this alleged reason were probably innocent.[35]

The permanent organization created by the convention, the Equal Rights Council, was to have a hierarchical organization with a unit in each county and with state and national bodies. Editor Knox described it as "one great protective body to fight, and resist under law, mobs, lynchings, railroad discrimination, jury denials, ballot discrimination and every species of injustice." Turner said that such an organization might "make it possible for a negro to remain here and be a man and citizen, and there is no African immigration in it." Though Turner finally gave up on the United States and went to Canada to die, he was willing in 1893 to give whites one more chance. The phrase, "resist under law," was a key to Turner's advice to Blacks who chose to remain in the United States.[36]

The Equal Rights Council hoped to collect one dollar from every Black and use the funds to fight in the courts, to hire detectives to hunt down lynchers, to lobby Congress and the state legislatures to pass indemnity laws to pay the families of mob victims. The fund would also pay lecturers and encourage race journals to become "a tongue of fire" in defense of the race.[37]

The National Equal Rights Council reported more victories than had the Afro-American League, but these were in the same areas as the Afro-American League victories--separate car laws and Northern discrimination. The Equal Rights Council also failed to exploit the interest in anti-lynching activity and passed from the scene even more quickly than the Afro-American League. After a long discussion, it merged with the League, but by that time there was no strength in either.

One of the factors influencing the timing of Turner's call for his convention was the snubbing of Blacks by the managers of the Columbian Exposition, the world's fair held in Chicago in 1893. Three bills introduced into the Fifty-second Congress would have provided for a statistical exhibit on Blacks in the United States which could have included data on lynching. All of the bills failed.[38]

Douglass, who had been placed in charge of the Haitian exhibit, and Ida B. Wells published a pamphlet, <u>The Reason Why the Colored American Is Not in the World's Columbian Exposition</u>. There were no funds for this project until Miss Wells arranged a series of emergency meetings with the Black women of Chicago and raised the $500 necessary to print 10,000 copies. These were distributed, and echoes came back from foreign countries. The pamphlet detailed the disabilities, including lynchings, that retarded Black progress, and at the same time noted great progress despite these disabilities.[39]

When the Fair management did set aside a "Negro Day," Douglass gave the main address, which was, in part, aimed at the Northern white conscience. He told the North:

> The South hates you. . . . Fourteen states have abandoned their courts, judges and juries, and a wild mob sits as a burlesque dispenser of justice to the Colored Man. . . . In your fawning on these cruel slayers, you slap us in the face. . . . Why in heavens name do you take to your breast the serpent that once stung, and crush down the race that grasped the saber that helped make the nation one and the Exposition possible?[40]

Several people, important to the anti-lynching reform later, heard Douglass speak and were influenced by him.

Ida B. Wells was the obvious co-worker for Douglass to have at the Columbian Exposition as she was already well known for her courageous opposition to lynching and her attacks on the rape myth. She wrote for both the white and the Black press and lectured widely. Her ability on the lecture platform won her invitations to visit England which led to a significant foreign reinforcement of the anti-lynching reform and to the organization of the National Association of Colored Women.[41]

The club movement among Black women had developed a strong social consciousness from abolitionist work. It continued and grew after the Civil War, as local groups organized for a variety of religious, social, and cultural purposes. These groups had strong feelings concerning lynching, but lacked a national organization. When Ida B. Wells started her career as an anti-lynching lecturer in 1892, she naturally turned to these groups for support. Her work tended to focus the interest of the clubs on anti-lynching activities. She was an able organizer who caused clubs to spring up in her wake, as in Chicago, where the women's groups that formed to raise money for the Exposition pamphlet continued as active organizations.[42]

The centers of club activity were Washington and Boston. Mary Church Terrell, Oberlin graduate, daughter of the rich and politically powerful Black Republican leader of Memphis, Robert Church, organized many of the Washington clubs into the Colored Women's League in 1892. In Boston, a move in the same direction was taken by the Black social leader, Mrs. Josephine St. Pierre Ruffin, who organized the New Era Club in January 1893, after she heard Miss Wells speak in New York. This New York meeting, in turn, was an outgrowth of the planning of Mrs. Victoria Earle Matthews and Miss Maritcha Lyons who had met Miss Wells that summer and had organized a series of successively larger groups of women to hear her story. In her autobiography, Ida B. Wells says that the Lyric Hall meeting in New York "was the real beginning of the club movement among colored women." Mrs. Ruffin went on to organize Black women in other New England cities to hear Miss Wells.[43]

In 1894, Miss Wells toured England to obtain support for the anti-lynching campaign, much as Frederick Douglass and other abolitionists had done before the Civil War to obtain support for their struggle. She told British audiences that the white press in the United States acknowledged that rape was alleged in only one-third of the lynchings, and she repeated the charges that had caused the Memphis mob to shut down her paper, Free Speech. William J. Stone, governor of Missouri, was also travelling in England at that time and learned of Miss Wells's activities. Stone publicly charged her with lying. John W. Jacks, editor of the Montgomery (Missouri) Standard and president of the Missouri Press Association, picked up the governor's charges and added an attack on the morals of Miss Wells in particular and on all Black women in general, which he mailed to the Women's Era, the publication of Mrs. Ruffin's New Era Club of Boston. Jack's letter was the catalyst that led directly to the formation of the National Association of Colored Women (NACW).[44]

The New Era Club sent copies of the letter to other Black women's clubs, and plans were made for a national organization to deal with the charges made by Jacks. A conference was called to meet in Berkeley Hall, Boston, in late July 1895, which was attended by about 100 delegates from ten states, representing twenty-five clubs. Mrs. Ruffin was elected president, Mrs. Helen Cook of Washington and Mrs. Booker T. Washington, vice-presidents. The new group issued a strong protest to the insults to Black women generally and to Miss Wells in particular, and they unanimously endorsed the course she had taken in agitation against lynching.[45]

The NACW always maintained an interest in anti-lynching work and the related problems of convict least, Jim Crow, and the franchise, but the protest was muted as it gradually came under the influence of Tuskegee. Fannie Barrier Williams, prominent Black clubwoman, was critical of some of the political activity of some of the Northern clubs. <u>National Notes</u>, the official organ of the NACW, said in 1903 that it would be undignified to engage in controversy. The following year, Mrs. Williams wrote, "Disfranchising the Negro in the South has been a great blessing in disguise; that since he is not permitted to vote, he is acquiring land and money."[46]

In 1897 the NACW met at Nashville September 15-17. Resolutions were adopted against rape, lynching, the "whole publication of crime in the newspapers," the convict lease system, and liquor."[47] In 1898, NACW President Mary Church Terrell, who had been an active anti-lynching lecturer, spoke before the National American Women's Suffrage Association in Washington on the subject, "The Progress of Colored Women." She spoke of the Black woman's fight against Jim Crow and the convict lease, but did not mention lynching. Ida B. Wells believed that Mrs. Terrell was deliberately snubbing her by ignoring the issue with which Miss Wells was so closely associated for fear that Miss Wells would defeat her for the presidency of the NACW. Miss Wells had met W. T. Stead, the editor of the British <u>Review of Reviews</u> during the Columbian Exposition and had responded to his query as to why Blacks were so ineffective in their opposition to lynching by pointing out the jealousies that divided Blacks and prevented the growth of one single, strong organization. His rejoinder was that perhaps Blacks had not been lynched enough to appreciate the overriding need for unity.[48]

The individual women's clubs continued to work on aspects of the lynching problem, especially the Ida B. Wells Club of Chicago. It wrote McKinley and Congress to protest lynching, only to receive the standard reply that the federal government had no authority to intervene with state problems. This club organized an Executive Committee on "Southern Outrages" which called on Governor John P. Altgeld in 1893 to protest the lynching of a Black who had been taken from a southern Illinois jail into Kentucky and lynched.[49]

The organizational efforts of Black women to halt the tide of lynching increased the number of people involved in the reform and laid the basis for the greater involvement of women later. Nevertheless, despite their hard work and good intentions, racial violence continued throughout the 1890s almost unabated. Possibly no event in the decade illustrated more forcibly the need for effective Black protest than the "riot" in Wilmington, North Carolina.

The Wilmington riot of 1898 illustrated the effective use of the racist's mythologies to maintain and increase white supremacy, and the energizing nature of such incidents to stimulate Black opposition to lynching. Republican-Populist fusion in North Carolina in 1896 had elected a white Republican governor, Daniel L. Russel, and a Black congressman, George H. White. A few Blacks were elected and appointed to lesser offices in the state. Wilmington had one Black officeholder, the Recorder of Deeds. In 1898, the North Carolina Democrats were determined to seize power, by a military coup, if necessary, and then re-write the state constitution to disfranchise Blacks.[50]

To disarm possible Northern opposition and to mobilize the racists, the true motives of this coup were hidden behind the twin myths of rape and "Black domination." When an editorial attacking the rape myth was published in Alex Manley's Black newspaper, the <u>North Carolina Record</u>, the event was seized on by whites to initiate the Wilmington riot.

The rape myth had been given much publicity throughout the South that summer when a speech by Mrs. W. H. Felton, a prominent Atlantan, received extensive coverage and much favorable editorial comment in the white press. She asserted that white men feared to go out of sight of their homes, so fearful were they that their wives would be molested. Mrs. Felton's ideas were not new. The same thing had been appearing in the white newspapers and opinion journals from the time the New South started its campaign to win the acceptance of the North for its concept of proper race relations. In August, Editor Alex Manley of the Record replied with the argument that he and other Black editors frequently used: that which whites called rape was often a liasion that had been exposed. Manley wrote:

> Meetings of this kind go on for some time until the white women's infatuation or the man's boldness brings attention to them and the man is lynched for rape. Every Negro lynched is called a "big burly black brute" when in fact many of these, who have been thus dealt with, had white men for their fathers and were not only not "black and burly" but were sufficiently attractive for white girls to fall in love with them as is well known to all.

It was not that the content of this editorial was unusual, but that the timing of it fitted in with the Red Shirts' plans to take total control of North Carolina and cover up their true motivation, which was to rid the state of the last vestiges of Reconstruction.[51]

The superior military force of the Democrats, organized block by block in Wilmington by the Chamber of Commerce, determined the outcome of the election by keeping Blacks from voting. Benjamin Tillman used the Manley editorial to mobilize Red Shirts in South Carolina to help in patrolling the polling places in North Carolina in order to insure a Democratic victory. The day after the election, the Democrats, in a mob led by armed ministers, attacked the Black community and burned the building that housed the Record. When Blacks defended themselves, the governor called in the state militia which "shot down in cold blood almost 100 Negroes." This brutality, coupled with white resolutions to employ only whites, resulted in an exodus of 1,400 Blacks according to the Wilmington Messenger, a white newspaper. The "Talented Tenth" was especially a target of the mobs. W. E. Henderson, a Black attorney, was forced to dispose of his property in a hurried sale which brought him one-tenth of its value. Manley's investment in the Record went up in smoke, and he barely escaped. When W. E. B. Du Bois, then at Atlanta, heard of the Wilmington riot, he said, "The clock is turned back! The Sixties are here again!"[52]

The continuing racial violence of the 1890s led to a revival of the Afro-American League shortly before the Wilmington riot. There had been over 1000 lynchings from 1892 through 1897 and 78 per cent of the victims were Black. In response to this, there had been several calls to revive the Afro-American League. Nothing was accomplished toward that end until the lynching of two postmasters in 1898 led Bishop Alexander Walters to pressure T. Thomas Fortune in March of that year to reactivate the Afro-American League in order to demand the prosecution of the lynchers of federal employees. Fortune temporized, so Walters arranged for a meeting in Rochester, New York, where the Afro-American League was re-organized as the Afro American Council on September 15, 1898. The Council had the same program as the League, but expressed it in more tactful terms.

Ida B. Wells precipitated a clash when she contended, in a speech on mob violence, that Booker T. Washington was mistaken in thinking that economic advances by Blacks would insure immunity from mob violence. She also criticized President McKinley for failure to act against the lynchers of the postmasters. The Wilmington riot that fall caused Walters to call an executive committee meeting in Washington over the Christmas holidays. Walter's call stated that lynching, discrimination, disfranchisement, and moral, financial, educational and economic blocks to progress made it necessary to organize for self-protection. A committee from the Council called on McKinley but received no satisfaction. The President knew that the Council was a weak organization.[53]

One reason for the Council's weakness stemmed from lack of agreement on the method of protest. Militants such as Miss Wells were in the minority. Washington made anonymous financial contributions to the Council in 1901 and 1902, by which time Emmett J. Scott, Washington's secretary, said that Tuskegee controlled the organization. This insured that the Council would not be too critical of the Republican-controlled federal government's continued failure to protect Black citizens in their fundamental rights. This led to the formation of other Black organizations which would be more outspoken. The split began to widen more rapidly after William Monroe Trotter founded the Boston Guardian in 1901. The Guardian provided a center for opposition to Washington who was increasingly regarded by the militants as acquiescing to lynching and discrimination. Washington, on the other hand, charged that the militants antagonized both the Republican administration and the white South, and diverted energies from self-improvement into sterile political channels.[54]

The roots of this division could be seen in the discussion over anti-lynching tactics which began in the 1880s when Fortune's calls for self-defense and even retaliation were greeted by Blacks in the South with dismay. Each group was as militant as it felt it could be and still survive. The far greater degree of oppression and open anti-Black terror in the South, where the whites believed they had more at stake in keeping the Blacks subservient, limited the Black initiative there.

The Council continued to meet annually, but it had an even smaller supportive network of state and local organizations than the earlier League had. The delegates at the annual convention in 1906, stirred by lynchings and the Atlanta riot, protested ballot restrictions, Jim Crow, and mob violence. This militancy resulted in the dropping away of support by Washington's followers. Resolutions of the Council in 1907 were equally militant and were noticed by even fewer people. The National Council last held an annual meeting in 1908, but it was barely mentioned in the press.[55]

The basic weakness of Black organizations lay in the nature of the whole society. Blacks were weak as a result of centuries of slavery and oppression. The ideas of the Black leaders were largely unheard by the impoverished and poorly educated Black masses. They were also largely unheard or ignored by the white power structure which had a vested interest in continuing things as they were. Nevertheless, Blacks continued to develop organizations, and even when they failed to achieve the goal of ending lynching, they contributed to small advances toward this goal.

There were numerous cultural and intellectual organizations formed in the 1890s. The American Negro Academy which met intermittently until 1924 was founded in 1897.

It published twenty-two papers, some of which dealt with lynchings. The Negro Historical Society of Philadelphia was also founded in 1897, as was the Negro Society for Historical Research, founded by John Edward Bruce and Arthur Schomburg in Yonkers. These organizations reinforced each other and provided forums for discussion and encouraged publications. William Ferris, a member of the American Negro Academy and one of the more influential militants of the 1890s, said that his two-volume work, The <u>African Abroad</u>, grew out of talks he gave at these organizations and at similar ones, such as the Boston Literary Society, the Bethel Literary Society, the Second Baptist Lyceum, and the Shiloh Baptist Lyceum. In 1899, the Academy published a work by John L. Love which may have been the first scholarly refutation of the Reconstruction myth of "Black domination."[56]

There were many individual meetings, both all-Black and interracial, that considered the problem of lynching. Almost any occasion that would interest Blacks, especially in the North, would hear the outrages protested. One example was the large gathering at Faneuil Hall which welcomed Ida B. Wells back from England. The Emancipation Proclamation celebrations, mass meetings on the Fourth of July and Thomas Jefferson's birthday are also examples of the tendency for all meetings of Blacks to become anti-lynching forums.[57]

Lynchings declined from a peak of about 230 in 1892 to 130 in 1901. This decline was in part due to the activities of the organized and institutionalized Black response. However, the relationship was indirect. Blacks failed in this period to achieve their main goals of Black unity and sufficient white support to win the battle against lynching. Disfranchisement of Blacks increased in the South, so there was little opportunity to unite with the less racist Southerners in seeking legislative relief. The federal government continued to be dominated by whites who did not care to be troubled by the problems of Blacks and used the constitutional argements of states' rights as their excuse for inaction. The attitude of most public figures was that when Black and white interests were in conflict the former must give way to the latter. White opposition to lynching was slow to develop, because, with a few exceptions, whites were not much troubled by lynchings.

The slow entry of whites into the anti-lynching reform was manifested in the development of interracial organizations to oppose lynching which began in the 1890s. The National Citizens Rights Association was organized by Albion B. Tourgee in October 1891. Tourgee was adamantly opposed to the Southern segregation laws and later served as attorney for Homer A. Plessy in the 1896 case, <u>Plessy</u> v. <u>Ferguson.</u> The Association's stated purpose was to expose "the maliciousness and discrimination imposed on the Colored People in the South." Tourgee, always a staunch Republican, included equally staunch Republican Blacks on the Association's Advisory Board such as S. Laing Williams, a Black Chicago attorney who was indebted to Booker T. Washington for help in his career. Such people were not inclined to give the lynching issue priority over partisal politics. The National Citizens Rights Association did not attract the militants because it did not question the Republican national leadership. The Association did, however, help develop the tactic of pressing court cases aimed at establishing the point that segregation equals discrimination, a tactic which was later used extensively by the NAACP.[58]

The Constitution League, a more important interracial organization, was organized in 1903 by William A. Sinclair, a prominent Philadephia physician and Black leader, backed by John Milholland, a wealthy anti-imperialist Republican from New York. The Constitution League attacked disfranchisement, peonage, and mob violence by means of court action, legislative proposals, and propaganda. Milholland had proposed a national interracial civil rights organization to Booker T. Washington in 1900 and had financed much of the Afro-American Council's legal work. In 1904 the League and Washington tried unsuccessfully to get the Republican party to strengthen its platform plank on lynching. In 1906 Washington's failure to defend the Black cause in the Brownsville affair moved the League to shift its support to the more militant opponents of lynching. By 1911, the Constitution League's position was so close to that of the NAACP that merger of the two groups was seriously considered.[59]

The Southern anti-lynching reform was always more conservative than the Northern reform. It was slower to get started among whites who were more hesitant in accepting Black inputs than were whites in the North. This reluctance in the South to consider suggestions from Blacks contributed to the backwardness of the region's anti-lynching efforts. No all-white organization ever developed any meaningful attack on lynching. However, white organizations which considered race relations could not ignore the subject, and there was a tendency for such organizations to become interracial. This confirmed the validity of the Black belief that whites would cooperate with Blacks to oppose lynching when they would not cooperate toward any other end.

Southern white participation in the anti-lynching reform began inauspiciously with the all-white Montgomery Race Conference of 1900. A few faint white voices in an occasional pulpit or school had been heard earlier, but these were largely ignored. The Montgomery delegates opposed any easing of the caste restrictions on Blacks and most of them justified lynching for rape. At the same time, they came to believe that lynching discredited the law, obtained sympathy for criminals, brutalized whites, increased race antagonism, and that the mistake of a frightened woman could lead to the lynching of an innocent Black.[60]

Those who thought as did the Montgomery delegates were faced with an insoluble problem: how to oppose some lynchings without opposing all lynchings. Attempts to resolve this dilemma forced some white Southerners to choose between the democratic and religious aspects of their characters and the racist support fo the caste society. Few were ever able to resolve this dilemma completely, but some were forced into more active support of the anti-lynching reform by factual criticism. The weakness of the Southern white input into the reform stems from the inability to reject the mythology of lynching; fortunately, total rejection was not necessary to make a small contribution. Clifton R. Breckenridge, Arkansas Republican and ex-Minister to Russia, told the Montgomery Conference, "We know that the origin of lynching was unspeakable rage at unspeakable crime," yet he also said that the security of society lay in orderly justice. The attempt to resolve the contradiction led him to a generalized plea for justice for Blacks. The Reverend Charles T. Walker, probably the best known Black minister at this time, seized on this plea for justice in an address to an audience of 8,000 at Carnegie Hall, May 27, 1900, and pointed out its logical implications required opposition to all lynchings.[61]

In contrast to the tentative white movement away from a total defense of lynching that the Montgomery Conference expressed was the total rejection of all lynchings by the all-Black Georgia Equal Rights Movement. The Georgia Equal Rights Movement was organized by William Jefferson White on February 13-14, 1906, when 500 Black leaders came to Macon to protest lynching. For thirty years White had been editor of the Georgia Baptist, which Du Bois said was "probably the most universally read Negro paper in the South." More than once White narrowly escaped lynching during Reconstruction because of his aggressive efforts in behalf of education for Blacks. The Georgia Equal Rights Movement was a response to continued lynching and to Benjamin Tillman's statement that Southern Blacks were content and only the Northern Blacks complained. The group issued a manifesto protesting the lynching of 260 Blacks in Georgia since 1885. Among the signatories were Bishop Turner, W. E. B. Du Bois, J. Max Barber, and John Hope. The Georgia Movement resolved to "agitate, complain and protest; besiege the legislature, go to court and above all, organize," and "work in peace with white brothers in this land of plenty." The Reverend Charles T. Walker attended, at the request of Booker T. Washington, to see that the movement did not become too radical.[62]

The Georgia Equal Rights Movement both expressed and increased the Black resolve to oppose the caste society more actively. This heightened determination was reflected in the self-defense initiatives taken by Blacks in the Atlanta riot which came seven months later.

As at Wilmington, eight years earlier, Georgia illustrated how effective use of the rape myth by demagogues elevated the most extreme racists to high political office. On September 22, 1906, the worst riot between 1900 and World War I occurred in Atlanta as an aftermath of Hoke Smith's campaign for governor of Georgia. This "riot" had been planned for months and was precipitated by false stories of rape carried in the Atlanta Journal, owned by Smith and edited by John Temple Graves. Clark Howells, editor of the Constitution, reinforced the Journal's campaign to increase race hatred.[63]

J. Max Barber, editor of the Voice of the Negro, a monthly Black literary and opinion journal founded in Atlanta in 1904, presented the Black version of the riot and paid for his temerity. The morning of the second day of the riots, September 23, the New York World telegramed Graves for a statement which was published the following day. It declared that the riot was in response to a "carnival of rape." Barber sent the World a reply to Graves's charges and asserted that three weeks before the riot, the Journal had offered $1,000 reward to mob leaders who would "lynch brutal Negro imps from hell." Barber also charged that Hoke Smith hired thugs to black their faces and knock down white women, and that when bloodhounds tracked the assailants to white homes, the evidence was ignored. James English, president of the Fourth National Bank of Atlanta, member of the Police Commission, and Governor Terrell's Chief of Staff, called Barber to his office and told him to deny publicly the letter to the World or go to the chain gang. Barber was not willing to do either, and moved the Voice of the Negro to Chicago instead. William Jefferson White was also driven out of Atlanta at this time for his remarks on the riot. Among other things, White had said that it was appropriate that the mob had piled the bodies around the statue of Henry Grady.[64]

The Atlanta riot had repercussions throughout the United States. Blacks met everywhere to discuss the massacre and listen to addresses breathing a bitter resentment against the enemies of their race. The riot temporarily revitalized the Afro-American

Council and led to its being taken over by the militants who used it to criticize Washington's leadership and to charge him with complicity in the Atlanta events. The National Negro Business League met in Atlanta shortly before the riot, and Washington was told by John Temple Graves to urge Blacks to give up their criminal ways and to cooperate with whites in bringing criminal Blacks to justice. He was told if he wished "to vindicate the reputation he has obtained for leadership and good sense he would not miss this opportunity to speak in thunder tones along these lines." The National Negro Business League dutifully passed resolutions against Black criminals and was praised by Graves. A letter to the Boston Guardian from Savannah, Georgia, signed, "the leading Negro Citizens," protested Washington's attitude toward Black crime and charged him with a share of the responsibility for the riot. The number of Blacks who believed that the mythology of rape should be met head on by denials and factual refutation was increasing, and they saw their effort being undermined by Washington's position that the problem was one of Black, not white, creation. Julius Taylor, editor of the Chicago Broad Ax, and one of Washington's most outspoken critics, said that Washington advised Atlanta Blacks not to defend themselves and to stop raping. The Columbia Southern Sun said, "Mr. Washington will have to get another remedy to cure the race problem, for his ownership of a brick-block house had, in this case, utterly failed."[65]

The Atlanta riot led to increased Black militancy and to more interracial cooperation. Both of these developments strengthened the anti-lynching reform. Following the riot, ex-Governor William J. Northern organized the Christian League, a statewide interracial organization to oppose mob violence. In Atlanta, Charles T. Hopkins, prominent white attorney, and the Reverend H. H. Parker, pastor of the First Colored Congregational Church, organized a Civic League to attack the conditions that generated the riot. As one of these conditions was the routine denial of judicial due process to Blacks accused of rape, both organizations joined in securing a trial for Joe Glann, a Black charged with assaulting a white woman. At the onset both thought him guilty and only wanted to establish a precedent for legal executions, but their investigation of the case proved him innocent.[66]

The Atlanta riot in late September, followed by the dismissal of the Brownsville soldiers the day after the November, 1906 election sharpened the division among Blacks. This division, which started in the 1890s with the discussion over the character of education, was basically a consideration of a more fundamental question. Would the logic of the economic maturation of the economy make an equal place for Blacks as Washington thought, or would Blacks have to take the leadership in forcing the development of society toward Black equality, as the militants believed?

This division was reflected in the early stages of the anti-lynching reform with Douglass and Turner as harbingers of the militant wing which was nourished in the literary, cultural, and historical societies. The conservative wing was represented by the fundamentalist clergy and the Southern educators, financed by white philanthropy and relying upon divine Providence and the development of liberal capitalist democracy to overcome the vestiges of slavery and to eliminate lynching.

The establishment of the Boston Guardian in 1901 provided a forum for the militants which they used to try to redirect white support from Tuskegee and other segments of Washington's organization to themselves. To do this required an attack on Washington's position that only low-class Blacks were lynched and that the accumulation of material wealth meant the acquisition of immunity from attack by whites. Illustrative of the Guardian's attack was a story in December 1902 concerning Black sharecroppers buying their own bits of land. They were terrorized by whitecappers for taking Tuskegee rhetoric seriously, and laws were passed prohibiting the sale of land to Blacks.[67]

William Ferris, William Monroe Trotter and his partner, George W. Forbes, challenged Washington for control of the Afro-American Council in July 1903 and lost. The militants had also been challenging Washington's leadership at the National Negro Business League meetings all over the country. This year (1903) saw a great increase in the number of protest meetings generally. When Washington came to Boston to address the NNBL, the militants demanded that Washington answer a series of embarrassing questions. The ensuing melee disrupted the meeting and resulted in Trotter's arrest and sentence to thirty days in jail. One of the questions was, "Is the rope and the torch all the race is to get under your leadership?" This Boston "riot" was the single most significant event directing Du Bois irrevocably away from Washington. The Carnegie Hall Conference of January 1904 was Washington's last major attempt to reverse the direction Du Bois was travelling. There Washington agreed to give up the "darky" jokes and speak more forthrightly against lynching. The conference resolved in favor of "vigorous denunciation of lynching and all punishments without due process of law." Booker T. Washington kept his agreement for a while, and in March 1904 issued the strongest statement against lynching that he ever made prior to the formation of the NAACP.[68]

Washington could not long continue to follow Du Bois's lead. If Washington talked to white audiences, as he did for a while after the Carnegie Hall meeting, and did not tell belittling "darky" jokes, the white audiences did not respond favorably, and his coverage in the white press declined. Washington soon saw that he had relinquished the tools he needed to keep the Tuskegee machine operating. Tuskegee's white friends praised disfranchisement and hailed what they reported to be an improved attitude of Southern leaders toward lynching. By affirming these statements, Washington increased his vulnerability to attack by the militants, who asserted that there was no improvement in race relations.[69]

A meaningful attack on lynching required an attack on all aspects of the exploitation of Blacks in the South and on the caste system. Washington could not do this as it would isolate him from the springs of his power--white philanthropy and the Republican machine. Rather than decline into a nonentity, he chose to continue on his familiar path. He rationalized the disfranchising state constitutions, saying that the Fifteenth Amendment was premature; he condoned the stereotype, saying that Blacks were grateful for crumbs; he misrepresented Black history and character, accepting too much of the mythology of lynching. To rationalize this behaviour, Washington developed his ideological commitment to the concept that the democratic implications of developing free enterprise would being an end to all proscriptions. He saw in the dialectic of capitalism, the synthesis of democracy.

On the other hand, lynching was so indefensible that Washington could not acquiesce in it. The lynching issue was the one with which he had least disagreement with the militants. Of all the issues, lynching was the one on which it was most necessary for a Black leader to be "right," if he were to have any followers. It would be incorrect to say, as some have, that Washington was uncompromising in condemning lynching, but it would be even more incorrect to say that he condoned it. He admitted being tempted into confrontation with whites in the early years of his work but decided that course would do no good; it would distract Blacks from cashing in on opportunities. "Besides that," Washington said, "I saw that the masses of the Negro people had no disposition to carry on any general war against white people." Washington opposed lynching as much as he could without jeopardizing his white support. Even the "darky" jokes that Du Bois found so offensive served their role. George Washington Carver was with Washington when he was scheduled to give a talk in Florida the night after a lynching. Carver related that the audience was segregated by means of a white sheet, and the white men were carrying guns, but Washington softened them up with jokes until they were ready to hear his message.[70]

Washington opposed lynching with many variations on his themes that injustice harmed its perpetrators as well as its recipients, and one could not keep a man down in the gutter unless one also stayed in the gutter to hold him there. Washington worked with the reformers crusading against the convict lease and prison brutality and other facets of Southern life which contributed to the climate that permitted lynching. He used his appointive influence to get sympathetic judges. However, as he had developed a vested interest in the concept that hard work and economic advancement would remove enterprising Blacks from the ranks of the lynchables, he fell into the trap of assuming that the mob victims were low-class Blacks who had not heeded his advice. In 1897 he said, "The men who are lynched are invariably vagrants, men without property or standing." Whites used such statements to countenance lynching, as they used other portions of Washington's rhetoric to sanction disfranchisement and the expropriation of political and civil rights.[71]

Washington held several misconceptions about society. He did not view lynching as a tool maintaining the caste system of the South, but as an aberration of that society. Washington misunderstood the convict lease system. He thought it existed to make money for the state and did not see it as an economic solution to the problem of great numbers of political prisoners. Washington would have been surprised if someone had suggested that the reason up to 90 per cent of all Southern prisoners were Black was because Blacks were the main protestors against the politics of caste. Washington also misunderstood lynching. He thought it was the work of poor whites venting their frustrations rather than the final resort of a society determined to preserve the caste oppression of Blacks at all costs. Washington expressed the fundamental fallacy in his world view when he wrote in 1905, "Every white man will respect the Negro who owns a two-story brick business block and has $5,000 in the bank." Clark Howells, editor of the Atlanta <u>Constitution</u> denied this in an editorial which stated that property holding was more apt to increase the Blacks' likelihood of getting "into trouble" because it made the Blacks more "insolent." Washington ignored Howells's statement because he had a vested interest in his particular view of society, much as whites who propagated the rape myth ignored the facts because they had a vested interest in the society which the myth upheld.[72]

Black militancy and activism constituted the fundamental force energizing the antilynching reform and Washington did much to disarm that force. When Washington enunciated the "Atlanta Compromise" in his address at the 1895 Cotton Exposition, he did not mention lynching, although there had been over 1,600 lynchings in the preceding decade and 113 already that year. In response to reporters' questions in Washington, D. C., four months later, as to whether lynching had stirred up Blacks to the point of race war or insurrection, Washington replied,

> No, not at all. God did not put very much combativeness into our race. Perhaps it would have been better for us if we had not gone licking the hand that had beaten us. But that is the way of our race.

Thus, Washington helped create the attitude which his statement could be construed as deploring. William Lloyd Garrison, son of the famous abolitionist, remarked in 1904 that he was no longer going to protest wrongs in the South because Washington told him two years earlier that protest only made things worse.[73]

While touring Europe in 1910, a year in which eighty Blacks were lynched, Washington enraged some Blacks by issuing Pollyanna statements concerning improving race relations in the United States. When he returned, Washington wrote in World's Work, "I felt that the millions of Negroes needed something more than to be reminded of their sufferings and of their political rights; that they needed to do something more than merely to defend themselves." This spirit lingered on at Tuskegee where a participant in a 1920 conference said, "A local lynching at the levee might dampen the spirits of a few Negroes who might be near enough to smell the powder," but the article continued with the thought that this was nothing compared to meeting an example of the Tuskegee ideal who worked hard, lived frugally and prospered.[74]

Washington overestimated the good will that Southern whites had for Blacks and was surprised and shocked by the intemperate fury of the Southern reaction to his dinner with Roosevelt in 1901. One Alabama congressman said that it would have been a good thing to have placed a bomb under the table and killed both the President and Washington. Senator Tillman said that the event would necessitate the killing of a thousand Blacks "before they learn their place again." Arthur Mitchell, a student at Tuskegee at this time and later a New Deal congressman from Illinois, stood guard over Washington at Tuskegee with a rifle when Washington was threatened with lynching because of the famous dinner.[75]

Prior to 1912, Washington's strongest statement against lynching was made in 1904, in compliance with the promise he made to the militants at the Carnegie Hall Conference. Then in 1912 in an even more frank statement he said that most lynch victims were Black, many were innocent of any wrongdoings, white girls gave false testimony, and white men blacked their faces to commit crimes for which Blacks were lynched.[76]

One area of the Tuskegee protest to lynching was in the work of its Department of Records, headed by Monroe Work until his death in 1938. Washington became aware of the value of sending out press releases on lynching statistics which became, for much of the white media, the only time the subject would be mentioned. This backfired, however. The Outlook, the most widely read opinion journal of the early 1900s, for example, had printed many lurid descriptions of, and comments on, lynching up to the time the Tuskegee releases became available. From that time on, it would not discuss lynchings except in connection with the publication of the Tuskegee press releases which were issued only every six months or annually. The rather dry statistical approach made the subject seem unreal and remote to the average reader because the vivid reportage that characterized many earlier accounts was lacking.[77]

When it became apparent in the summer of 1904 that Washington would not be able to keep his pledge to maintain a more militant public posture against the proscriptions and outrages, the Northern militants increased their attacks on him and formed the New England Suffrage League in October. The Suffrage League functioned as a lecture bureau to promote agitation. Its speakers exhorted the crowds to sign petitions, write letters to Congress, and to condemn Southern brutalities. This organization, led by William Monroe Trotter, evolved into the National Equal Rights Association which was active until the New Deal.[78]

In an attempt to create an organization with a broader base than the Suffrage League, Du Bois and other militants founded the Niagara Movement in 1905. The Niagara Declaration of Principles did not deal with lynching specifically, because there was little disagreement with Washington's position taken in March 1904. The Declaration did state, "The Negro race in America . . . needs protection and is given mob violence." J. Max Barber, one of the original members, said that the purpose of the Niagara Movement was "to rebuke the race leaders who seek the applause of the white mob."[79]

The New England Suffrage League, the Georgia Equal Rights Movement, the Afro-American Council, and the American Negro Academy all supported the Niagara Movement. Du Bois suggested that the all merge in 1908. This was accomplished for all practical purposes by the formation of the National Association for the Advancement of Colored People.

The decision of the Supreme Court in 1883 voiding the Civil Rights Act of 1875 was believed by Black leaders to mark a reversal of the trend toward the equality of the races that began with the Civil War. The decision encouraged segregation and strengthened caste divisions and indirectly supported second-class citizenship for Blacks. To exploit any people requires their debasement and this decision led to perpetuation of the patterns of exploitation and debasement which Blacks continued to protest. As protest often resulted in a lynching, the lynch mob was viewed by many Blacks as the most important obstacle to their progress. To oppose lynching, a large variety of Black organizations were created to foster Black pride, unify the race, improve the image whites had of Blacks and to work for equal justice. At the same time, the older institutions and organizations were used to promote the anti-lynching reform. One of the most traditional channels which Blacks used to promote the reform was the political process.

FOOTNOTES--CHAPTER II

[1] The basic sources for lynching statistics are derived from the records collected by Tuskegee and the NAACP. See Daniel T. Williams, "The Lynching Records at Tuskegee Institute; with Lynching in America: A Bibliography," in Eight Negro Bibliographies, comp. by Daniel T. Williams (New York: Kraus Reprint Co., 1970); NAACP, Thirty Years of Lynching in the United States: 1889-1918 (New York: Arno Press and the New York Times, 1969). The Crisis periodically published updated NAACP statistics and the Negro Year Book and Annual Encyclopedia of the Negro, ed. by Monroe N. Work (Tuskegee, Alabama: Tuskegee Institute, 1912-1952) published the annual Tuskegee lynching statistics. There are minor discrepancies between the Tuskegee and the NAACP data but both sources agree that their records are incomplete. See Williams, "Lynching Records," p. 4; NAACP, Thirty Years, p. 6.

[2] Report of the Committee on Grievances at the State Convention of Colored Men of Texas, 1883," in Afro-American History: Primary Sources, ed. by Thomas R. Frazier (New York: Harcourt, Brace & World, Inc., 1970), pp. 178-83; Mifflin Wistar Gibbs, Shadow and Light: An Autobiography (Washington, D.C.: n.p., 1902), pp. 175-76.

[3] New York Globe, September 15, 29, 1883, p. 1.

[4] Loren Miller, The Petitioners: The Story of the Supreme Court of the United States and the Negro (New York: Random House, 1966), pp. 136-47; Alfred H. Kelly & Winifred A. Harbison, The American Constitution: Its Origins and Development (New York: W. W. Norton & Co., 1955), pp. 489-90.

[5] W. E. Burghardt Du Bois, Black Reconstruction (New York: Harcourt, Brace and Co., 1935), pp. 690-92.

[6] Edwin S. Redkey, ed., Respect Black: The Writings and Speeches of Henry McNeal Turner (New York: Arno Press and the New York Times, 1971), p. 60; Frederick Douglass, Life and Times of Frederick Douglass (New York: Collier, 1962), p. 540.

[7] Charles T. Gorham, Robert G. Ingersoll (London: Watts & Co., 1921), p. 7; Eva Ingersoll Wakefield, ed., The Letters Of Robert G. Ingersoll (New York: Philosophical Library, 1951), pp. 181, 687; New York Globe, November 24, 1883, p. 1.

[8] For one such meeting see Peter Gilbert, ed., The Selected Writings of John Edward Bruce: Militant Black Journalist (New York: Arno Press and the New York Times, 1971), p. 19.

[9] New York Globe, December 15, 1883, p. 1; January 5; February 16; March 15, 1884, p. 1; Valeria W. Weaver, "The Failure of Civil Rights, 1883, and Its Repercussions," Journal of Negro History, 54 (October, 1969), 368-82.

[10] New York Globe, February 16, 23, March 1, 8, May 3, 1884.

[11] Ibid., May 3, p. 2, 4.

[12] New York Freeman, July 4, August 8, November 7, 1885; August Meier, Negro Thought in America: 1880-1915 (Ann Arbor: The University of Michigan Press, 1963), p. 70.

[13] New York Freeman, November 28, December 5, 12, 1885, March 13, 1886.

[14] Meier, Negro Thought, pp. 128, 70.

[15] Frederick Douglass, "The Lessons of the Hour," Indianapolis Freeman, March 31, 1894, p. 5.

[16] New York Freeman, February 7, p. 2; November 14, 1885, p. 2; New York Age, December 22, 1888, p. 2. Louis Filler, The Crusade Against Slavery, Harper Torchbooks (New York: Harper and Row, 1960), p. 80; New York Age, December 20, 1890, p. 6.

[17] For T. Thomas Fortune's early political thought see his two books Black and White: Land, Labor, and Politics in the South (New York: Fords, Howard & Hulbert, 1884); The Negro in Politics (New York: Ogilive & Rowntree, 1885); and the editorials in the New York Globe. For an analysis of the Afro-American League and Fortune's change in attitude see Emma Lou Thornbrough, "The National Afro-American League: 1887-1908," Journal of Southern History, 17 (November, 1961), 494-512; T. Thomas Fortune, "A Proposed Afro-American National League," New York Freeman, May 28, 1887, p. 1. This first statement by Fortune places the need to suppress mobs clearly at the top of the list of things needing done.

[18] New York Freeman, July 9, 1887, p. 1.

[19] Ibid., June 6, September 10, 1887, p. 2.

[20] Leslie H. Fishel, Jr., and Benjamin Quarles, The Negro American: A Documentary History (Glenview, Ill.: Scott, Foresman, 1967), p. 325; New York Age, November 12, December 17, 1887; February 11, 18, 1888; October 5, November 23, 1889: Each December 1889 and January, 1890 issue of the Age carried numerous stories concerning the organization of locals.

[21] New York Freeman, October 18, 1889, p. 1; The letter was from William E. Matthews, prominent Black banker of Washington. He had just returned from Europe. See I. Garland Penn, The Afro-American Press and Its Editors (Springfield, Mass.: Wiley & Co., 1891), p. 526.

[22] "An Appeal from the National Afro-American Council to set aside a day of fasting as a protest against lynching," New York Tribune, May 4, 1889, cited in Chronicles of Negro Protest, ed. by Bradford Chambers (New York: Parents Magazine Press, 1968), pp. 179-81.

[23] New York Age, November 23, 1889, p. 1.

[24] Ibid., September 7, 1889, p. 2.

[25] Ibid., July 9, 1887, p. 2; November 23, 30, 1889, p. 1; March 9, 1889, p. 2.

[26] U. S., Congress, House, Congressional Record, 51st Cong., 1st sess., 1890, 21 pt. 3: 2039 (mentions disposition of the petition). For Fortune's keynote address see John H. Bracey, Jr., August Meier, and Elliott Rudwick, Black Nationalism in America (Indianapolis: Bobbs-Merrill, 1970), pp. 212-222. For the League's Constitution and Address to the Nation see Fishel, The Negro American, pp. 325-27.

[27] Indianapolis Freeman, September 26, 1891, p. 4.

[28] New York Age, October 3, 1891, p. 2; Robert L. Factor, The Black Response to America: Men, Ideals, and Organizations from Frederick Douglass to the NAACP (Reading Mass.: Addison-Wesley Pub., Co., 1970), p. 126.

[29] New York Age, July 25, 1891, p. 1.

[30] The best known of these cases was Fortune, v. Trainor in which T. Thomas Fortune won a judgment of $1,016.23 arising from the failure of the Trainor Hotel in New York City to serve him, see New York Age June 7, 1890, p. 1; November 14, 1891, p. 2; Indianapolis Freeman, March 31, 1894, pp. 1, 4; Penn. Afro-American Press, p. 535. The Reverend W. H. Heard won $250.00 damages from the Pullman Company after he was forced into a Jim Crow coach July 20, 1891, see New York Age, September 5, 1891, p. 1. See also, for other cases, New York Age October 10, 1891, p. 2; Indianapolis Freeman, October 3, 1891, p. 6; July 22, 1893, p. 4.

[31] Penn, Afro-American Press, p. 551.

[32] Redkey, Respect Black, pp. 57, 145, 159.

[33] Indianapolis Freeman, March 19, 1892, p. 4; August 5, 1893, p. 4; September 30, 1893, p. 2.

[34] Ibid., November 25, 1893.

[35] Ibid., December 9, 1893, p. 4.

[36] Ibid., January 13, 1894, p. 1.

[37] Ibid., April 21, 1894, p. 1.

[38] Indianapolis Freeman, January 13, 1894, p. 1; Redkey, Respect Black, p. 151; New York Age, February 21, 1891, p. 1; for Congressman Cheatham's speech on one of the bills see U. S., Congress, House, Congressional Record, 52d Congl, 1st sess., 1892, 23 pt. 5: 4683-84; New York Age, October 24, 1891, p. 4.

[39] Alfreda M. Duster, ed., Crusade for Justice: The Autobiography of Ida B. Wells (Chicago: The University of Chicago Press, 1970), pp. 116-17; Indianapolis Freeman, March 25, 1892, p. 4; April 8, 1893, p. 4.

[40] Indianapolis Freeman, September 9, 1893, p. 1.

[41] Ida B. Wells was a journalist who was driven from her home in Memphis by a mob angered at her attacks on the rape myth in the Black newspaper, Free Speech. For her career as an anti-lynching pioneer see her three pamphlets: "Southern Horrors: Lynch Law in all its Phases" (1892); "A Red Record: Tabulated Statistics and Alleged Causes of Lynchings in the United States: (1895); and "Mob Rule in New Orleans: Robert Charles and His Fight to the Death" (1900). These have been reprinted as Ida B. Wells-Barnett, On Lynchings (New York: Arno Press and the New York Times, 1969). For Miss Wells's Memphis experience see "Southern Horrors," p. 18.

[42] Duster, Crusade, pp. 117, 121.

[43] Mary Church Terrell, A Colored Woman in a White World (Washington: Ramsdell Publishers, 1940), p. 148; Booker T. Washington, N. B. Wood, and Fannie Barrier Williams, A New Negro for a New Century (New York: Arno Press and the New York Times, 1969), p. 121; Duster, Crusade, pp. 78-81, 117, 121.

[44] Washington, Wood, and Williams, A New Negro, pp. 396-97; for Ida B. Wells in England see Duster, Crusade, pp. 87-223.

[45] Washington, Wood, and Williams, A New Negro, pp. 399-400; Duster, Crusade, p. 282.

[46] Factor, Black Response, p. 114; Chicago Broad Ax, October 15, 1904, p. 1.

[47] Indianapolis Freeman, October 2, 1897, p. 2.

[48] Mary Church Terrell, "The Progress of Colored Women," Library of Congress, Mary Church Terrell Papers, Box 47; Duster, Crusade, pp. 258, 123.

[49] Indianapolis Freeman, July 29, 1893, p. 1.

[50] The riot was lauded by Southern spokesmen as a defeat of a "Black Domination" which never existed. Three per cent of the 1896 legislators were Black. See the Chicago Broad Ax, December 10, 1898, p. 1. For a white view approving the riot see Richard Hofstadter and Michael Wallace, American Violence: A Documentary History, Vintage Books (New York: Random House, 1971), pp. 230-236.

[51] Mrs. Felton was a well-known outspoken white supremacist who led the attack on Professor Andrew Sledd which resulted with his resignation from Emory College in 1902. Sledd had presumed to question the rape myth in the July, 1902 Atlantic Monthly. See Harry V. Warnock, "Andrew Sledd, Southern Methodists and the Negro," Journal of Southern History, 31 (August, 1965), 251-71. See W. Laird Clowes, Black America:

A Study of the Ex-Slave and his late Master (London: Cassell & Co., Ltd., 1891), p. 141, for similar earlier editorials in the Black press that went relatively unnoticed because they did not fit into larger white plans. For the Manley editorial see Chicago Broad Ax, December 3, 1898, p. 1; and Maurine Christopher, America's Black Congressman (New York: Thomas Y. Crowell, 1971), p. 163.

[52] Factor, Black Response, p. 182; Christopher, America's Black Congressman, p. 163; Indianapolis Freeman, November 19, December 3, 1898, p. 1; Chicago Broad Ax, December 31, 1898, p. 1. October 19, 1904, p. 1; Jay Saunders Redding, The Lonesome Road: The Story of the Negro's Part in America (Garden City, N.Y.: Doubleday & Company, 1958), pp. 92-93.

[53] Indianapolis Freeman, July 22, 1893, p. 4; December 5, 1896, p. 4; Meier, Negro Thought, p. 172; Chicago Broad Ax, December 17, 1898, p. 1; Ida B. Wells-Barnett, "The National Afro-American Council," Howard's American Magazine, 6 (May, 1901), 415-18, Library of Congress, Mary Church Terrell Papers, Box 47.

[54] Meier, Negro Thought, pp. 172-74; Factor, Black Response, pp. 128-30.

[55] The fact of continuing organized Southern Black militancy should not be overlooked; for example, there were ten streetcar boycotts in the South from 1898 to 1906. See Meier, Negro Thought, p. 175. For the last throes of local Councils see Chicago Broad Ax, May 23, 1908, p. 1.

[56] The American Negro Academy Occasional Papers 1-22 (New York: Arno Press and the New York Times, 1969); William Ferris, The African Abroad: Or His Evolution in Western Civilization, 2 vols. (New Haven: Tuttle, Morehouse, and Taylor Press, 1912); John L. Love. "The Disfranchisement of the Negro," ANA Occasional Papers No. 6.

[57] Indianapolis Freeman, September 8, 1894, p. 1; Chicago Broad Ax, March 16, 1898, p. 1.

[58] Indianapolis Freeman, March 19, p. 1; May 21, p. 4; December 9, 1893, p. 4; Theodore L. Gross, Albion W. Tourgee (New York: Twayne Publishers, 1963), pp. 117-18; George M. Fredrickson, "Introduction," in A Fool's Errand by Albion W. Tourgee, Harper Torchbooks (New York: Harper & Row, 1961), p. xx.

[59] Factor, Black Response, pp. 313-14; Chicago Broad Ax, May 18, 1907, p. 1; Charles Flint Kellogg, NAACP: A History of the National Association for the Advancement of Colored People (Baltimore: The Johns Hopkins Press, 1967), p. 40; Voice of the Negro, 3 (April, 1906), 242-3.

[60] The Southern Society for the Promotion of the Study of Race Conditions and Problems in the South, Race Problems of the South (New York: Negro Universities Press, 1969).

[61] Ibid., pp. 170-77; Silas Xavier Floyd, Life of Charles T. Walker, D.D. (Nashville: National Baptist Publishing Board, 1902), p. 149.

[62] For background on White see Ridgely Torrence, The Story of John Hope (New York: MacMillan Co., 1948), pp. 54-56. For the conference see Voice of the Negro, 3 (February, 1906), 90; 3 (March, 1906), 175-76; Meier, Negro Thought, p. 222.

[63] Chicago Broad Ax, October 6, 1906, p. 2.

[64] Ibid., October 6, 1906, pp. 1-2; Voice of the Negro, 3 (November, 1906), p. 470; Crisis, 5 (December, 1912), 72; William P. Pickett, The Negro Problem: Abraham Lincoln's Solution (New York: G. P. Putnam's Sons, 1909), pp. 195-97; Hofstadter, American Violence, pp. 237-40.

[65] Chicago Broad Ax, September 29, 1906, pp. 1-2; October 13, 1906, pp. 1-2; December 3, 1910, p. 1; Ferris, African Abroad, 2:906 for Southern Sun citation.

[66] Booker T. Washington, The Story of the Negro: The Rise of the Race from Slavery (New York: Doubleday, Page & Co., 1909), vol. 2, p. 107.

[67] Factor, Black Response, pp. 275-76.

[68] W. E. B. Du Bois, The Autobiography of W. E. B. Du Bois: A Soliloquoy on Viewing My Life from the Last Decade of Its First Century (New York: International Publishers, 1968), Ch. 14, "The Niagara Movement,"; Factor, Black Response, pp. 292-306.

[69] Factor, Black Response, pp. 309-10, 319.

[70] As an example, "Uncompromising in his condemnation of lynching, Booker T. Washington was more pliable on other issues," appears in Nathaniel Weyle and William Marina, American Statesmen on Slavery and the Negro (New Rochelle, New York: Arlington House, 1971), p. 275; Booker T. Washington, My Larger Education, (Garden City; Doubleday, Page & Co., 1911), p. 63. Rackam Holt, George Washington Carver: An American Biography (Garden City, N. Y.: Doubleday, Doran & Co., 1943), pp. 210-11.

[71] Washington made the statement about the low status of lynch victims in an interview with the press in Indianapolis. See Indianapolis Freeman, August 28, 1897, p. 4; for white use of Washington's rhetoric see Factor, Black Response, p. 263.

[72] The Voice of the Negro, 2 (March, 1905), 194-95.

[73] Washington's statement in Minneapolis Journal, February 2, 1896 cited in Emma Lou Thornbrough, ed., Booker T. Washington (Englewood Cliffs, N. J.: Prentice Hall, 1969), p. 72; for Garrison statement see Chicago Broad Ax, May 21, p. 1.

[74] S. P. Fullinwider, The Mind and Mood of Black America (Hometown, Ill.: The Dorsey Press, 1969), p. 82; Booker T. Washington, "Chapters from my Experience," World's Work, 21 (November, 1910), 13633-35; "Conference at Tuskegee," Competitor, 1 (April, 1920), 29.

[75] James F. Morton, Jr., The Curse of Race Prejudice (New York: Published by the Author, 1906), p. 27; Tillman statement cited in Thornbrough, Washington, p. 87; Mitchell account in Christopher, Black Congressmen, p. 176.

[76] Washington's 1904 statement is in Voice of the Negro, 1 (April, 1904), 166-67; and Ralph Ginzburg, 100 Years of Lynchings (New York: Lancer Books, 1962), pp. 64-65; Voice of the Negro, 1 (October, 1904), 489. Booker T. Washington, "Is the Negro Having a Fair Chance?" Century, 75 (November, 1912), 46-55.

[77] Jessie P. Guzman, "Monroe Work and His Contributions," Journal of Negro History, 34 (January, 1949), 428-461.

[78] Stephen R. Fox, The Guardian of Boston: William Monroe Trotter, (New York; Atheneum, 1970), p. 78; Factor, Black Response, p. 273.

[79] Leslie H. Fishel, Jr. and Benjamin Quarles, The Negro American: A Documentary History (Glenview, Ill.: Scott, Foresman and Co., 1967), p. 357. For two views of the Niagara movement see "The Significance of the Niagara Movement," Voice of the Negro, 2 (September, 1905), 600-04; and Elliott M. Rudwick, "The Niagara Movement, Journal of Negro History, 42 (July, 1957), 177-200; for the Niagara Movement's "Declaration of Principles," see Francis L. Broderick and August Meier, Negro Protest Thought in the Twentieth Century (Indianapolis: Bobbs-Merrill, 1965), pp. 48-52.

CHAPTER III

POLITICS AND LYNCHING

Most of the nineteenth century political activities in support of the anti-lynching reform were initiated by Blacks. The reformers tried to influence political parties, to influence executives at all levels of government, and to obtain the passage of legislation. The Republican need for Black support insured that the party would at least issue statements opposing lynching. This rhetoric encouraged Blacks to try to influence the Republican party to abandon its equivocation and to implement its promises. In this connection, Blacks were particularly sensitive to presidential attitudes. The development of the Progressive movement in the twentieth century strengthened the reform and brought more whites into the movement. The events associated with World War I increased the significance of the anti-lynching reform to the nation which was seeking unity in order to prosecute the war more effectively.

In the 1880s, the white South argued that the disfranchisement of Blacks would reduce racial violence because whites would no longer perceive Blacks as a threat. Disfranchisement, however, did not bring racial peace. Blacks did not accept the place assigned to them by whites in the post-Reconstruction society, and consequently, disfranchisement only reduced the areas in which Blacks could strive for justice. At the same time disfranchisement increased the role of the white racist-demagogue who encouraged the mobs. The process of disfranchisement which increased the susceptibility of Blacks to mob attacks, was greatly accelerated when the United States Supreme Court overturned most of the Civil Rights Law of 1875 in the decision on the Civil Rights Cases in 1883. After this decision, both lynchings and disfranchisement increased. George Knox, editor of the Indianapolis _Freeman_ noted that each reinforced the other.[1]

The revised Southern constitutions, which were designed to disfranchise Blacks, did not reduce racial violence. In 1898, when the United States Supreme Court ruled in favor of the 1890 Mississippi Constitution, it ignored the use of violence to keep Blacks from the polls and this encouraged other states to follow the example of Mississippi. As Blacks became weaker politically, the penalty for protest increased. Some of the older white patricians expressed surprise that this should be so. William D. Oates, ex-Governor of Alabama, said in 1901 that he could not understand why whites wanted to kill Blacks now that they had been rendered harmless. Congressman Romulus Z. Linney, Republican from North Carolina, speaking against the impending disfranchisement in his state in 1900 said, "In exact proportion as people are deprived of their votes, in that exact proportion you have lynching and assassinations." Francis Grimke, Black militant minister, wrote in 1905, that in the areas where Blacks were disfranchised, "The life of a Negro isn't worth as much as that of a dog. He may be shot down, murdered, strugn up to a tree, burnt to death, by any white ruffian, or band of law-breakers and murderers with impunity. . . . If he goes to law, there is no redress."[2]

Seventeen years after Mississippi had led the way in 1890 to the constitutional disfranchisement of Blacks, Senator James K. Vardaman of Mississippi said that every Black in the state would be lynched if that was what was necessary to maintain white supremacy. Actual disfranchisement by violence, followed by legal and constitutional means, was very effective and led to white political apathy, a one-party, machine-controlled system, and "rotten boroughs." An extreme example of machine control was in the Sixth Congressional District of South Carolina, where the Democrats received 100 per cent of the vote in 1896 according to Congressman George H. White. No Iron Curtain country had such apparent electoral unanimity in more modern times.[3]

Blacks resisted this process of disfranchisement and some became victims of lynch mobs for their temerity. In the mid-1880s, six Blacks were lynched in Texas because they were serving as election officials and resisted white attempts to destroy the ballots. No legal action was taken against any of the lynchers, but Norris Wright Cuney, the Black Republican leader of Texas, was threatened with death for organizing meetings to protest the lynchings. George Swayze, former state senator and Black political leader of East Feliciana Parish, Louisiana, was lynched in 1890 for advising Blacks to vote Republican.[4]

Even after they were barred from state and local political activity in the South, Blacks continued to try to influence the federal government to act against lynching and cheered every evidence of presidential support. The possibilities of anti-lynching reforms would appear to increase at presidential election time as Democrats tried to allay Black fears and as the Republicans made efforts to maintain their hold on Black loyalties. These waves of concern would peak every four years and then break in a foam of rhetoric. Bishop Henry McNeal Turner described this process in 1890 in an open letter to former Senator Blanche K. Bruce, Black Reconstruction leader from Mississippi. Turner wrote: "Mobs have broken open jails by scores and by hundreds, and the lynch-law victims could be counted by the thousands, . . . but beyond a little thunder during the presidential campaigns, nothing has been said or done about it."[5]

President James Garfield might have been more sympathetic toward Blacks than was his successor; he at least consulted with his old friend Albion Tourgee about education for Blacks after his election in 1880. Chester A. Arthur, who became president when Garfield died in September, 1881, supported the policy of excluding Blacks from the political process. When Grover Cleveland was inaugurated in 1885, he assured Blacks that he had no intention of limiting their freedom and chided Calvin Chase, editor of the Washington <u>Bee</u> for stating that a Democratic victory would mean the death of millions of Blacks. Cleveland was correct in the sense that it made no difference which party occupied the White House; each was equally disinclined to protect Blacks from illegal violence. There were more lynchings in Arthur's last full year than in any of Cleveland's first term. Some Blacks blamed the Republican defeat of 1884 on Republican treachery in failing to defend the Black franchise in the South. Others detected a silver lining in the cloud of Democratic victory. Bishop Turner thought the Democrats might reduce the number of lynchings, because, if they did not, "it might recoil upon them and drive them from power." However, there were 579 lynchings during Cleveland's first term as president, so most Blacks welcomed the return of the Republicans under Benjamin Harrison in 1889.[6]

Some Blacks believed the Democratic party held greater possibilities than the

Republican party. A national conference of Blacks endorsed Cleveland in 1888 on the grounds that splitting the Black vote would ease tension in the South. T. McCants Stewart, one of the Black Democrats, issued an appeal for the white men of influence in the South to join hands with the law-abiding Blacks for the suppression of lynching and for the "honor of the South." Stewart said that if the offer was rejected, Blacks would fight back until this coalition was achieved and by self-defense make the cost of lynchings too high for the whites to pay.[7]

Harrison entered the White House after his successful 1888 campaign which included some vague statements about justice for everyone. However, he was careful not to touch on Jim Crow or lynching when he campaigned in the South in 1891. In April 1892, when the campaign was heating up, a delegation of Black leaders met with Harrison to ask for some anti-lynching action. The president advised them to collect the facts on lynching for a year and then give them to him and the public press. He promised to use the material collected to create an anti-lynching public sentiment. Harrison's caution resulted from his awareness of the racist attitudes of many Northerners and his relationship with the lily-white Republicans in the South. The postponement of any statement on lynching until after the election, he believed, would avoid alienating any voters and would enhance his chances of defeating Cleveland.[8]

Not long after he talked to the delegation of Black leaders, Harrison wrote members of the Virginia State Baptist Convention that "lynchings are a reproach to any community." He added, "I am, in a large measure, without the power to interfere for the prevention or punishment of the offenses." He did promise to speak out and make "every effort to arouse the conscience of our people," and support due process in the courts. This turned out to be just one more broken promise and lynchings increased to their all-time peak in 1892.[9]

In his second term, Cleveland was no more inclined to act against lynching than Harrison had been. When Cleveland accepted his party's nomination in 1888, he had promised to "guarantee to our colored citizens all of their rights of citizenship," but he never mentioned the subject of lynching to Congress. During his second term, although he used federal power to break the Pullman strike, Cleveland repeatedly claimed that he lacked the constitutional authority to quell racial strife. He did not even attempt to investigate any of the numerous deaths in the South during the 1892 election when the Democrats used terrorism against the Populists. In the state of Georgia, alone, fifteen Blacks were killed in the election violence.[10]

Cleveland's apathy toward anti-lynching reform in part reflected the success of the emissaries of the New South in winning national acceptance of their views on race relations. Cleveland had considerable contact with these Southern spokesmen. It was not surprising that when T. Alex Beckum, a leading white Democrat in Stamford, Connecticut, wrote Cleveland requesting an anti-lynching statement for use in the 1894 campaign, Cleveland responded with his customary evasiveness. "I am in favor of law and order," he wrote Beckum, "and opposed to mob vengeance in any case. . . . The laws of the land are, or ought to be, sufficient for the protection of any citizen . . . and to punish any crime."[11]

The failure of the Democratic party to free itself from the influence of Southern white racial thought resulted in continued support of the Republican party by most Blacks. The hope which revived among Blacks whenever a new Republican president took office was strong when William McKinley was elected in 1896. McKinley had been outspoken against lynching while governor of Ohio. He praised three men who had lost their lives preventing a lynching, and told the Ohio Assembly in 1896 that "lynchings must not be tolerated in Ohio." This advanced position resulted in part from the fact that Blacks voted in significant numbers to influence elections in Ohio. Ohio also had one of the country's most successful and outspoken Black newspaper, the Cleveland <u>Gazette</u>, which was owned and edited by H. C. Smith. The <u>Gazette</u> had considerable influence on the Black electorate. According to I. Garland Penn, historian of the early Black press, Judge J. B. Foraker "owed his first election as Governor of Ohio more to the <u>Gazette</u> than to any other newspaper, white or colored." Smith was several times elected to the state legislature and has as one of his constituents, Mark Hanna, McKinley's political advisor.[12]

The development of imperialist policies by the United States is closely associated with the presidency of McKinley. The doctrines of imperialism drew support from the white supremacists and, in turn, strengthened the doctrines of white supremacy. When the imperialists argued that the darker peoples in the areas newly won from Spain were not ready for self-rule, the white Southern leaders agreed and said this applied equally to the darker peoples already in the United States. When the Supreme Court decided in the Insular Cases, beginning in 1901, that the new subjects of the United States were not entitled to the protection of the Bill of Rights, the advocates of white racial superiority said that by the same reasoning, the Bill of Rights did not apply to Blacks either.[13]

McKinley supported imperialism and the racist ideology of white supremacy which accompanied it. When he visited Atlanta in 1898, he had nothing to say about the frequent lynchings, although the party platform had contained an anti-lynching plank. This plank was largely the result of the work of Blacks in the National League of Republican Clubs. When this interracial league met in 1897, it was going to ignore the lynching issue, but Blacks from Ohio, with help from D. Augustus Straker, a Black Republican leader from Detroit, were able to force reconsideration and to obtain a resolution stating that lynching was a denial of justice and destructive of good morals.[14]

The Black press was almost one in pressing the claim that Black support of and valorous participation in the Cuban war should be recognized and rewarded by extending the protection of the Constitution to Blacks in the United States. McKinley had encouraged this claim in his first Inaugural when he said, "Lynching must not be tolerated in a great and civilized country like the United States," and "Equality of rights must prevail."[15]

McKinley fully accepted the view of his predecessors that the federal prerogative did not extend to influencing the states to prevent lynchings. This opinion, which had been growing since the Compromise of 1876, became more deeply embedded in the philosophy of the Republican party during the McKinley incumbency. The theory which held that the federal government could not intervene against the interests of the white supremacists to influence the course of race relations was extended to the world of business where a papallel theory was elaborated that the federal and state governments could not act against the corporate interests. The connection between these two paralled theories was not lost on the leaders of the developing trusts. As a consequence, the business leaders, who were also important backers of the Republican party, helped to uphold the white supremacist's vested interest in maintaining a caste society. Both the trusts and white supremacy were strengthened by the laissez faire attitudes at the federal level. At the same time it was also important to the Republicans to keep the Black voter loyal. This contradiction was resolved by deepening the gulf between the party's rhetoric and its practice in race relations. This was only a temporary solution and led to an increase in tensions that were successfully utilized by Blacks later to advance the anti-lynching reform.[16]

The actual Republican attitude toward lynching was illustrated in the reaction to a particularly brutal lynching in Georgia in 1899. Sam Hose, a Black agricultural worker who was charged with rape, was publicly tortured and burned alive before a crowd of thousands of cheering whites. Reverdy C. Ransom, a liberal Black activist, then minister of the A. M. E. Institutional Church in Chicago, financed an investigation of this lynching. The investigation disclosed that Hose's real crime was the killing of his employer in a fight which grew out of a dispute over wages, and the rape charge was only used to obscure the facts. Because of the great size of the crowd viewing the lynching and because of the extreme sadism in the method of execution, this lynching received more publicity than most. Accounts appeared in most newspapers, the journals of opinion, and the religious press. It was also a subject for congressional debate. It is unlikely that McKinley did not know of it, just as it was unlikely that he did not hear of lynchings when he campaigned in the South. Ransom, incensed at high level apathy, asked McKinley to treat such lynchings as he would if Black mobs were killing whites. McKinley did not respond, but in his December message to Congress he dwelt at length on the lynching of Italian nationals in Louisiana but said nothing about Blacks except to make a brief reference to lynching in general. "What I said in my Inaugural Address of March 4," he said, "I now repeat: The constituted authorities must be cheerfully and vigorously upheld, lynchings must not be tolerated." Julius Taylor, editor of the Chicago Broad Ax, reported that McKinley's attorney general remarked shortly after the burning of Sam Hose that it was no concern of the federal government how many Blacks were lynched.[17]

When P. B. S. Pinchback led a delegation of prominent Blacks to the 1900 Republican Convention, they obtained a platform plank supporting the enforcement of the Fifteenth Amendment and the protection of Blacks. This, too, was only rhetoric, and McKinley did not mention the subject in his Second Inaugural or in his last Message to Congress.[18]

Even in death, McKinley was associated with the lynching issue. On September 6, 1901, James Parker, a large and muscular Black, was standing next in line behind Leon Czolgosz to greet McKinley at a reception at the Pan-American Exposition at Buffalo. Parker knocked Czolgosz down before the assassin could fire a third shot into the president, but because he was Black, Parker was not called as a witness and was even excluded from the trial. Czolgosz was tried and convicted, but he was not lynched. The Black press used the trial of Czolgosz to emphasize the racist nature of lynching and to stimulate discussion of the subject by commenting that though many innocent Blacks were lynched, this fate did not befall a white even if he assassinated the president.[19]

The failure of both major parties to oppose lynching led some Blacks to reconsider the possibilities of a third party. Frederick Douglass had been unanimously nominated for the vice-presidency by the 500 delegates of Victoria Woodhull's Equal Rights Party in 1872. No campaign was mounted, but the tradition of Black national candidates was started. C. H. J. Taylor was the leading advocate of a Black third party in the late 1890s. As a distinguished attorney, he had been admitted to practice before the Supreme Court in 1868. He had been an editor in both Kansas City and Atlanta and served a brief term as Minister Resident in Liberia in 1887. Earlier, Taylor had been critical of Reconstruction and had advised Blacks to vote for their sectional interests rather than for the Republican party. He advocated race pride and supported Bishop Turner's 1893 Civil Rights Convention. Like Turner, he also eventually abandoned hope in both parties. In 1897 he said that the Black position was worse than under Grant and pointed out that the Blacks appointed by McKinley were not the leaders of the race, that Mark Hanna's barber had a better chance of getting a job than a Black bishop. Taylor wanted a Black political organization that would extend from a national headquarters down through each state and into each community. By 1897 he was planning to call a convention to meet in 1900 after the Republican and Democratic conventions. Taylor announced that he would then support the better of the two parties. If they were both equally bad, as in the past, he was prepared to advocate a separate ticket. He believed that through such independent political action, Jim Crow, the convict lease, and lynching could be wiped out within ten years. Taylor maintained that if such an organization had existed in time to support the Populists, Populism would have triumphed. There was little support for Taylor's third party, and he died before his plans for a convention in 1900 could be realized. The idea of an all-Black party did not die with Taylor. The National Liberty Party actually did appear in August, 1904, but it was no stronger than the Equal Rights Party of 1872.[20]

The National Liberty Party finally endorsed Theodore Roosevelt for president but nominated George E. Taylor for vice-president. Taylor was born in Little Rock of a free mother and a slave father. He was editor of the LaCrosse (Wisconsin) Evening Star and the Wisconsin Labor Advocate. He was also a thirty-third degree Mason and prominent in the Knights of Pythias. Taylor led the anti-Harrison faction at the 1892 Republican convention and was president of the Negro National Democratic League from 1896 to 1900. He stated that his party aimed to revive the Whig party and that it grew out of the civil and personal Liberty Leagues among Blacks in the South and East. It advocated pensions for ex-slaves, enforcement of the Constitution, and support for the principles of the Declaration of Independence. The October 1904 issue of the Voice of the Negro was banned in parts of the South because it gave the new party some publicity.[21]

The amount of concern the Progressive movement had for Blacks is a matter for debate. Booker T. Washington thought Blacks shared in the Progressive movement, but Black historian Rayford Logan denied this. John Hope Franklin, also a prominent Black historian, took an intermediate position which received support from Dewey Grantham who contended that the progressives supporting imperialism were apathetic to Black problems. Certainly most of the progressive whites who worked with Blacks opposed the United States' picking up the "white man's burden." Theodore Roosevelt, who saw the new imperialism of the United States as a positive good, his his racism from the public until after he had won the 1904 election.[22]

Roosevelt concealed his personal conviction that Blacks lacked "sufficient intelligence and moral vigor" because he valued the support at the polls that Blacks gave him. Mark Hanna and the Republican election analysts were convinced that a solid Black vote made the 1900 victory possible. This was one reason for Roosevelt to temper his racism.

Another reason was the pressure from liberal white Republicans such as Albert Pillsbury, Morefield Story, Thomas Wentworth Higginson, Frank Sanford, Albion Tourgee, and John Milholland, who were in the abolitionist tradition and all staunch opponents of lynchings.[23]

Roosevelt's position on lynching was ambivalent. As governor of New York, he had commuted the sentence of a white man convicted of rape. Two days later, while unveiling a statue of Frederick Douglass at Rochester, Roosevelt spoke at length on the need for swift and drastic punishment of Black rapists. He also advocated punishment for lynchers but expounded more on the crimes of Blacks than the crime of lynching. He urged Blacks to cooperate in the capture and conviction of Black criminals. Roosevelt continued to maintain throughout his life that the Black's worst enemy was the Black rapist, even though he would sometimes acknowledge that 75 per cent of all lynching was for other reasons.[24]

Roosevelt's first Message to Congress was unusually long but did not mention lynching or disfranchisement. He resisted the efforts of historian James Ford Rhodes and Henry Pritchett, president of the Massachusetts Institute of Technology, to work for the repeal of the Fifteenth Amendment, but then neither did he support the efforts of Senators Edgar D. Crumpacker and Thomas Platt to enforce it. Unlike previous presidents who stated that they did not have power to enforce the Civil War Amendments, Roosevelt thought that he did have the power but did not think it wise to exercise it.[25]

In July, 1903, Governor Winfield Durbin of Indiana ordered the militia to fire on a mob attacking the Evansville jail where sixteen Blacks were held, some only for petty theft. Evansville was excited by the recent news of a Black school teacher who was accused of murder and burned at the stake in nearby Belleville, Illinois. A similar fate was planned for the sixteen. Judge Thomas Jones, a Tuskegee-recommended Roosevelt appointee, active in opposing lynching and peonage in Alabama, requested the president to issue an anti-lynching statement. Roosevelt responded with a letter of praise to Governor Durbin, but half of the letter was taken up with the horrors of rape, the need for the swift trial and conviction of rapists, and the need for Blacks to cooperate in the apprehension of Black criminals. In his Annual Message that year, the president noted that it was the rich who escaped justice, and that the law was "easy of enforcement against the man who had no money," yet when Roosevelt wrote Durbin that Blacks should act against their criminals, he ignored the fact that Blacks were largely excluded from the judiciary, the profession of law, police forces, and juries. On the positive side, Roosevelt took notice of the fact that few lynchings were for rape. On the day following the release of the president's letter, John Temple Graves, a spokesman for the New South who shared the views of Henry Grady and Benjamin Tillman, speaking on the Chautauqua circuit, said that white and Black were equally subject to lynching for rape and that lynchings were only for rape. As far as the New South was concerned, the president might as well not have spoken.[26]

Roosevelt's statement opened the door to an extensive press comment on lynchings which resulted in advancing the anti-lynching reform since the following positive points were reiterated: most lynchings were for causes other than rape; sometimes innocents were lynched; and the mob struck at the foundations of law and order. The Voice of the Negro reported in September, 1904 that many newspapers and preachers were opposing lynching, but the editor thought that these voices would relapse to silence after the election. Part of the Black press was critical of the president's statement. The Broad Ax advised

Roosevelt that he was begging the question; instead of writing letters for swift trials, the president should urge Congress to pass legislation to execute everyone involved in a lynch mob, for "that is what will stop lynching."[27]

With the election of 1904 approaching, Republicans made extensive use of this publicity to nourish Black hopes that Roosevelt would increase his commitment to the anti-lynching reform. Because of this and the fact that he kept the patronage door open, Black support of the Republican party continued strong.

The single event which did the most to indicate that Roosevelt had little or no firm commitment to the principle of equal justice for Blacks was his handling of the Brownsville affari. When units of the Black Twenty-fifth Infantry Regiment stationed at Brownsville, Texas, in 1906 were subjected to harrassment and discrimination by the town's citizens, only the soldiers were blamed for a disorder in which one civilian died. A Southern-conducted investigation recommended that three companies be discharged without honor because they were shielding the guilty individuals. Roosevelt had often commented on what he called the problem of Blacks' sheilding their criminals and implemented the recommendation on the day after the 1906 election. Adam Clayton Powell, Sr., pastor of Harlem's largest Baptist Church, responded to this action in the New York Times:

> After suffering all manner of insults and indignities a half-dozen soldiers, it is claimed by the municipal authorities, "shot the town up." The President promised to turn the guilty over to the State of Texas. He knew when he made the promise that within forty-eight hours after they were turned over to the Texas authorities, they would be burned at the stake and their charred bones sold for souvenirs. Under these conditions who can blame them if they did "stand together in a determination to resist the detection of the guilty?"

John T. Campbell, a Civil War veteran living in the Lafayette, Indiana, Soldier's Home, wrote Roosevelt a letter about Brownsville which summed up much of the criticism that was also appearing in the Black press. He said that a citizen of Brown County, Indiana, was almost beaten to death by whitecappers, and Roosevelt should say that if the people of the county do not tell who did it, "They shall all be dismissed from citizenship in the United States . . . without honor." Evidence against the soldiers was inconclusive and there were strong indications that the incident was a frame-up executed by Brownsville whites who were enraged by the sight of Blacks' wearing their country's uniform.[28]

Roosevelt's Message to Congress in 1906 considered the subject of lynching in a manner that did not help the anti-lynching reform. The only departure he made from the standard mythology of the New South was to conclude with a plea for equal justice for Blacks and whites. Henry Grady would have siad that that happy condition already existed. Kelly Miller, Professor of Sociology at Howard University and no radical, said that this message was "calculated to do the Negro more harm than any other State Paper ever issued from the White House." It demeaned the Blacks and at the same time assumed that they had a certain power to control criminals which no other group had. The Voice of the Negro said that the Message was Roosevelt's way of helping the white South hide the fact that lynching was caused by the desire to keep Blacks in slavery.[29]

Roosevelt continued to illustrate his ambivalence about lynching. In 1911, yearning for the White House again, he called for stronger laws against rape but not against lynchers. In the 1912 campaign, he charged the Democrats with brutality towards Blacks and the Republicans with hypocrisy for attacking lynching in the South but doing nothing nothing about the lynchings and race riots in the North. In 1917, Roosevelt criticized President Woodrow Wilson for ignoring the race riot in East St. Louis that summer. He also attacked Samuel Gompers, president of the American Federation of Labor because Gompers blamed the industrialists and the Black labor they were recruiting.[30]

Theodore Roosevelt helped the anti-lynching reform by giving the subject a great deal of publicity. He could have done a great deal more if he had given it honest publicity, but he reflected the prevailing white racism of his time and did not care to rise above it except for the period when he needed the Black vote in the election of 1904. Nevertheless, lynchings declined every year he was in office except for 1903 and 1908.

The election of 1908 placed William Howard Taft in the White House. As Roosevelt's secretary of war, Taft had fully approved his chief's handling of the Brownsville matter. This made some Blacks apprehensive concerning race relations under the new president. Following the election, the Broad Ax predicted an increase in lynching and advised more effective organization among Blacks for self-protection. What little doubt some Blacks might have had about Taft's attitude was dispelled six weeks after his inauguration when he told a Black audience at Biddle University in North Carolina that Blacks should stay in agriculture and not be concerned about political rights. This complete acceptance of caste meant that Taft would also fail to oppose lynching. He saw no inconsistency between the Fifteenth Amendment and disfranchisement and ignored racial violence. When Oswald Garrison Villard persuaded Taft to intercede in behalf of Pink Franklin, a Black South Carolina agricultural laborer who shot a nightrider attacking his home, all Taft would do for an innocent man was to get his death sentence commuted to life imprisonment.[31]

The participation of whites in the anti-lynching reform was closely associated with the trend in the frequency of lynchings. The reform tended to lag, especially among whites, when lynchings were declining, and the complacent presumption was made by many that time would heal all and therefore no effort on their part was required. When lynchings increased, the tendency to despair by those interested in the anti-lynching reform was overshadowed by a heightened determination to reverse the upward trend. These periods in which lynchings increased were also the periods in which the greatest number of whites joined the reform movement.[32]

With the exception of a few small reversals, there had been a fifteen year decline in lynchings from 230 in 1892 to sixty in 1907. This had lulled many whites into thinking the problem would soon vanish. However, in 1908 there was a 66 per cent increase over 1907. Each presidential term after Benjamin Harrison's had been marked by fewer lynchings than the preceding term. Under Taft this trend was reversed and there were more lynchings during his presidency than during Roosevelt's second term. In no year of Taft's incumbency did the number of lynchings drop down to the level of 1907, and the increase in 1908 marked the beginning of a period of several years in which the anti-lynching reform expanded significantly. The period of increasing lynchings before 1893 saw the original organization of the reform as a result of Black initiatives. The increased interest in the reform beginning with 1908 was, in part, due to the increased white participation.

The Progressive period was one in which the belief grew that man was in charge of his destiny. At this time more people began to believe that many of the defects of society were the result of selfishness and stupidity and not the result of the operation of vast, vague, and enigmatic natural forces. The period of the Muckrakers was one of increased questioning of the evils of society. With the questioning, the belief grew that the evils could be controlled. Before the Progressive period, many who thought that lynching was wrong did not think that there was anything they could do about it. During the Progressive period, more people began to believe that lynching was a social problem about which they could do something constructive. Unfortunately, anti-lynching reform was not only one of the last reforms to attract the white progressives, but it attracted fewer than most of the other reforms promoted in this period.[33]

The event which galvanized these progressives into action was the race riot in Springfield, Illinois, in 1908, when eight Blacks were killed (two by lynching) and fifty were injured. Brutal though this riot was, it was far from the worst that the United States had experienced. Its timing and its location gave it unique importance. It came at a time when white progressives were beginning to define lynching as a social problem, and the site had symbolic significance. Not only was Springfield the home of Abraham Lincoln, but lynchings there seemed to prove that the Southern spokesmen were correct in their repeated statements that lynching was a national problem not confined to the South. Some progressives accepted this and set about to create a national organization to deal with it.[34]

The Springfield riot led to the formation of the National Association for the Advancement of Colored People two years later. The NAACP was the single most important organization participating in the anti-lynching reform. It was formed by the union of the Black militants, many of whom had been in the Niagara Movement, and the few white progressives who were disturbed by the Springfield riot. William English Walling, writer, settlement house worker and socialist, was one of the progressives responding to events in Springfield. His now famous article, "The Race War in the North," focused the attention of progressives on the problem of race relations. Similar articles had appeared frequently in response to specific acts of racial violence in the past, but it was the growing white concern over the increase in lynchings in 1908 that made the Springfield riot a landmark.[35]

After 1908, the number of lynchings again began to decline, although it was not until 1913 that the low record of 1907 was broken. As this decline occurred, the rate of recruitment of new people to the reform also declined. However, those who had joined remained active, helped found the NAACP, and prepared the basis for future progress. When lynchings increased during Wilson's second term, white support for the anti-lynching reform also increased and the earlier base of the movement was broadened.

The election of Woodrow Wilson in 1912 was an opportunity to test the theory that Democrats in power could do something about lynching because they were in control in those areas where most lynchings occurred. This idea had been advanced since C. H. J. Taylor advocated in the 1890s that Blacks vote their sectional interests instead of remaining tied to the national Republican machine. The theory proved fallacious. Although president of Princeton for eight years and governor of New Jersey for two, Wilson was by birth, upbringing, and sympathy, a Southern Democrat, but he was able to conceal the extent of his commitment to the caste system until after the election of 1912. Perhaps the history of the period would have been different had a Northern, urban-oriented candidate been selected by the Democratic party. This latter choice had been the one consistently advocated by Black Democrats for decades as they totally rejected the Tillman-Vardaman-Blease wing of their party. Alexander Walters, in his capacity as president of the National Colored Democratic League in 1912, placed a two-page advertisement in the Crisis which urged Blacks to vote for Wilson because only the Democrats could restore their rights in the South. Walters further noted that in the strongly Democratic Sixty-first Congress there had been only two "hate" speeches and that no legislation adverse to Black interests had been passed.[36]

The record of the Wilson administration in the field of race relations is well known. A thoroughgoing white supremacist himself, he chose outspoken racists as advisors. A. S. Burleson, the new postmaster general and leader of the anti-Black cabal in Washington, was publisher of the Harpoon, a Texas racist weekly even more vitriolically critical of Blacks than Vardaman's Weekly. As dispenser of patronage, Burleson saw to it that of the thirty-one most important government jobs held by Blacks in 1913, only eight were filled by Blacks in 1917. This reduction was particularly obvious because it occurred during a period of an expanding federal government.[37]

Oswald Garrison Villard, one of the progressive organizers of the NAACP and publisher of the New York Evening Post tried to interest Wilson in the establishment of a National Race Commission which would have studied the status of Blacks and given publicity to lynching. Wilson was to appoint the Commission, but refused to do so "because," he said, "of the feeling that there is some sort of an indictment involved in the very inquiry itself."[38]

Pressure on Wilson to take some positive action against lynching, even if it were only a public statement of pious platitudes, was unrelenting. In 1916, he dispatched a note to Carranza protesting lawlessness and loss of lives of United States citizens in Mexico, and Du Bois suggested that the same type of note should be sent to the governor of Georgia. As lynchings increased, more and more people pressured Wilson to do something. The bloody East St. Louis riot of 1917 did not outwardly move him, nor did he issue any public statement on lynchings during his first five years in office. Wilson was finally moved to issue a statement because of the growing criticism of the United States by agents of the Central Powers who were repeatedly pointing out the contradiction between the wartime slogans of making the world safe for democracy and the undemocratic race relations. In addition, mob activity was disrupting the national unity Wilson wanted for the war effort. In the guise of patriotism, mobs were attacking citizens of foreign descent, workers, and political dissenters. In May, 1918, the Nation cited over 100 such cases which had occurred since the United States had entered the war in April 1917. The Nation concluded, "Social intolerance, private grudges, industrial tyrannies, political intrigues--all have wrapped themselves in the flag."[39]

The government made several half-hearted efforts to stem the tide of increasing domestic violence. Wilson made a statement July 26, 1918, calculated to reduce the divisiveness which was weakening the war effort. He spoke of the honor of the nation and of democracy. He asked for positive cooperation to end lynching in order to disprove "German lies about the United States." Difficult to evaluate but impossible to ignore was the cumulative effect of the Black protest on Wilson. Several cities held NAACP-sponsored parades in the summer of 1917 in protest of the East St. Louis riot. Ten thousand marched in New York City alone. The following spring, the War Department and the Committee on Public Information called a conference with Black leaders who asked for an end to lynching in return for support of the war effort. The "Close Ranks" editorial by Du Bois in the Crisis was a result of this conference. The editorial advised Blacks to "forget your grievances and stand by your country." Wilson's weak anti-lynching statement and Black patriotism did no good. Lynchings increased further as the fury of the "Red Summer" of 1919 broke upon the country. By that time there were few Blacks who would disagree with James S. Stemons, a Black Philadelphian, who wrote Wilson regarding his failure to reduce lynchings in November 1920, "The verdict of the masses . . . has long been that while you were vigorously preaching one thing, you were, when expediency demanded it, as vigorously practicing the direct opposite."[40]

Neither the unstinting Black support of the war nor the government's ceaseless incantation of "democracy" resulted in any automatic improvement in the Black status. W. S. Scarborough, president of Wilberforce, said that the reason there was no extension of democracy in World War I was because the South was in the saddle. Nevertheless, the war did accelerate changes which altered the patterns of race relations in the United States and set in motion forces which resisted restoration of the pre-war condition of Blacks and augmented the anti-lynching reform. The new mood of the urban Blacks, the Great Migration, and the overseas experience of 200,000 Black troops, all combined to create the "New Negro" who raised the price whites had to pay for the practice of lynching.[41]

Although the South was successful in forcing most Blacks away from the ballot box, they remained an important part of the Republican party machinery there. This factor, combined with the gradually increasing Black vote in the North to create pressure for anti-lynching pronouncements by the Republican party. From 1883 to 1919, the anti-lynching reform movement made efforts to influence all the presidents. It was hoped that both of the major parties would make a contribution to the reform, but greater hopes were placed in the Republican party. When major party interest in opposing lynching was least, some Black interest in a third party appeared. Although not successful in eliminating lynching, these Black pressures on the parties helped to educate the public and the nation's leaders and contributed to the belief that federal anti-lynching legislation was necessary.

FOOTNOTES--CHAPTER III

[1] Indianapolis Freeman, December 14, 1895, p. 4.

[2] Williams v. Mississippi, 170 U. S. 213 (1898); C. Vann Woodward, Origins of the New South: 1877-1913 (Baton Rouge: Louisiana State University Press, 1951), p. 353; John Dollard, Caste and Class in a Southern Town (New Haven: Yale University Press, 1957), p. 216; U. S. , Congress, House, Congressional Record, 56th Cong. , 1st sess. , 1900, 33 pt. 2:1364; F. J. Grimke, "The Negro and His Citizenship," in American Negro Academy Occasional Papers: 1-22 (New York: Arno Press and the New York Times, 1969), 11:80. For lyncher as hero, see Carter G. Woodson, A Century of Negro Migration (Washington: Association for the study of Negro Life and History, 1918), p. 156.

[3] Ray Stannard Baker, Following the Color Line: American Negro Citizenship in the Progressive Era, Harper Torchbooks (New York: Harper & Row, 1964), p. 264. U. S., Congress, House, Congressional Record, 55th Cong. , 3d sess. , 1899, 32 pt. 2:1125.

[4] Maud Cuney Hare, Norris Wright Cuney (New York: Crisis Publishing Co. , 1913), pp. 69-71; Indianapolis Freeman, June 28, 1890, p. 1.

[5] Edwin S. Redkey, ed. , Respect Black: The Writings and Speeches of Henry McNeal Turner (Arno and the New York Times, 1971), p. 79.

[6] George M. Frederickson, "Introduction," in A Fool's Errand by Albion Tourgee Harper Torchbooks; (New York: Harper & Row, 1966), p. xix; Vincent P. De Santis, "Negro Dissatisfaction with the Republican Party in the South: 1882-1884," Journal of Negro History, 36 (April, 1951), 148-159; Vincent De Santis, "The Republican Party and the Southern Negro, 1877-1897," Journal of Negro History, 45 (April, 1960), 71-87; Chase cited in New York Freeman, April 18, 1885, p. 1; Redkey, Respect Black, p. 71.

[7] Indianapolis Freeman, July 28, 1888, p. 1; September 28, 1889, p. 1. This appeal by Stewart was "republished by request," October 5, 1889.

[8] Indianapolis Freeman, April 25, 1891, p. 4; April 30, 1892, p. 1; Mary Church Terrell, A Colored Woman in a White World (Washington: Ramsdell Publishers, 1940), pp. 409-10.

[9] George Sinkler, Racial Attitudes of the American Presidents: From Abraham Lincoln to Theodore Roosevelt (Garden City, N. Y.: Doubleday & Co. , 1971), pp. 277-78.

[10] Indianapolis Freeman, September 18, 1888, p. 2; Sinkler, Racial Attitudes, p. 278; Mary Frances Berry, Black Resistance/White Law (New York: Meredith Corp. , 1971), pp. 114-15; Hanes Walton, Jr. , The Negro in Third Party Politics (Philadelphia: Dorrance & Co. , 1969), p. 94.

[11] Indianapolis *Freeman*, September 22, 1894, p. 4.

[12] Sinkler, *Attitudes*, p. 295; I. Garland Penn, *The Afro-American Press and Its Editors* (Springfield, Mass.: Wiley & Co., 1891), p. 282; Indianapolis *Freeman*, September 19, 1896, p. 5.

[13] Christopher Lasch, "The Anti-Imperialists, the Philippines, and the Inequality of Man," *Journal of Southern History*, 24, (August, 1958), 319-31. Rubin Francis Weston, *Racism in United States Imperialism: The Influence of Racial Assumptions on American Foreign Policy, 1893-1946* (Columbia: University of South Carolina Press, 1972), pp. 37-55.

[14] Chicago *Broad Ax*, December 24, 1898, pp. 1, 4; Indianapolis Freeman, July 31, 1897, p. 2.

[15] For examples see Chicago *Broad Ax*, December 17, 1898, p. 1.

[16] Dewey W. Grantham, Jr., "The South and the Politics of Sectionalism," in *The South and the Sectional Image*, ed. by Dewey W. Grantham, Jr., (New York: Harper & Row, 1967), pp. 45-46.

[17] On the lynching of Sam Hose see Chicago *Broad Ax*, April 25, 1899, p. 1; May 9, 1899, p. 4; June 6, 1899, p. 4; July 7, 1903, p. 1; Outlook, May 27, 1899, pp. 200-201; September 7, 1901, p. 10; *Christian Advocate*, May 4, 1899, p. 693; For justification and defense of the lynchings see Congressman James M. Griggs of Georgia in U. S., Congress, House, *Congressional Record*, 56th Cong.; 1st sess., 1900, 33 pt. 2:1413; NAACP, *Thirty Years of Lynching in the United States: 1899-1918* (New York: Arno Press and the New York Times, 1969), pp. 12-13; Ralph Ginzburg, *100 Years of Lynchings* (New York: Lancer Books, 1962), pp. 10-21; Alfred Holt Stone, *Studies in the American Race Problem* (New York: Doubleday, Page & Co., 1908), pp. 460-75; Carter G. Woodson, ed., *The Works of Francis James Grimke* (Washington: The Associated Publishers, Inc., 1942), 1:296-7, 308; William Ferris states that Archibald Grimke gave his most eloquent speech at the Boston mass meeting protesting the Hose lynching, see William H. Ferris, *The African Abroad: Or His Evolution in Western Civilization* (New Haven: Tuttle, Morehouse, and Taylor Press, 1913), 2:892. For Ransom's investigation see New York *Age*, June 22, 1899; for his contact with McKinley see Sinkler, *Racial Attitudes*, p. 298; *Broad Ax*, December 9, 1899, p. 1; October 5, 1901, p. 1.

[18] Chicago *Broad Ax*, September 24, 1904, p. 1; December 23, 1899, p. 1; Berry, *Black Resistance*, p. 123.

[19] Washington *Bee*, September 14, 1901, pp. 1, 4; September 21, 1901, p. 1; October 12, 1901, p. 4.

[20] "Frederick Douglass, 1872," The *Liberator*, October 1, 1932, cited in Nancy Cunard, *Negro Anthology* (New York: Negro Universities Press, 1969), pp. 22-24; Indianapolis *Freeman*, September 15, 1888, p. 1; April 27, 1889, p. 1; October 23, 1897, p. 5; December 25, 1897, p. 1; February 19, 1898, p. 4; Chicago *Broad Ax*, July 15, 1899, p. 1; August 6, 1904, p. 1; August Meier, *Negro Thought in America: 1880-1915* Ann

Arbor Paperbacks; (Ann Arbor: The University of Michigan Press, 1966), pp. 32, 36, 51, 82, 128.

[21] Voice of the Negro, 1 (October, 1904), 479, 491.

[22] Alton Hornsby, Jr., In the Cage: Eyewitness Accounts of the Freed Negro in Southern Society, 1877-1929 (Chicago: Quadrangle Books, 1971), p. 7; Dewey W. Grantham, Jr., "The Progressive Movement and the Negro," South Atlantic Quarterly, 54 (October, 1955), 461-477.

[23] Letter Theodore Roosevelt to John Byrne, September 19, 1904 cited in Sinkler, Racial Attitudes, p. 349; Robert L. Factor, The Black Response to America: Men, Ideals and Organizations from Frederick Douglass to the NAACP (Reading, Mass.: Addison-Wesley Pub., Co., 1970), p. 208.

[24] Sinkler, Racial Attitudes, p. 355.

[25] Chicago Broad Ax, December 7, 1901, p. 1; Sinkler, Racial Attitudes, pp. 348-50.

[26] "Civilization at Evansville," Independent, July 16, 1903, pp. 1694-5; Sinkler, Racial Attitudes, pp. 356-58; The Works of Theodore Roosevelt, 16 vol. Presidential Addresses and State Papers (New York: P. F. Collier & Sons, n.d.), pp. 523-28; message to Congress in J. D. Richardson, ed., A Compilation of the Messages and Papers of the Presidents. 20 vols. (n.p.: Bureau of National Literature, 1897), 15: 6858-6889.

[27] Voice of the Negro, 1 (November, 1904), 513; Chicago Broad Ax, August 15, 1903, p. 1.

[28] New York Times, December 18, 1906, p. 5-3; Broad Ax, June 29, 1907, p. 1; Henry R. Pringle Theodore Roosevelt: A Biography A Harvest Book (New York: Harcourt, Brace & World, 1956), pp. 322-27. See also Emma Lou Thornbrough, "The Brownsville Episode and the Negro Vote," Mississippi Valley Historical Review, 44 (December, 1957), 469-83; James F. Tinsley, "Roosevelt, Foraker, and the Brownsville Affair," Journal of Negro History, 41 (January, 1956), 43-65.

[29] Roosevelt: State Papers, 15:351-54; Kelly Miller, Race Adjustment: Essays on the Negro in America (New York: Neale Publishing Co., 1908), pp. 299-300; Voice of the Negro, 3 (December, 1906), 520.

[30] Theodore Roosevelt, "Lynching and the Miscarriage of Justice," Outlook, November 15, 1911, pp. 706-7; Sinkler, Racial Attitudes, p. 358; Roosevelt did offer himself as Republican standard bearer in 1918, see Pringle, Roosevelt, p. 424 and Joseph Bucklin Bishop, Theodore Roosevelt and His Time: Shown in His Own Letters (New York: Charles Scribner's Sons, 1919-1920), 2:431-34. See also Bernard Mandel, "Samuel Gompers and the Negro Workers, 1886-1914," Journal of Negro History, 40 (January, 1955), pp. 34-60. On Roosevelt and Gompers see Crisis, 14 (August, 1917), 164; and Bishop, Roosevelt, 2:431-34.

[32] The large increase was in 1908, before Taft took office. Under Taft there was a reversal of the long term trend of declining numbers of lynchings, by four-year presidential terms, that began with Cleveland's second term. For a convenient table of lynchings per year from 1882 to 1951 see Jessie Parkhurst Guzman, "Lynching," in Racial Violence in the United States, ed. by Allen D. Grimshaw (Chicago: Aldine Publishing Co., 1969), pp. 56-69.

[33] The Progressives who were concerned by the race problem were mostly Northern urbanites more interested in settlement house work than lynching. See Gilbert Osofsky, "Progressivism and the Negro, New York 1900-1915," American Quarterly, 16 (Summer, 1964), 153-68; Allen F. Davis, Spearheads for Reform: The Social Settlements and the Progressive Movement 1890-1914 (New York: Oxford University Press, 1967).

[34] Kellogg, NAACP, p. 9.

[35] Mary White Ovington, The Walls Came Tumbling Down (New York: Arno Press and the New York Times, 1969), pp. 100-103; William English Walling, "The Race War in the North," Independent, September 3, 1908, pp. 529-34; This article led to the National Negro Congress of 1909 which in turn developed into the NAACP. See National Negro Congress, Proceedings (Arno Press and the New York Times, 1969). Ovington, "The National Association for the Advancement of Colored People," Journal of Negro History, 9 (April, 1924), 107-16. James L. Crouthamel, "The Springfield Race Riot of 1908," Journal of Negro History, 45 (July, 1960), 164-181.

[36] Crisis, 4 (September, 1912), 306-07; see also Arthur S. Link, "The Negro as a Factor in the Campaign of 1912," Journal of Negro History, 32 (January, 1947), 81-99; August Meier, "The Negro and the Democratic Party, 1875-1915," Phylon, 17 (Summer, 1956), 173-91.

[37] William B. Hixson, Jr., Moorfield Storey and the Abolitionist Tradition (New York: Oxford University Press, 1972), p. 129; see also Kathleen DeLong Wolgemuth, "Woodrow Wilson's Appointment Policy and the Negro," Journal of Southern History, 24 (November, 1958), 457-471; Henry Blumenthal, "Woodrow Wilson and the Race Question," Journal of Negro History, 48 (January, 1963), 1-21.

[38] Ray Stannard Baker, Woodrow Wilson: Life and Letters (Garden City, N.Y.: Doubleday, Doran & Co., 1931), 4:222-23; for the first publication of the commission plan see Oswald Garrison Villard, "A Race Commission--A Constructive Plan," Nation, April 27, 1921, p. 612.

[39] Crisis, 10 (September, 1915), 226-27; Nation, August 3, 1918, p. 114. Reports sent back to Germany during the war note lynching as proof of lypocritical United States war aims, see Earl R. Beck, "German Views of Negro Life in the United States, 1919-1933," Journal of Negro History, 58 (January, 1963), pp. 22-32.

[40] U.S., Congress, Senate. Mob Violence: Statement of the President of the United States, S. Doc. 272, 65th Cong., 2d sess., 1918; Crisis, 16 (July, 1918), 111. For Du Bois' second thoughts on this position see W. E. B. Du Bois, The Autobiography of W. E.

B. Du Bois: A Soliloquy on Viewing my Life from the Last Decade of its First Century (New York: International Publishers, 1968), p. 274; Stemons cited in Dewey Grantham, "The Progressive Movement and the Negro," p. 472.

[41] Chicago Defender, August 30, 1919.

CHAPTER IV

NATIONAL AND STATE ANTI-LYNCHING LEGISLATION

In addition to attempts to influence national policy through the application of pressure on the political parties and the presidents, Blacks attempted to obtain federal and state legislation that would at least curtail the lynching problem. Efforts at the state level were initiated first and were more successful in the sense that legislation was actually passed and signed. However, the state legislation was seldom enforced and much that had been passed represented an effort to undermine proposals for federal legislation; especially was this true after World War I when passage of the federal anti-lynching legislation appeared possible.

The first congressional proposals concerned with lynching dealt indirectly with it. It was hoped that by the establishment of investigative and study commissions, publicity would be generated which would reduce lynchings. The proposals drew on the experience of the investigations of the racial violence associated with the Ku Klux Klan and the various "riots" related to the overthrow of Reconstruction. As little of immediate practical good came from these earlier studies, the proposals for later commissions were not universally cheered by anti-lynching advocates for some viewed them as election "gimmicks." Even so, others saw the value of the publicity of the earlier studies and supported efforts to initiate more commissions in the realization that even though they would not lead to legislation, they would at least initiate some discussion. On the grounds that all the members of the proposed commission would be Blacks, T. Thomas Fortune supported Senator John A. Logan's bill of 1884 which would set up such a commission. From time to time Logan presented petitions from Black groups supporting his bill, but like all such proposals until 1922, it died in committee.[1]

Thomas E. Miller voiced one of the first complaints against lynching coming from a Black congressman. Miller was born in South Carolina in 1849 and served three terms in the South Carolina legislature before he was elected to Congress in 1888. A fraudulent count kept him from taking his seat until the House of Representatives ruled in his favor just before adjourning in 1890. He was permitted to sit in Congress only from January to March 1891, the last two months of his term. Given five minutes to speak on federal supervision of elections, he said that the most important thing was "the infernal lynch law. That is the thing we most complain of."[2]

On August 3, 1894, Republican Congressman Henry W. Blair of New Hampshire introduced a joint resolution to provide $25,000 to investigate lynching and all alleged rape cases since 1884 which had resulted in unlawful violence against the accused, "by whipping, lynching or otherwise." As such an investigation would undermine the mythology of the New South, it was strenuously opposed by Southern leaders. On four different occasions, Blair presented to Congress petitions of Blacks supporting his Resolution, but it also died in committee.[3]

The first federal anti-lynching bill was introduced by George H. White, Black Republican congressman from North Carolina. White's career paralleled Miller's. White was born a slave in 1852, graduated from Howard in 1877, and was admitted to the North Carolina bar. He served two terms in the state legislature and worked eight years as Solicitor of the Second Judicial District. He was elected to Congress in the Republican-Populist fusion of 1896 and remained there two terms. The disfranchisement of Blacks in North Carolina prevented his election to a third term. Instead of being intimidated by the Wilmington riot of 1898, the device by which the Democrats drove the Republicans from power, White became even more race conscious.

In the 1900 session of Congress, White interrupted a debate on the impending constitutional disfranchisement of Blacks in North Carolina. The Democrats claimed that this action was necessary to end "Black domination" and the fear white women had of Blacks. On this occasion White said: "Not more than fifteen per cent of the lynchings are traceable to that crime [rape] and there are many more outrages against colored women by white men than there are by colored men against white women."[4]

Editorial comments similar to White's remarks had resulted in the suppression of Black newspapers by mobs in Memphis, Atlanta, and Wilmington where mobs had used the editorials as the excuse for pogroms that devastated the Black communities. This particular comment of White's did not go unnoticed. As typical of the Southern response, White read into the Congressional Record, the Raleigh (North Carolina) News and Observer editorial replying to White's statement that rape was charged in only 15 per cent of all lynchings:

> This utterance of White's is sufficient to show the absolute necessity of permanent white rule in this state. It makes plain the fact that the Negro has learned nothing from experience and that he is utterly devoid of all sense. . . . He becomes a menace . . . and a danger to the safety of both races.[5]

White made an eloquent "farewell" speech in Congress on January 29, 1901, which included a plea for his anti-lynching bill which was still languishing in committee despite an organized nationwide petition drive supporting it. He then applied for a federal position and was told that an endorsement from Booker T. Washington would help his application. His appeal to Washington was unsuccessful. Democracy had deteriorated so much in North Carolina after the disfranchisement of Blacks that George H. White and other Black Republicans were driven from the 1904 State Republican Convention with clubs. After his congressional service, White helped found the all-Black town of Whitesboro, New Jersey, worked with the Constitutional League in the Brownsville case, practiced law in Philadelphia, and became a member of the Executive Committee of the NAACP branch there.[6]

In another effort of Blacks to use the legislative process to attack lynching, William A. Pledger, first vice-president of the Afro-American League in 1890, testified in 1902 before a congressional committee considering the establishment of a Negro Study Commission. His testimony held that Blacks "have been lynched simply that their crops might revert to the landlord. You will find instances of that kind in nearly any Black belt of the states South." Senator Jacob H. Gallinger of New Hampshire, speaking in behalf of this Negro Study Commission, introduced lynching statistics into a Senate debate. Senator George F. Hoar of Massachusetts used the occasion to suggest that lynchers be tried in federal courts. Both senators expressed dismay at what they described as the increasing brutality with which the mob victims were tortured.[7]

Although there were no Blacks in Congress from the forced returement of George H. White in 1901 until the election of Oscar DePriest in 1928, a number of bills were introduced in both houses dealing with race relations and lynching. Fifteen measures were introduced from 1901 to 1920 relating to the lynching of foreign nationals, and almost one million dollars was paid out to compensate their dependents. This concern was primarily for Italians and never carried over to Blacks. There was a flurry of interest in Congress in 1915 when it was thought that the percentage of whites among mob victims had gone up startingly. Eight per cent of the persons lynched from 1904 through 1918, excluding the year 1915, were white; in 1915, 45 per cent were white. This increase created concern until it became known that all but six of the forty-nine whites lynched that year were Mexicans or Mexican-Americans. Of these, twenty-six were lynched in Texas.[8]

In this same period--1901-1920--sixteen bills were introduced into the Senate and the House to investigate or to punish those responsible for lynchings and race riots. All of these proposals received support from Blacks and the interracial anti-lynching groups whose effectiveness and impact were slowly increasing. By 1918 some of the proposals were considered with sufficient seriousness to be the subject of legislative hearings, but they all died in committee. It was not until 1922 that a bill on lynching reached the floor of either house for a vote. Practically all of the Black organizations and the Northern-based interracial anti-lynching forces formed a coalition in 1922 to force a vote on the Dyer bill in the House of Representatives. A combination of Republican inaction and Southern Democratic action by means of a filibuster prevented the Senate from voting. The measure was carried over in 1923, but the Senate did not act then, either, and the bill died with the session. Even though the Dyer bill was H.R. 1 in the next session, it did not even come up for vote in the House.[9]

One of the reasons that there was no effective federal action against lynching was the skillful use of the doctrine of "states rights" by the opponents of anti-lynching reform. A part of the price demanded by the South in the Compromise of 1877 was that there should be no federal interference in the police powers of the state. The state alone would deal with all problems of law and order. The tradition developed that the federal government was powerless to enforce due process, or other aspects of the Bill of Rights, if the state chose to violate the Constitution when dealing with its citizens. Rather than give up the struggle because of this unbenign federal neglect, Blacks chose to seek action on the state level.

Some of the militants among Northern Blacks believed that the white South was monolithically opposed to all Black civil rights. It was from this Northern group that the stirring calls for an eye-for-an-eye retaliatory self-defense came. Other Blacks, especially some in the South, saw the whites there as divided, and they hoped that the more moderate whites would curb the more violent racists. Some Blacks occupied a middle position. They held that the white South was divided, but that the better whites needed to realize that their society would be disturbed by Black militant self-defense before such whites could be prodded into acting on their convictions. It was to these Southern whites who could be expected to show sympathy for the victims of the more brutal racism that the Black legislators appealed. Their success was limited, but it was greater than that achieved at the federal level.

All the states had laws on the books which could have been used to protect prisoners and to punish the members of mobs. The fact that such laws were seldom used for these purposes strengthened the arguments of those who believed that not more legislation but enforcement of existing laws was the major need. Many of these early laws were passed during Reconstruction, and subsequent state governments did not improve them. The 1872 Louisiana Constitutiton had a "Hood and Mask" provision patterned after the anti-KKK Act of Congress. This was re-enacted in 1924, but the NAACP review of state legislation in 1931 disclosed that this was all Louisiana had enacted in this area.[10]

One of the first post-Reconstruction attempts to enact state anti-lynching legislation was in Tennessee. S. A. McElwee, a Black delegate to the 1887 legislature, introduced a bill which died in committee. In 1898 Tennessee did provide for the removal of sheriffs who permitted prisoners to be lynched. Thomas Dudley, Memphis correspondent of the Indianapolis Freeman suggested that it would be better if the legislature paid $500,000 to the survivors and a like sum in the way of a fine to the federal government for each lynching. In 1916 the Republicans wished to keep the Black vote without giving Blacks any recognition. To counter this, Republican leader R. R. Church fielded an all-Black ticket in Western Tennessee and used the anti-lynching issue to mobilize support. In 1918 the governor asked the NAACP for help in drafting a measure, but it was not enacted. In 1924, the Church faction in Tennessee was even stronger, and the Blacks stayed and fought the 200 Klansmen who invaded the 1924 State Convention to a bloody draw.[11]

When Georgia passed an anti-lynching law in 1893, Bishop Henry McNeal Turner called for an expression of special thanks to the "noble and Christian-hearted Governor," at the January 1, 1894, Emancipation Proclamation celebrations. However, as enforcement of this law was left to the initiative of the local sheriff, the main beneficiary of the caste system, it was not used. This 1893 law was part of the Democratic campaign led by Governor William J. Northern to deal with the Populist challenge. The Populists had denounced lynch law and were attracting Black support. When fifteen Blacks and several whites were killed in the 1892 election, the Populists began to organize nightriding societies for self-protection. Governor Northern expected two things from this anti-lynching legislation. It would provide a weapon to use against Populist nightriders, and it would counter the Populist's appeal to Blacks and encourage Blacks to look to the Democrats for protection. When the next threat to Georgia's white supremacists came from the World War I migration, this measure was strengthened in 1914 by defining lynching as murder. Governor Hugh M. Dorsey requested that anti-lynching legislation be made more effective by giving the governor authority to remove derelict sheriffs and to send troops even if the sheriff did not request them. Dorsey's term expired in 1921 before he could effect any change, and the new governor, Thomas W. Hardwick, was opposed to any anti-lynching legislation.[12]

The attempts to obtain effective anti-lynching legislation in Texas were no more successful than those in Georgia. In the 1890s while most Black leaders were pressing for legislative and executive anti-lynching action, some believed that there was no way to control lynching by law or decree. Norris Wright Cuney, the Black Republican leader in Texas, belittled the governor's power to act constructively against lynching. Cuney said in 1892:

> There is no power lodged in the Governor to stop lynching. He can call out the militia, and shoot down the mob if they refuse to disperse, but the lynchers do their work quietly and retire to their homes and if the community is in sympathy with them, that is the law. The only way to stop lynching is to build up a healthy public sentiment all over the State, which will condemn it as a crime against the law, humanity and God.

Cuney was opposing Governor James S. Hogg's second term. Although Hogg had declaimed against lynching, he had never acted to oppose it. Hogg's faction of the Democratic party won the election on a "3-C" campaign, against "Clark, Cuney, and Coons." Judge George Clark headed the liberal Texas Democrats who were interested in fusion with Blacks.[13]

When whites did act against violent manifestations of racism, they had the support of Blacks. In 1897 when the sheriff of Palo Pinto County, Texas, organized resistance to a band of 117 Regulators who wanted to drive all Blacks out of the county, Blacks held a mass meeting at Dallas to thank the officers for their law enforcement activities.[14]

Texas passed an anti-lynching law in 1897 which Lawrence D. Rice says reduced the number of lynchings considerably. The number of lynchings did decline in Texas after 1898, but this also was the trend in states which had no legislation. Texas had seventy-five lynchings in the twenty years after the law was passed, but the law was never revoked. One of the more striking failures to use the 1898 law occurred in 1918 when a mob, unable to find George Cabaniss, a Black accused of threatening a white man, lynched his wife and their five sons on June 4 at Huntsville. One congressional witness, recalling her youth in Texas, charged that the Texas Rangers "became themselves instruments of mob rule on many occasions." Some Texans petitioned Governor Samuel Lanham in 1905 to legalize lynching and planned community meetings over the entire state in support of this proposal. The governor said that his oath of office forced him to oppose lynchings.[15]

Isaiah Reed, Black delegate to the South Carolina Constitutional Convention of 1895, introduced a resolution which would empower the governor to call out the state militia to prevent a lynching and to remove a sheriff who did not protect his prisoner. This proposal failed, but another was adopted which would pay $2,000 to the family of each person lynched and remove culpable sheriffs. This Act was never enforced, and in 1899, the governor, in a message to the legislature, proposed that the indemnity be increased to $5,000 and that any sheriff who lost a prisoner to a lynch mob would be removed from office, disfranchised and barred from all future offices. The governor said that the sheriff should be willing to die to defend his prisoner.[16]

The first test of the South Carolina law occurred in 1896 when an effort was made to convict a white physician and his four accomplices who whipped to death a Black and his mother for allegedly stealing from a church a Bible worth $5.00. The Black's wife was also whipped but survived to testify. Her testimony was ignored, and all the defendants were acquitted. In 1922 the state added a provision requiring that a county pay $2,000 to the mob victim's heirs. The State Supreme Court upheld this provision in at least two instances. The law simply stated that it was only necessary to prove that a lynching had taken place in the county, whereupon the judge was required to give a directed verdict against the county. In this way the prejudice of juries was bypassed.[17]

In 1893 the North Carolina State Legislature passed a weak act intended "to protect prisoners confined in a jail." The provisions requiring witnesses of a lynching to testify and granting them immunity to prosecution was upheld in 1908. In a rare exception to the general practice, this law was enforced once in 1918. Governor Thomas A. Bickett used troops to prevent a lynching in Winston-Salem, and fifteen members of the mob which attempted to storm the jail were convicted. Additional anti-lynching legislation was passed in 1921 which waived the requirement that a prisoner had to be present at any hearing on a motion for a change of venue. This was to keep mobs from lynching prisoners to prevent their being moved to areas where a more fair trial was possible.[18]

There was a wave of anti-lynching legislation initiated in the 1890s when the Democratic party was threatened by interracial unity in the South. This wave subsided in the late 1890s. By then Blacks had less political influence and not enough of them voted to influence the state legislators to enact anti-lynching legislation. The most important legislative action between this wave and the next occurred in Illinois where Edward Green, a Black legislator, got his bill passed in 1908 as the state was reeling under the shock of the riots of that year.[19]

Black initiatives in this era had been successful even earlier in Ohio where the passage of an anti-lynching bill was a personal triumph for H. C. Smith, influential Black editor of the Cleveland Gazette, who mobilized Black pressure to support the inclinations of progressive Governor Asa S. Bushnell. This law provided that the county in which a lynching occurred should pay $5,000 to the heirs of the mob victim. The 1897 lynching of Clark Mitchell put the law to the test. A Circuit Court upheld the law in behalf of the heirs of this victim of a mob in Urbana, Ohio, but the state's Supreme Court overturned it.[20]

The next wave of state anti-lynching legislation occurred in the 1920 when Southern society was threatened by the new militancy of the post-World War I Blacks and by the exodus which hurt its economy. To defuse the militancy and stem the migration, the South made some token efforts to improve race relations. One of these was in the area of anti-lynching legislation.

Kentucky was one of the first states to act, passing legislation in 1920. Governor William O. Bradley had asked a special session of the legislature to consider the problem of mobs in 1897, but nothing was accomplished. The governor could not even offer a reward unless a local judge requested this type of action. Governor Edwin P. Morrow, possible heeding President Wilson's 1918 advice, used the militia to suppress mobs. He also refused to reinstate John H. Edgar, jailer of Woodford County, who, in March, 1921, turned the keys of the jail over to the mob which lynched Richard James. Morrow said, "It is the duty of a jailer to resist a mob until he is beaten into insensibility or killed." The Norfolk <u>Journal and Guide</u> said that the South needed good and brave governors like Edwin P. Morrow of Kentucky, Albert H. Roberts of Tennessee, and Thomas W. Bickett of North Carolina, because "they stand for law and order."[21]

The NAACP supported state anti-lynching legislation except where such legislation was a ruse to discredit attempts to obtain a federal anti-lynching law. H. J. Capehart, a Black state legislator of West Virginia, proposed a measure which became law in 1921 with the full support of the state's Blacks and the national NAACP. This law provided for $1,000 fine and a year's imprisonment for all convicted lynchers and a $5,000 fine for any official guilty of negligence. Oliver Randolf, son of a slave, graduate of Wiley College in Texas and the Howard Law School, was active in the NAACP when he introduced anti-lynching legislation in New Jersey which passed in 1922.[22]

By the 1930s some states were still like Florida, where, according to an NAACP consultant, "the word 'lynching' was simply not used in the statutes." Florida had considered anti-lynching legislation in the period of the first wave of state legislation and Governor William D. Bloxham's message to the legislature in 1897 supported such legislation, but it did not pass. A weak law aimed at unlawful assembly was passed in 1914, but like most state legislation, was not used against lynch mobs.[23]

When state action was taken against mob violence, it was due more to the influence of officials who had state-wide responsibilities than it was due to actions and attitudes of the local officials. Those who had the broader perspective of the entire state were quicker than more locally oriented officials to realize that lynching was doing more harm than good. State officials were in a better position to feel the adverse effects of the economic losses that followed when Black workers left for safer climes. Such officials were more exposed to the criticism of the growing anti-lynching reform movement than was the local sheriff, and if they had ambitions for national office, a reputation for being out of sympathy with mob action was helpful. State officials were more subject to the pressures from the manufacturing and financial interests than were the county officials dependent on a largely agricultural constituency. The former were more inclined to consider the value of the reputation of the state as a place of order and stability that would attract outside capital than the more rural local officials. In many instances, however, the state officials were not the most important figures in law enforcement.

The sheriff was a key figure in many of the Southern states because he was independent of the governor who usually did not have a state constabulary which could override a sheriff's inclinations. Alabama and Tennessee were exceptions to this by 1923. The sheriff was often the head of the courthouse ring than ran the county. His friends and relatives had a vested interest in maintaining caste. His pay derived from the fee system and could be as high as $80,000 a year around 1900. This made harassment of Blacks profitable, and his office depended on his playing the role of kingpin of white supremacy. To be "soft" on the race question was usually political suicide. Theodore Roosevelt tried to find a job for a Southern law enforcement officer who had saved a Black from a lynch mob and who had been promptly turned out of office at the next election.[24]

Because of the sheriff's key role, most of the anti-lynching legislative proposals included provisions to remove him from office if he did not actively try to prevent the lynching. Some proposals provided for a fine and imprisonemnt for a derelict official. Proponents believed that these measures would encourage the sheriff to resist the mob, and that he would be actively aided by all those who were dependent upon him. There are enough examples of determined sheriffs thwarting mobs to indicate that they could do so if they wished. In 1888 the Birmingham, Alabama, sheriff killed ten and wounded eleven members of a mob intent on lynching a white charged with murder. Four years later Deputy Sheriff Meredith of Green County, Arkansas, rescued a Black from a mob of fifty by threatening to have the prisoner back or die in the sttempt. The Voice of the Negro saw "hopeful signs in Mississippi," when a sheriff held off a mob in 1904 by threatening to shoot to kill. In 1913 South Carolina Sheriff W. J. White stood off a mob bent on lynching Will Fair, a Black accused of rape. Fair was later tried and found not guilty. After World War I, the opponents of lynching gave considerable publicity to officials who protected their prisoners. By casting them as heroes, the reformers hoped to encourage similar actions by others. The publicity had the additional effect of controverting the myth that no whites opposed lynching. This show of sincerity by officials increased the willingness of Blacks to work with whites in opposing lynching and the added Black interest and pressures helped reform-minded whites to counter the pressures from others who did not want any official action against mobs. One result of this process was that actions by local officials to protect their prisoners became more the rule and less the exception.[25]

Although the legislative process on both the state and national level was dominated by representatives who were apathetic or hostile to the goals of the anti-lynching reform, there were some tentative steps taken in the direction of enactment of laws to curtail lynching. None of the federal proposals were seriously considered before 1922, yet the precedent of suggesting that lynching was a matter for federal legislation was established. Laws were actually passed at the state level but they were seldom enforced, especially in the early period of the reform when few whites were troubled about lynchings. The matter was of such concern to Blacks that whenever they had an opportunity to introduce an anti-lynching bill, they usually would do so. This strengthened the reform because it served to initiate some dialogue on the lynching problem. When the occasional sheriff or governor would use force against the mob, the effect was salutary and emphasized the point, long made by Blacks, that militancy and force would dissuade lynch mobs.

FOOTNOTES--CHAPTER IV

[1] New York *Globe*, February 16, 1884, p. 1; February 23, 1884, p. 2; U. S., Congress, Senate, *Congressional Record*, 48th Cong., 1st sess., 1884, 15 pt. 1:978, pt. 3:2994; pt. 5:4545.

[2] Maurine Christopher, America's Black Congressmen (New York: Thomas Y. Crowell, 1971), p. 113; U. S., Congress, House, *Congressional Record*, 51st Cong., 2d sess., 1891, 22 pt. 2:1216.

[3] U. S., Congress, House, *Congressional Record*, 53d Cong., 2d sess., 1894, 26 pt. 8:8182.

[4] Samuel Denny Smith, *The Negro in Congress: 1870-1901* (Chapel Hill: University of North Carolina Press, 1940), p. 125; U. S., Congress, House, *Congressional Record*, 56th Cong., 1st sess., 1900, 33 pt. 2:1365; Chicago *Broad Ax*, March 18, 1899, p. 1.

[5] U. S., Congress, House, *Congressional Record*, 56th Cong., 1st sess., 1900, 33 pt. 2:1507.

[6] U. S., Congress, House, *Congressional Record*, 56th Cong., 2d sess., 1901, 34 pt. 2:1634-38. Chicago *Broad Ax*, September 24, 1904, p. 1; August Meier, *Negro Thought in America: 1880-1915* (Ann Arbor: University of Michigan Press, 1963), pp. 112, 147, 249.

[7] U. S., Congress, House, *Commission to Enquire into the Condition of the Colored People*, H. Rept. 2194, 57th Cong., 1st sess., 1902, to accompany H. R. 12940; U. S., Congress, House, *Congressional Record*, 57th Cong., 1st sess., 1902, 35 pt. 6:5903, 05.

[8] Congressman L. C. Dyer of Missouri pointed out the high number of Mexicans and Mexican-Americans lynched in 1915. U. S., Congress, House, *Congressional Record*, 65th Cong., 2d sess., 1918, 56 pt. 6:6177.

[9] Robert Lewis Zangrando, "The Efforts of the National Association for the Advancement of Colored People to Secure the Passage of a Federal Anti-Lynching Law, 1920-1940," (unpublished Ph.D. dissertation, University of Pennsylvania, 1963).

[10] Letter, A. P. Tureaud to William Andrews, March 6, 1931, Library of Congress, NAACP papers, Admin. file, C205.

[11] New York *Freeman*, March 5, 1887, p. 4; March 19, 1898, p. 7; *Messenger*, July, 1925, pp. 252-3.

[12] Indianapolis Freeman, January 6, 1894, p. 3; C. Vann Woodward, Origins of the New South (Baton Rouge: Louisiana State University Press, 1951), pp. 259-60. Chicago Defender, July 1, 1921.

[13] Maude Cuney Hare, Norris Wright Cuney (New York: Crisis Pub., Co., 1913), p. 161.

[14] Nation, September 30, 1897, p. 253.

[15] Lawrence D. Rice, The Negro in Texas: 1874-1900 (Baton Rouge: Louisiana State University Press, 1971), p. 250; Charles Flint Kellogg, NAACP: A History of the National Association for the Advancement of Colored People (Balitmore: Johns Hopkins Press, 1967), p. 230. Broad Ax, November 11, 1905, p. 1.

[16] George Brown Tindall, South Carolina Negroes: 1877-1900 (Columbia: University of South Carolina Press, 1952), p. 253-54; Chicago Broad Ax, January 28, 1899, pp. 4; See also Tindall, "The Question of Race in the South Carolina Constitutional Convention of 1895," Journal of Negro History, 37, (July, 1952), 277-303.

[17] Indianapolis Freeman, March 21, 1896, p. 4; on court enforcement see testimony of Walter White, U.S., Congress, Senate, Committee on the Judiciary, Punishment for the Crime of Lynching, Hearings before a subcommittee on the Judiciary, Senate, on S. 1870, 73d Cong. 2d sess., 1934, pp. 19-20; Letter, N. J. Frederick to Oliver Randolph, February 20, 1931, NAACP papers, Admin. file C-204.

[18] Frenise A. Logan, The Negro in North Carolina: 1876-1894 (Chapel Hill: University Press, 1964), p. 187; Immunity to witness upheld see State v. Bowman, 59 SE 74 and American Law Review, 42 (January-February, 1908), 130; Kellogg, NAACP, p. 230; Norfolk Journal and Guide, January 29, 1921, p. 1.

[19] Alfreda M. Duster, ed., Crusade for Justice: The Autobiography of Ida B. Wells (Chicago: The University of Chicago Press, 1970), p. 309.

[20] Chicago Broad Ax, November 19, 1898, p. 4.

[21] Chicago Broad Ax, February 13, 1897, p. 4; American Law Review, 34 (March-April, 1900), 238-39; on the influence Wilson had on Morrow see Competitor, 1 (March, 1920), 3; and Chicago Defender, February 14, 1920; Norfolk Journal and Guide, January 1, 1921, p. 4; March 2, 1922, p. 1.

[22] Norfolk Journal and Guide, April 23, 1921, p. 4; The NAACP particularly supported the New Jersey effort, see NAACP papers, Admin. file C-207.

[23] Letter, S. D. McGill to William Andrews, February 19, 1931, NAACP papers, Admin. file C-205; Indianapolis Freeman, April 24, 1897, p. 4.

[24] George Sinkler, Racial Attitudes of the American Presidents: From Abraham Lincoln to Theodore Roosevelt (Garden City: Doubleday, and Co., 1971), p. 356.

[25] New York *Times*, December 10 (4-2), 11 (4-4), 1888; Indianapolis *Freeman*, June 11, 1892, p. 1; *Voice of the Negro*, 1 (April, 1904), 173; Ralph Ginzburg, *100 Years of Lynchings* (New York: Lancer Books, 1962), p. 85.

CHAPTER V

THE ROLE OF THE PRESS, EDUCATION, AND

THE CHURCH IN THE ANTI-LYNCHING REFORM

One common opinion that influenced the anti-lynching reform throughout was that executive, legislative, and judicial attempts to control lynching would fail if they were not backed up by a popular consensus that lynchings were wrong. In 1883 there was no such consensus among whites. Few whites at that time were even aware that the number of lynchings was increasing, and most of those who were aware regarded the custom as a needed supplement to the official judicial process. Fifty years later the popular consensus had been reversed and the majority opinion had changed to one which encouraged the decline of lynching. Three institutions which contributed to this change were the press, the school, and the church.

The Press

In the 1880s the press was divided on the question of lynching along the same lines that the country was divided. The Black press uniformly opposed lynching, while the white press usually ignored it, excused it, or sometimes encouraged it. The Black press was weak, its readership small, and its editors and printing plants were subject to violence if the protest was too vehement. By the 1890s the larger metropolitan white newspapers started to become more factual in their coverage then developing that lynching was a form of anarchy which could spread to threaten white society if not checked. This idea grew slowly because of the wide circulation of basically false stories of Black crime which presented the mob victim as one who received his deserved punishment. Although opposition in the white press to lynching increased, much of its credibility and effectiveness was lost because it did not challenge the underlying racist assumptions that made lynching possible. In contrast to the general tendency of the white press to support lynching, or at least not to oppose it effectively, was the small but determined Black press which had both Black and white readers.

The Black editors were reformers who were not content with the status of their people. All of them wanted social change and suffered from a dual disability. As reformers, they were ahead of their times and had the problems of acceptance that all reformers have. In addition, they were espousing the reform least popular among whites, the elimination of racism. When the communications revolution created a national market for the reform ideas of the Muckrakers, there was still no equivalent dissemination of the Black critique in the white world.

The Black editors also had a problem getting their message to Blacks. Circulations were small and the editors blamed their financially precarious positions on the fact that the Black community did not support them sufficiently. T. Thomas Fortune thought the "hundreds of thousands of dollars we squander every year." would have been better spent on subscriptions. In 1886 he said that he had to borrow $10,000 a year to keep the Freeman in existence. The Freeman's circulation of 5,000 at that time was one of the sources of his frequent despair; he thought that it should have been 100,000. In the 1890s, George Knox's Indianapolis Freeman's claimed circulation of 10,000 was the largest. Circulation of the Black press remained small until World War I.[1]

The Black editors and publishers saw themselves as the vanguard leading the anti-lynching movement and they took their responsibilities for the advancement of the race seriously. Their awareness of common problems and a common enemy made them the first Black professional group to organize. But once organized, the National Afro-American Press Association went through the same evolution that the Afro-American Council and the National Association of Colored Women's Clubs had gone through. It came to be dominated by the Tuskegee machine, and like the Afro-American Council and the NACW, though it never ceased to oppose lynching, it became more cautious in its protest and more tolerant of Republican policies. John Mitchell, Jr., President of the Afro-American Press Association, and editor of the Richmond Planet spoke of Republican treachery in 1891, but by the early 1900s the organization was an appendage of the National Negro Business League, and no longer an outspoken critic of the Republican party. Like Booker T. Washington, it continued to denounce lynchings as did the regional groups. Ida B. Wells delivered a paper on lynching at the first meeting of the Southern Afro-American Press Association in 1892. The Western Negro Press Association was organized in 1895, and papers on lynching were regularly presented at its conventions.[2]

The fact that the Black press organizations became less outspoken and militant in their opposition to lynching did not mean that individual editors tempered their opposition. In fact, some protested lynching so vehemently that they became targets for attacks by mobs. John Mitchell of the Planet called for the prosecution of the mob which lynched Dick Walker of Prince Edward County, Virginia, in 1886. He then received a warning from one of the mob members, "If you will poke that infernal head of yours in this county long enough for us to do it, we will hang you higher than he [Walker] was hung." That same year the correspondent of the New York Freeman was driven out of Salisbury, North Carolina, by a mob, for denouncing mobs and "civilian ruffians and judicial sneaks," and the editors of the Atlanta Defiance were jailed and fined for what Fortune called, "defending the race."[3]

White violence against the Black press was not uncommon. Jesse Chisolm Duke, editor of the Montgomery (Alabama) Herald lost his position for attacking the rape myth in 1886. Whites used his editorials to drive Black professionals out of Montgomery and to attack a proposal then before the legislature to support higher education for Blacks. When the Atlanta Constitution tried to start a race riot over the appointment of a Black postal clerk in 1889, the editor of the Selma (Alabama) Independent was threatened with death because he wrote that if there was a race war, he hoped all the whites would be wiped out. Mobs destroyed the Memphis Free Speech in 1892 and forced Ida B. Wells to leave the state. One of the acts of the mob in the Wilmington riot of 1898 was to burn out the building housing the Planet. J. Max Barber's Voice of the Negro was driven from Atlanta to Chicago as an aftermath of the 1906 Atlanta riot. These physical attacks on the Black press all followed challenges to the rape myth.[4]

The Black press was the victim of a double standard which left the white press to blame Blacks for all racial trouble but intolerant of Black rebuttals. Washington attorney, Archibald Grimke, in a paper prepared for the American Negro Academy in 1913, said that if a Black editor wrote about whites as whites did of Blacks, the press "will give the grim facts relating to the end of that editor."[5]

Historically, the white press in the United States had functioned to maintain the status quo in race relations. The abolitionists believed that the press sided with or abetted every anti-abolitionist mob. Later, the anti-lynching reformers said that the press also encouraged lynching mobs with stories of Black contentment and criminality.[6] Benjamin Mays, President of Morehouse College, said, "For decades much of the white South argued that Southern Negroes were satisfied with their plight. They said this when lynching was widespread." Mary Church Terrell, a leading Black clubwoman, wrote that the white press always had space for her people's vices and defects but engaged in a conspiracy to keep stories of self-help and progress out of the appers on the grounds they were "controversial propaganda." Speaking of the press support of lynching, P. B. S. Pinchback, Black Republican leader, said, "To justify it at home, and palliate it abroad, the docile, efficient and peaceful Negro was transformed into a demon." J. W. Hood, presiding Bishop of the A. M. E. Church in 1903, charged that in the early 1890s,

> A concerted effort was entered upon to prepare the minds of the American people for the contemplated disfranchisement of the Negro; and to that end, the best writers obtainable were employed to prepare articles for such journals as are willing to publish that kind of matter.

Hood noted that lies repeated became accepted as truth. A. M. E. Bishop James C. Embry was pessimistic about the future because of the newspaper distortions that went as a matter of course with the coverage of lynchings. He said, shortly before he died in 1897:

> The frequent newspaper accounts of lynchings with the prejudicial descriptions of the victim of the mob, and his reported crimes, are fast converting the white women of America into enemies of every Negro man by causing them to regard every Negro as a possible rape-fiend.[7]

An 1889 Mississippi case illustrates this routine distortion by the white press. When two wagons met on a road, the one driven by a Black did not get out of the way of the white driver quickly enough. The white threatened to lynch the Black, who gathered his friends and resisted the mob when it came. Some of the whites were shot and the Blacks escaped, but the mob destroyed the property of the Blacks, including buildings and cattle. This was reported as an occasion where Blacks made a sudden, unprovoked, and murderous attack on innocent whites.

Such press treatment was the rule, not the exception, in the North as well as in the South. The New York _Tribune_ described Blacks who resisted a lynch mob in 1898 as "vengeful assassins." Change came slowly. Herbert J. Seligmann, a member of the editorial staffs of the New York _Evening Post_ and the _New Republic_ before he joined the NAACP staff as publicity director, wrote in 1920 that Blacks were still "at the mercy of brutal and vituperative editors."[8]

Of all the segments of the white press, the one selected for the most criticism by Blacks was the Associated Press. William Ferris charged that it advertised the Black as a criminal and kept silent about his progress. The Indianapolis Freeman said in 1889, "It is about time we were awakening to the vast amount of injury that is being done to us and how we are losing favor with the Northern people." The Freeman attributed this change to the Associated Press which "cooked up" reports. John Dancy, editor of the Star of Zion, told an Emancipation Proclamation celebration in Massachusetts that the Associated Press constantly bolstered the corrupt Democratic party, excused lynching, and vilified Blacks. Fortune thought the election of Benjamin Harrison had led to a resurgence of anti-Black violence in the South:

> A virtual state of terror prevails . . . men are shot down by the score on pretense of a race rising; others are lynched for assault and others are roasted alive. . . . The Associated Press Association, through its lying agents in the South, places the blame on the defenseless Black victims of white barbarians.

Just two months before his death, Frederick Douglass wrote George C. Knox, editor of the Indianapolis Freeman, regarding the bad press Blacks were getting. In speaking of the Associated Press' defense of lynching, he said, "When one lie in its defense had lost its ability to deceive, another is invented." Monroe Trotter, editor of the Boston Guardian, said that the Associated Press was a part of a Southern conspiracy to defame the character of the Black man "in order to render him odious to the white people of the North . . . to better undo the work of Reconstruction."[9]

When Black papers discussed the distortion and suppression of facts that were an integral part of most white coverage of all stories dealing with race relations, especially those tinged with violence, they would call attention of the readers to the fact that the cumulative impression given the whites would produce a transition from initial revulsion toward lynchings to acceptance of the custom. A poem by Alexander Pope in many a Black editor's arsenal was often used to illustrate this.

> Vice is a monster of such frightful mien,
> As, to be hated, needs but to be seen;
> Yet seen too oft, familiar with her face,
> We first endure, then pity, then embrace.[10]

The distortions by the white press were a serious obstacle to the second major Black strategy in the war against lynching. The first, Black resistance, could be achieved despite the white press campaign. In fact, the vilifications strengthened the implementation of this strategy, because as the knowledge grew among Blacks that the white press was not to be trusted when it reported matters of concern to Blacks, so also grew the presumption of the innocence of any Black charged with any crime by the white press, and the sense of injustice deepened with each additional lynching. However, the second major strategy, coalition with whites to oppose lynching, would suffer a severe setback if a campaign such as that conducted by the Associated Press were to succeed. The problem of how to deal with the distortions had to be met. Some Black editors met it head on by denying white charges, some ignored the specifics of the lynchings and generalized on the denial of due process, and the bad result this could have on whites if it spread to the white world. Others vacillated. The Indianapolis Freeman illustrated some of the varied tactics attempted. Originally, its first editor, E. E. Cooper, followed the line of cooperating with what he termed the "good South" and until 1889, indicated that lynching, which he rarely mentioned, was an aberration and not really a built-in feature of Southern life. In the fall of 1889, the Freeman started to publicize the Southern outrages more, and in one of its first detailed lynching stories reached the conclusion that the situation was growing worse. The lynching of one of the leading intellectual and upright Blacks in a Southern town was his evidence. Cooper decided that John Mitchell's Planet was correct in attempting to expose the reasons for lynching. However, additional publicity did not seem to help, either, and the earlier policy of playing down lynching was resumed. When George Knox became publisher of the Freeman, he went through the same cycle of first playing down lynching stories, but by July 1897, he admitted to his readers that this did not seem to help, either, and he began to feature them more often, with stories and illustrations.[11]

Black hopes for assistance in the struggle against lynching, from at least part of the white press, was a rational one which bore fruit. Blacks had not been without white allies in the past, and many whites could agree that lynching was wrong even if they could not go farther into the fields of equal opportunity and brotherhood. I. Garland Penn, the historian of the Black press in this period, divided the white papers into three groups: Friendly, half-friendly, and unfriendly. Much of the "friendly" white press that denounced lynchings did it in such a way as to vitiate the force of the criticism by adding, "as long as Negroes violate white women, there shall be mobs in spite of our denunciations."[12]

The Atlanta Constitution best exemplified the spirit of the New South. Of all the Southern papers it had the largest circulation and the most national influence. Penn was not the only Black to place it in the "friendly" group. In 1896 Bishop William B. Derrick of the A. M. E. Church listed the Constitution as an exception to the rule that "the Southern Press in an engine of great danger" to Blacks. In 1905, the Voice of the Negro gave the Constitution credit for not being blatantly racist, but noted that Clark Howell, the managing editor was silent on lynching then because he was campaigning for office and wanted the votes of the lynchers. E. Franklin Frazier, later recognized as the most prominent Black sociologist, wrote in 1924, "The Atlanta Constitution speaks against lynching occasionally, and poses as a friend of the Negro, but has no real appreciation of Negro manhood." Frazier supported his contention by noting that the Constitution consistently refused to print "Mr." or "Mrs." before the names of Blacks and consistently spoke of "contented darkies."[13]

The Constitution exemplified the basic weakness of the liberal white South's input into the anti-lynching reform. William Skaggs, one of these liberals, writing the same year as Frazier, was at loss to understand why the decades-long campaign of the Constitution had "accomplished nothing" against lynchings. The failure of the liberal white South to admit that lynching was associated with caste, and to realize that no meaningful attack on lynching could be mounted without an attack on the caste system, meant that the white South would always be the weak link in the anti-lynching reform. Its press was unable to undermine the social structure that produced economic, psychological, and sexual benefits to whites.[14]

In the 1890s the metropolitan white newspapers began to reflect the view that lynchings were no longer necessary to maintain a caste society. As caste became imbedded in the law of the land, through Supreme Court interpretations of the Constitution and in the many states codes sanctioning unequal and discriminatory treatment for Blacks, extra-legal enforcement of caste strictures became gradually less necessary. The beneficiaries of the caste system controlled the white press, and they came to realize that lynching weakened the entire structure because it energized opposition that might go on to attack underlying fundamentals. To avoid this, the white press began to attack lynching qua lynching, not as a manifestation of a sick society. As the white press did this, it was encouraged by Blacks who continued to view the elimination of lynching as the first step to general reform. The evolution of the press in several states illustrated this growth of white realization that lynching, a tool to institute caste after Reconstruction, had been replaced later by legal tools which usually functioned quite effectively.[15]

The white press was never monolithic in support of lynching. In addition to its questioning the positive value of lynching as a bulwark of caste, there were politically inspired attacks on lynching in both Republican and Democratic newspapers. The Republicans attacked lynching when and where the Democrats were in power in an effort to hold the allegiance of Black voters. Democratic newspapers published stories indicating that lynching accompanied Republican administrations as well as Democratic ones. Other attacks on lynching appearing in the white press were from Black contributors and from whites who wished to move white society in the direction of more integration with Blacks. Robert Ingersoll, George Washington Cable, Albion Tourgee, and the New England abolitionists were included in this group, some of whom were readers of the Black press.[16]

There were always white subscribers to the Black press. The tradition established by the Black abolitionist papers carried over after the Civil War. A study of the circulation of the Black press in 1904 stated that of the total 118,000 subscribers, 3,000 were white. Many libraries had subscriptions to the Black press and thereby made these publications available to more white readers. The first Black daily, founded in 1882, had a subscriber list that was 80 per cent white. As the anti-lynching movement grew stronger in the progressive period, the circulation of the Black press among whites increased. One factor contributing to this was the greater scope of coverage and interest in general problems and national issues that characterized the Black weeklies. This policy in which the editors took pride had been forced on the Black editors by virtue of the fact that they had a greater portion of their circulation outside the county of publication than the equivalent white weekly. The thesis that lynching was unjust, unchristian, undemocratic and contrary to the Anglo-Saxon juridical tradition was constantly seen by the white readers, and it reinforced their pre-existing tendencies to accept the Black view.[17]

The Black view of lynching also made inroads on the white awareness through its appearance in the white press. One of the criteria I. Garland Penn used in categorizing the white press was its policy with regard to accepting contributions from Blacks. Some of the Northern white papers had Blacks on their staffs and a greater number printed Black materials. The St. Louis Globe-Democrat printed Bishop Turner's remarks of 1883 in which he characterized the decision of the Supreme Court in the Civil Rights cases as "barbarous." Newspapers further North were even more open to Black contributions. Blacks were well aware that the white press was not uniform in its coverage of Black activities. The Afro-American League originally planned to hold its first convention in Nashville but changed the site to Chicago, one of the reasons for this being to get a better white press.[18]

The circulation of Black views in the white world should not be overestimated. The weakness of this current was largely responsible for the slow start of the anti-lynching reform which was over a decade in showing even the first small successes of the 1890s. On the other hand, some interracial dialogue did exist, and the Black editors were initiators of and participants in it. The existence of this dialogue contributed to the early success of the reform and led to the readiness of the progressives to respond to the Springfield, Illinois, riot in 1908.

Before World War I, the white South scarcely noticed the Black press except when the mythology of lynching was attacked by a hometown Black editor. Whites had little understanding of the national distribution of the more important Black newspapers. The Indianapolis Freeman, for example, was distributed by a network of agents in over 500 cities and towns as early as 1891. A white editor might read the local Black newspaper in order to keep abreast of signs of discontent so that he could point with alarm and alert other whites to impending challenges to white supremacy, but most Southern whites who read newspapers, read only those which reflected their own prejudices.[19]

The Great Migration increased awareness of the Black press which was blames for creating discontent among the Black masses in the South. The migration also brought increased awareness of the Black press among Blacks. The Chicago Defender, the largest and most influential Black newspaper affecting the migration, attained a circulation of a quarter million through a network of 2,500 agents, despite extensive Southern efforts to suppress it. The Defender prospered because it expressed the growing militancy of the times.[20]

The urbanization of Blacks resulting from the migration led to great increases in the circulation of the Black press. There were many Black newspapers and magazines by 1920 with circulations exceeding the Indianapolis Freeman's record of 10,000 in the 1890s. The migration also led to more and better coverage of Black activities in the enlarged urban ghettos. Not only did the white press seek subscribers and customers for its advertisers, but it wished to influence the greatly augmented Black electorate. One way to do this was to cover the continuing lynching story more fairly.

Education and the Anti-Lynching Reform

Education and lynching were associated in a dual manner. Whites used lynching to limit education, and Blacks used education to reduce lynchings. The white objection to the education of Blacks was based on the belief that "book learning" made the agricultural work animal discontented with his status and hence a threat to the caste society. Blacks believed that education would remove the stigma of the "dense-brute" stereotype and would obtain for Blacks the respect of whites which would mean the end of lynching. Education was viewed by both Blacks and whites as the key to upward mobility and to the acquisition of property and influence. This in turn was believed to remove the white from the mob-forming rabble and the Black from the rank of the lynchables. To believe this required at least a limited acceptance of the white myths as to why lynching existed. Blacks who did not accept the myths could also see education's contribution to the reduction of lynching, for they argued that education would produce the leaders who would organize the Black masses and inspire them to the necessary opposition to lynchings. They believed education would produce a ministry that was alive to the Social Gospel, that it would produce teachers who would inspire a greater sense of self-worth, that it would produce leaders who could articulate the Black position to other Blacks and also to the white world, and that it would produce lawyers who could fight for justice in the courts.

W. E. B. Du Bois said in 1949, "Of all the civil rights that the world has struggled and fought for, for five thousand years, the right to learn is undoubtedly the most fundamental." The freedmen and their white allies realized this, and one of the first activities of the Reconstruction legislatures was to establish public schools that would be open to all. The education of Blacks, which had been proscribed before the Civil War, was bitterly opposed after the war by those who could not see any new role for Blacks in the society. W. H. Crogman, president of Clark University, said in 1883 that such people felt that it was bad enough to be deprived of their slaves, but to see the freedmen getting an education was simply intolerable, "Hence it is easy to account for the burning of so many schoolhouses, and the cruel and brutal treatment of so many teachers during those early days of Reconstruction." A typical victim was a Mr. Scoby who came to Bostrop County, Texas from Massachusetts in 1873, to teach. A drunken mob came to his home in May, 1874, called him out and killed him.[21]

The close relation between lynching and education may be seen in the alignment of support and opposition to the Blair bill. The socially progressive forces favored this federal aid to education in the 1880s, and the apologists for lynching were the most bitter in attacking the concepts of the bill. Fortune thought it would help to end Southern violence because, under the bill's provisions, "the ignoramus of either race becomes a rare bird." There were many Black-initiated memorials and petitions supporting the Blair bill. Bishop Turner arranged for an address, "National Aid to Education," by the Reverend Charles Walker, to be printed so that a copy could be sent to every member of Congress. The fight for the passage of this bill continued through several Congresses until its final defeat and abandonment in 1890.[22]

The root of the opposition to the Blair proposal was in the South where most of the benefits of the bill would go. There the objection centered around the provision that the funds for education be divided fairly between Black and white children. The de facto disfranchisement achieved through the intimidation that had accompanied the overthrow of Reconstruction enabled the white South to allocate the educational resources in favor of white children. They did not want Blacks educated, even if it meant giving up the prospects of even greater improvements in the education of whites. Educated Blacks were a threat to the caste system. As Governor Joseph F. Johnston of Alabama said: an educated Black would not work for the prevailing wage of six dollars a month. Augustus Straker, Black Detroit attorney, wrote of a Southern senator who counseled whites to "keep the spelling book and the land from the possession of the Negro, if you hope to control him."[23]

Even a slight education could arm a Black worker so that he could resist some of the less sophisticated oppression. Mary McLeod Bethune--Black educator, clubwoman and political figure--was the first member of her family to go to school. She learned to read and cipher quickly, and one day a few months after her formal education began, she accompanied her father on a short trip to the merchant who traditionally bought the Bethune cotton. The bale was weighed as usual, and the merchant said that it was 280 pounds, again as usual. Young Mary's quick eyes had read the scales, and she blurted out that the correct weight was 480 pounds. In this case the merchant laughingly acknowledged his mistake and made the correction, but there was no retroactive adjustment for all the past "mistakes" that her illiterate father had not been aware of. The Bethunes were fortunate. In many areas of the South, any challenge of the white man's record keeping would have resulted in eviction of the Black tenant, whipping of the "sassy" laborer, or in many cases the lynching of the Black worker as an object lesson to others.[24]

Despite all the white-erected obstacles to the education of Blacks, many attended schools where they were inculcated with the Puritan virtues of thrift, work, cleanliness, and morality. These virtues were said to be admired by whites; therefore Blacks who possessed them would be more acceptable to whites and less subject to mob violence. To a certain extent this was true. However, sometimes an upwardly mobile Black was lynched because he refused to play the subservient role assigned by whites, and because he became an economic threat as he became more able to compete with whites. A common remark in the Black press from the late 1880s was that the new generation was too educated to take the treatment handed out to slaves, "that is why so many get killed here in the South." Three aspects of "the treatment handed out to slaves" which were most likely to lead to lynching involved the access of white men to Black women, the failure of whites to pay for Black labor, and the white demand for obsequious deference in all social contacts.[25]

Although there was great Southern opposition, schools for Blacks proliferated with much Northern help. The idea of education for Blacks was most appealing to the Northern philanthropists who, according to Lerone Bennett, Black historian and journalist, were in part salving their consciences, troubled by the abandonment of the Blacks. Bishop Turner conceded that in this area, whites had been the most helpful. He pointed out, however, that education alone did not give manhood. Turner knew that most of the educational opportunities offered Blacks were designed to produce graduates who would accept second-class citizenship and contribute to the economy of the South, but who would not challenge the distribution of the fruits of this economy in any meaningful way.[26]

The difference of viewpoint on the function of Black education was one of the roots of the Washington-Du Bois split. Washington's conception was embodied in the Tuskegee Farmer's Conferences which started in 1890 and were patterned after similar conferences held earlier at Hampton. They were concerned with the means by which the farmer could improve his moral, religious, and economic condition. The conferences were in line with Social Darwinist intellectual currents and tended to place all the blame for their condition on Blacks themselves. These improvements were all things which Washington thought would lead to white acceptance of Blacks. He thought this would reduce lynching immediately and would eventually eliminate the caste aspects of society. Du Bois had no quarrel with this indirect approach, but felt that those who could, should challenge the injustice more directly.[27]

Du Bois's theories on the vanguard role of the Talented Tenth were confirmed by the

Black attorneys who appeared on the scene in increasing numbers from the 1880s. By providing counsel for Blacks who would otherwise be "railroaded" through a trail and on to legal execution, Black attorneys increased their career opportunities and helped to strengthen the confidence of Blacks in the possibility of obtaining justice in the courts. This, in turn, tended to counter the feeling among Blacks that arrest was often tantamount to death in the hands of the law or the lynch mob. Black distrust of the law often had led to resistance to arrest, the death of law officers, and the formation of lynch mobs. The confidence in the courts which Black attorneys helped develop contributed to the anti-lynching reform. S. A. McElwee, Black attorney and Tennessee legislator, believed that "a great deal of injustice to the Negro from courts comes from our lack of competent advocates." R. J. Smith, a Black attorney of Montgomery, Alabama, enlisted the governor's interest in a lynching case where the mob could not find the man they were after and lynched his father instead. Smith said, "This proves the great need for colored lawyers who will sympathize with their race and assist in such and similar matters." Black attorneys could sometimes find employment as counsel for white clients where the latter were being tried for the rape of Black women. One who did so in Baltimore in 1891 was both praised for being nondiscriminatory and blamed for lack of racial solidarity.[28]

The increasing number of educated Blacks made many contributions to the anti-lynching reform movement. The Black professionals began to organize, starting with editors in 1880. Black teachers organized nationally in 1889 and lawyers in 1890. Even in Mississippi, Black attorneys were organized by 1891. In 1893, a Black lawyer's convention sent anti-lynching resolutions to Congress to reinforce the Turner Civil Rights Convention's lynching protests which were arriving in Washington, D. C., at this time.[29]

The educated ministry was one of the most important sections of the Talented Tenth. The ministers not only had great influence in the Black community, but they voiced the protests in terms that whites could understand, and many were in the fore-front of the civil rights struggle. An outstanding example was Francis Grimke, who sometimes was ahead of Du Bois in urging resistance to wrongs. Part of Grimke's influence was due to the fact that he not only was very articulate, but he wrote all of his sermons and made copies of many which were circulated among the Black intellectuals. These sermons were not only critical of lynching and lynchers but were also critical of those who did not forthrightly condemn it. Grimke particularly attacked the white myth that all lynch victims were guilty of rape. His brother Archibald was a member of the American Negro Academy and was also outspoken in his condemnation of lynching.[30]

The inadequate education of the rank and file Black preacher reduced, but did not eliminate, his ability to influence both races. The Messenger believed that an aroused and united Black community was required for progress. It attributed the failure of the Black ministry to achieve this goal to their relatively poor education. The majority of Black clergymen may not have engaged in protest sufficiently to bring the wrath of whites down on their heads, but enough did to constitute a significant trend, illustrated by the Mississippi Black minister who was fined $500 for selling race literature. One of the earliest memories of Shirley Graham, W. E. B. Du Bois's second wife and daughter of an A. M. E. minister, was the sale of the Crisis at the church.[31]

The increase in educational opportunities was greater than the increase in job and career opportunities for the Black graduates; therefore the level of discontent among the Talented Tenth increased, especially in the 1890s. At this same time the pathological social strictures which limited communication between the races were also increasing. Much of this discontent was channeled into the reform movement and helped to overcome the weakness engendered by the lack of interracial cooperation and communication.[32]

The fact that the educated Blacks became the leaders of the Black protest in the United States was attributed by Carl N. Degler, historian, to the absence of the "mulatto Escape Hatch." Degler contrasted the United States with Brazil and stated that Brazil defined as "Negro" only those who were pure Africans. Lighter Blacks, whose phenotype was altered from pure African by an infusion of other genes, did not find their upward mobility as restricted as the darker Blacks. In contrast, the United States defined anyone with an observable trace of any African phenotypes as "Negro," and imposed the same restrictions on all Blacks. As a result, the realization grew among Blacks in the United States, that they all shared a common destiny, that they were all "in the same boat." This meant ultimately that no Blacks could advance in the United States unless all did. This realization contributed greatly to the racial solidarity of the Talented Tenth with the Black masses and kept the educated Blacks interested in the problems of the rank and file. Degler concluded that the "Mulatto Escape Hatch" operated in Brazil to attenuate protest by permitting middle-class Blacks to enter into the mainstream more fully than in the United States. Degler stated that there is no organization in Brazil comparable to the NAACP, that the protest to lynching has been a factor contributing to the general progress of Blacks in the United States, and that struggle, not time, changes things. The legislative sanction of caste, which gained momentum after 1883, did much to increase racial solidarity in the United States.[33]

The militants saw the need for more educated Blacks. William Ferris said that Booker T. Washington was wrong to stand in the way of developing higher education as that disarmed the race for the struggle with the leaders of the New South. At the same time Du Bois threatened the New South with revolution if the Talented Tenth was not encouraged to guide the masses. In a 1902 <u>Atlantic Monthly</u> article, he said:

> And as the black third of the land grows in thrift and skill, unless skillfully guided in its larger philosophy, it must more and more brood over the red past and the creeping, crooked present, until it grasps a gospel of revolt and revenge and throws its new-found energies athwart the current of advance.[34]

Either way, the anti-lynching cause would be advanced. Implied was a choice between an orderly reform led by the Talented Tenth, or a mass uprising.[35]

Education did not make Blacks militant automatically, nor did lack of education make them docile. However, many of the leaders of the anti-lynching reform came from the growing number of Black college graduates who had numbered thirty-three per year in the 1875-1880 period but had increased to 120 per year in the 1895-1900 period. These college graduates, and other Blacks with less education, directly attacked lynching, or indirectly attacked the underlying conceptions of the society which produced the mobs. This was more true of Northern-educated Blacks, but some of those educated in the South also participated in the struggle. The Black teachers of Georgia objected to using Charles A. Smith's *A School History of Georgia*, in 1896 because it accepted all the stereotyped of Blacks. Over 3,000 heard President John P. Hawkins of Kittrell College, North Carolina, "lift the audience off its feet," in 1903 in a demand for equality in education and equality under the law. J. R. E. Lee, President of the National Association of Teachers of Colored Youth, stated in 1905 that one of the goals of education was elimination of mob violence. Students struck at Talladega in 1906 against racial slurs. A Louisiana educator was killed in the early 1900s for advising students to be more than servants. Thomas H. Amos, President of Harbison College, Abbeville, South Carolina, was ordered to resign and leave town or else face death and the total destruction of the college. He had also told his students to aspire. Some Black doctors also became prominent civil rights advocates.[36]

The enemies of education for Blacks were motivated by a desire to defend the caste system and they faced the same dilemma that those opposing other Black advances faced. They resolved the problem of opposing equality, in a society theoretically committed to democracy, by developing the rationalizing mythology that was so useful in defending racism on other fronts. One effort was made to establish that criminality among Blacks was increased by education. Senator Vardaman of Mississippi was eloquent on this point. Many Blacks made great efforts to refute this idea and one of the aims of the Atlanta University studies was to show that the opposite was true. The Law and Order League, an all-Black organization formed in Baltimore in response to the Atlanta Riot of 1906, believed that self-defense required the publication of the information that in twenty-five years only one Baltimore Black high school graduate had been convicted of any offense.[37]

Professor William H. Crogman was an example of the educated Black who devoted considerable effort to the seemingly impossible task of undermining the mythology with facts. He gave many talks dealing with the problem of racial slander by pointing to thousands of Black school teachers and usefully employed college graduates. Such arguments as these did not influence the hard-core white supremacist attitude which was summed up by the Raleigh *News Courier* in 1910: "It is hard to tell which is the worst enemy of the Negro race--the brute who invites lynching by the basest of crimes, or the social-equality hunting fellow like Du Bois." Although the prevalence of this attitude toward education for Blacks declined some, there were many who agreed with Cole Blease, a leading South Carolina Democrat. Blease said in 1925 that the greatest mistake whites ever made was to educate Blacks, because they were created to do only menial labor.[38]

The Church and the Anti-Lynching Reform

By 1883 it was clear that the white church which had supported slavery was to be one of the pillars maintaining the post-Reconstruction caste society. It was also apparent by then that the Black church would use the contradiction between racism and brotherhood to drive in a wedge and split off some white support for the anti-lynching reform. This process of appealing to the white conscience continued for decades with ever-increasing success as the religious institutions learned that segregation would not be disturbed if lynchings became less frequent. By 1933 no organized church failed to condemn officially all lynchings. Throughout the period, however, Reinhold Neibuhr's observation remained correct: "If there were a drunken orgy somewhere, I would bet ten to one a church member was not in it. . . . But if there were a lynching, I would bet ten to one a church member was in it." The white church did not take the lead in denouncing lynching as unchristian and immoral, but did respond to attacks on its basic hypocrisy. Blacks pioneered on the religious front of the anti-lynching reform as they had on other fronts. Their attack was weakened by lack of resources and lack of unity on tactics, programs, and methods; but, as in other areas of Black thought, there was agreement on the goal of ending lynchings. The whites who joined this reform movement for religious reasons were compelled by logic to work with Blacks, and this interracial activity carried over into other fields.[39]

In common with most other Christians of the day, Blacks, after the Civil War, saw the divine hand of God directing the course of history. Had not a war been fought to end slavery? Were not the Emancipation Proclamation and the post-Civil War Amendments to the Constitution proof that a better day was dawning? The belief that God was just and the wicked were punished, was a fundamental religious belief, as was the belief that white western civilization represented the highest political, moral, social, intellectual, and religious level that man had yet achieved.[40]

Blacks generally accepted these beliefs and based much of their criticism of white society on the fact that whites did not put their beliefs into practice. Black leaders called on the wrath of the Lord to smite the apostates. Archibald Grimke put it thus:

> One need not be a prophet to foresee that out of all this injustice and inequality God's avenging angel will come some day with sword, double-edged and deadly with disease and crime, to smite and to blight this land where white people having eyes refuse to see whither all their race injustice is leading.

Many of the accounts of lynching in the Black press conclude with the thought, "America take warning; the Lord God omnipotent reigneth, and He is a just and jealous God."[41] This apocalyptic vision is also reflected in some of the Black literature of the time.

The Black clergy could be divided into three ideological groups: the conservative-minded and often poorly educated shepherds of small flocks of agricultural peasants; the better educated, but still conservative, leaders who rose to control the religious and educational institutions of their denominations; and the more cosmopolitan liberal arts oriented, and basically urban, clergy who accepted the social gospel and had the greatest influence on the anti-lynching reform. Few of the ministers opposed anti-lynching activities, but the first group, largely in the rural South, was in no position to breathe fire and brimstone down on the heads of the mobs, though they were often capable of acts of self-sacrifice and heroism when directly attacked. They did not preach resignation. Oliver Cromwell Cox, Black sociologist, said:

> Probably no one who has seen the Negro preacher in his cabin church of the deep South, marching triumphantly over the King's English amid great surges of "Amen, Amen," and "Yes, Lord," lifting his congregation in repeated affirmations of faith and hope, could fail to realize that these people are far from being resigned in spirit.

Clearly the exception was the Black Baptist minister of Montgomery, Alabama, who in

1897, justified lynching for rape. The prototype of this minority was characterized by Black journalist W. Allison Sweeney as that "bellowing ass, who . . . somewhere in the South, is going up and down the land telling the natives why they should be content."[42]

The group of clergy in the ideological middle shared much of Booker T. Washington's belief in the gospel of wealth as holding the key to the acceptance of Blacks by whites, which would end the lynching problem. Bishop J. J. Moore, of the A. M. E. Zion Church, Bishop B. T. Tanner of the A. M. E. Church, and the Reverend Charles T. Walker, prominent Baptist, are examples of this middle group. At the 1886 National Baptist Convention, Walker, angered by the vehemence of the attacks on the Southern white Christians, acquired a small measure of fame by defending them. He clinched his argument by noting that the whites had recently donated $10,000 for missionary work among Blacks, thus proving their brotherly love. This scene was repeated three years later. In 1899 he served as a vice-president of the International Sunday School Convention of which Hoke Smith, prominent white racist demagogue, was president. Walker certainly did not support lynching, as Smith did, yet his belief in the unfolding of God's plan did not lead him into a position of active opposition to lynching.[43]

The third group of Black clergy furnished the real drive to the religious opposition to lynching. In addition to the tendency of the more militant Black clergy to be well educated, they usually had the support of the richer congregations in the urban centers. August Meier included James D. Corrothers, A. T. Waldron, Sutton Griggs, Reverdy C. Ransom, and Adam Clayton Powell, Sr., in this group, to which many might be added, such as Francis Grimke, Alexander Walters, John H. Sengstacke, Henry McNeal Turner, and R. R. Wright, Jr.[44]

Under the influence of the A. M. E. members of this third group, the A. M. E. Quadrennial Conferences became more outspoken. Somewhat conservative in 1900, by 1908 the Conference protests the Brownsville decision as a "monstrous injustice," and also attacked disfranchisement, lynching, peonage, and the convict lease system. By 1912 the Episcopal address favored outspoken protest against mob violence, and Reverdy C. Ransom, Niagara Movement pioneer, was made editor of the Review. In 1924, reflecting disappointment in the failure of the Dyer bill, the Quadrennial Conference, "the most powerful single body of Negroes in the world" according to the Messenger, advised, "We cannot longer be satisfied with the Republican Congresses meeting year after year and adjourning without passing one protective measure."[45]

The organization of the anti-lynching reform within the Black church got its start in the Northern urban centers. There many local efforts were initiated which gradually worked upward to become national policies later. In 1884, the Black ministers of Washington, D. C., led by the Baptists, held a convention to protest Southern outrages. In 1889, a North Ohio Conference of the A. M. E. Church resolved that if the government would not stop lynching, Blacks must rely on self-defense. The following year, the Philadelphia Annual A. M. E. Conference adopted a similar tone. In Wilmington, Delaware, in 1903 the A. M. E. ministers denounced lynching. As the migration to the North and urbanization increased, cities became even stronger centers of the anti-lynching reform.[46]

In his work, The Mind and Mood of Black America, S. P. Fullinwider stated that two trends were forming at this time, "rebellion against the white man, and a tendency to submit the tenets of fundamentalism to scrutiny." The more militant ministers led in both of these tendencies. One of the fundamentalist tenets was the belief in religious determinism, which was disarming in any struggle against lynching because it left the reform of society to God. The militants, while not distrusting God's intentions, believed that it was up to man to help God shape man's destiny; and as social activists, they condemned those Blacks who would excuse the whites or who sat patiently on the sidelines waiting for the better day to come. Professor Lewis D. Easton, a Black writing in the American Catholic Tribune, did not accept the idea that time, not struggle, changes things. In 1890 he said, 'One of our unfortunate peculiarities is a too forgiving spirit. We need . . . more vindictiveness toward those who do us injury."[47]

The more fundamentalist Blacks in the South used their religious understanding more to endure than to protest. They did not have the option of open defiance to white supremacy that was available to their Northern brethren. Black theologian Joseph R. Washington stated that "insurmountable obstacles" to protest decreed that the ministers accommodate to the caste society. According to James H. Cone, another Black theologian, any other course would have led to the lynching of the pastors and the burning of the Black churches. Accommodation was the only course by which they could protect their people. "Endurance now, liberty later," was the theme of these ministers.[48]

The slaves had faced "insurmountable obstacles" and developed theological beliefs that contributed to their survival. One of these was that they were more Christian then their masters. This led to two contrasting world views, one guided by love, and the other which equated fighting ability with virtue. The implication was that the latter, described by Howard Odum as "grounded in the religious intensity of the New England forefathers to convert or to kill," characterized the white community, whereas the Blacks were guided by love which enabled them to turn the other cheek.[49]

This attitude persisted and even increased while the conditions that gave rise to it were weakening. As the anti-lynching reform developed, inroads were made on the freedom to lynch, but the ministers had acquired a vested interest in an accommodative life style and continued to promote the idea that the Black was naturally meek and long-suffering and was duty bound to endure lynching until such time as God would end it. "We must suffer on," the Southwestern Christian Advocate said, "and be killed a while yet; the end is worth the means; . . . patience, prayer, and faith will conquer all things." Alexander Crummel, organizer of the American Negro Academy, said, "The lynching of the negroes in the South occurs because they, as a class, are degraded." Crummel's just God would not help those who did not deserve it. In June, 1892, the National Baptist Convention refused to pass an anti-lynching resolution, although the white Methodists had done so a month earlier. A survey made by Benjamin Mays revealed that by the early 1900s, less than 4 per cent of the Black ministers taught their parishioners to demand their rights.[50]

This accommodation retarded the development of the Black unity that the anti-lynching reform needed. Whites used accommodative statements of Blacks to deflect the criticism of the white church that came from the liberal branch of the Black church, just as white political figures used Washington's acquiescent rhetoric to disarm the critics of the political status of Blacks. Many of the Black ministers would have done more, but they were perplexed by the same dilemma that frustrated Washington. H. S. Doyle, fraternal delegate for the C. M. E. Church to the A. M. E. 1904 General Conference, explained this dilemma:

> We stand between embittered peoples inflamed by race hatred on the one side and goaded to desperation on the other. The one will strike us down if we attempt to save our people--our own people will strike us down if we attempt to restrain them from retaliation. Between these antagonisms, precarious indeed is our position.[51]

The traditional white view of the white church was that it tended to reflect current racial attitudes rather than to try to mold them. Actually the church was an active supporter of the social milieu that led to lynching, not just a passive supporter of the status quo. John Hope Franklin said, in his presidential address to the Southern Historical Association in 1871, that the white church was the "principal bulwark" against any change in race relations in the South. This Black view is of long standing. Frederick Douglass, speaking of lynching in 1883, said, "On these abuses the pulpit is dumb." John Edward Bruce, widely read Black journalist, wrote in 1891 that the first allegiance of white clergy was to caste prejudice and that white Christianity was a religion of lies, hypocrisy, and "humbuggery." The "humbuggery" was underlined from time to time by headlines in the Black press, such as one in 1901, "5000 Christians in Leavenworth Kansas Burned a Negro at the Stake." At the time of the 1906 Atlanta riot, an article in the <u>Voice of the Negro</u>, entitled, "The Church and the South," expressed the thought held by many Blacks that not only did the white church fail to oppose lynching in this period, but it was an active component of the intellectual climate that supported and encouraged lynching. The author stated, "Much of the blame for the narrowness of the South must be laid to the peculiar stripe of religion which so many Southerners set up as Christianity."[52]

The criticisms of white Christianity went on unrelentingly. Blacks knew that the contradiction between the stated white religious beliefs and the actual racist practice was a source of tension in the white community which Blacks worked unceasingly to heighten. One way this was done was to point out repeatedly that professing Christians lynched. In 1893, the editor of the <u>Christian Recorder</u> asked, "Where and when had the Christianity of the land recorded its protest against mob violence, and lynchings, and outrages?" The Indiana A. M. E. Church Conference of 1895 heard Dr. William B. Derrick speak of the cowardice of white ministers who failed to speak against mobs. The following year, R. C. Morris, president of the National Baptist Convention, said, "A large majority of the Christian people of America are silent upon the evils that we suffer daily." He also warned that the United States, as ancient Babylon, would be weighed in the balance and found wanting. Booker T. Washington criticized the white church in his 1904 anti-lynching statement. "Worst of all," he said, "these outrages take place where there are Christian churches." The Reverend William Jefferson White of the Georgia Equal Rights Movement rebuked the white Baptist Association of Atlanta a month before the 1906 riot. "It has been a distress to me," he said, "to find ministers who are as bitter against the Negro as any politician ever dared to be."[53]

The impact of Black appeals to the white conscience gradually increased. In 1890,

Roman Catholic Archbishop Ireland preached a sermon in Washington, D. C., reflecting the views of Pope Leo XIII, in which the Archbishop said that some congressmen spoke racial nonsence, as all men are equal in the sight of God. John Cardinal Gibbons, of Baltimore, in an article in the <u>North American Review</u> called attention to the lynching of innocents, but weakened his attack by saying, "I admit that there are exceptional times and circumstances when summary executions may be tolerated and condoned."[54]

This was the period of the beginning of the acceptance of the Social Gospel, the religious manifestation of the belief that social problems required collective, not just individual solutions. Walter Rauschenbusch, leading Social Gospel exponent, said repeatedly that it was necessary "to get rid of laws, customs, maxims, and philosophies inherited from an evil and despotic past." Although the Social Gospel exponents were weak in racial theory, they did recognize injustice. The Reverend Josiah Strong criticized Anglo-Saxons for mistreatment of "weaker" races. Washington Gladden in an 1890 Emancipation Proclamation address said, "I can see how the black man has been from the beginning the victim of wrongs unspeakable, at the hands of whites."[55]

The Methodist Episcopal Church North opened the gates to what would later develop into a flood of anti-lynching resolutions, statements, and pronouncements. Because of the work of Albion Tourgee, a prominent Methodist layman, the Northern Methodists passed a resolution condemning the burning to death of two Blacks in 1892. In 1896 the American Baptist Home Mission Board financed a lecture tour by John Hope, a young teacher at Roger Williams University in Nashville, and thus gave him an opportunity to present his views on the need for higher education for Blacks. Hope opposed the Washington view that "mere wealth" would solve any problems. Hope understood that Washington's gospel of wealth would disarm Blacks in the struggle against lynching and other disabilities unless it was leavened with broader concepts of human development and social progress. Hope and the other militant Black leaders who contributed the most to the anti-lynching reform were not the graduates of the agricultural and industrial schools that Washington promoted.[56]

Some churches confirmed the Black belief that whites would oppose lynching even though they were unwilling to take any other action to promote better race relations. The first racial problem to concern the Presbyterians after the Civil War was lynching. They condemned mob actions in 1899 on the grounds that such violence disturbed the social order and undermined constituted authorities. They were then generally silent on the problem until 1919. In 1906 the Southern Baptist Convention condemned lynching because it might lead to anarchy. The statement also contended that Black criminality was the real cause of lynching. The Alabama Baptist published editorials against lynching in 1904 and 1907. The Southern Baptists then joined the Presbyterians in silence. One reason the Methodist Church North was the earliest Protestant denomination to join actively the anti-lynching reform was that it had not become insulated from Blacks to the extent that other denominations had. In 1920, there were 300,000 Blacks with the M. E. Church, and they exerted a constant pressure to Christianize Methodism and the religious institutions Methodism supported.[57]

Many Jews understood prejudice and oppression, and Jewish merchants who aided the freedmen after the Civil War were a particular target for whitecappers and the Klan. Typical of the thought of the more progressive rabbis around the turn of the century was that of Rabbi Joseph Silverman who said in 1899,

> If the state authorities are incapable of putting down lynch law and forcing respect for regular proceedings, then some way must be found for instituting a Congressional investigation into these barbarous practices, and for providing remedial legislation as was done in respect to the Ku Klux Klan immediately after the Civil War.

The lynching of Leo Frank, a Jewish manufacturer in Atlanta, Georgia, in 1915, increased the support of Jews for the anti-lynching reform. This probably received more publicity than any lynching to date and impressed the fact on many, that although most mob victims were Black, some were not. This knowledge tended to strengthen the reform. The lynching of Frank led to the formation of the Anti-Defamation League of B'nai B'rith. B'nai B'rith, a Jewish fraternal organization, was founded in 1843. The Anti-Defamation League was vigorous in opposing all lynchings and cooperated with the NAACP. Charles Kellog found that rabbis and Unitarian ministers were the clergy most helpful to the early NAACP.[58]

The Southern Baptists, Methodists, and Presbyterians had become concerned about lynching around the turn of the century because they believed they were in a period of increasing violence that might lead to social disruptions with consequences that could not be foreseen. When the awareness that lynchings were declining became general, these churches turned to other problems in the early 1900s. The Federal Council of Churches, organized in 1908, went through the same evolution two decades later. It adopted the Methodist's "Social Creed," and like all the white denominations, paid little attention to Blacks until after World War I, although some of the local Councils passed resolutions against the discrimination in the federal government under President Wilson. In 1916 Bishop Alexander Walters joined the executive committee. The Houston riot of 1917 led to an investigation by the Federal Council of the treatment of Black soldiers.[59]

The sharp increase in racial violence and lynching that came to the United States in the "Red Summer" of 1919 moved the Federal Council to increase its anti-lynching activities. In October 1919 the Council issued a "Call to the United States People," which stated, "Communities that have expressed horror over the atrocities abroad have seen, almost unmoved and silent, men beaten, hanged, and also burned by the mob." The "Call" contained an eight-point program for the improvement of race relations. The following month the Federal Council asked each governor to investigate each lynching and make recommendations. Several denominations, including the Presbyterians, Methodists, Baptists, and Congregationalists, spurred by the same violence that moved the Federal Council, made anti-lynching pronouncements in the immediate postwar period. A number of churches followed the lead of the Federal Council and developed interracial committees, pulpit exchanges, and a literature which brought more people into the anti-lynching reform. Once again it proved true that whites moved to improve racial relations by first becoming interested in anti-lynching activities.[60]

When lynchings again began to decline after 1922, the rate at which people joined the reform movement also declined. However, many who had joined, stayed so that when lynchings again increased in the 1930s, the reform had not lost much of the broader base it had acquired in the 1919-1922 period.

In the early 1920s the white church was not yet ready to oppose lynching effectively. One study concluded that it was "quite remarkable that so little concern was expressed." Too many church members still shared the belief that there was nothing wrong with segregation, disfranchisement and the other facets of society that led to lynching. Major Jones of the Gammon Theological Seminary held that the theology of segregation must rationalize lynch mobs.[61]

The evolution of the white Protestant attitudes toward anti-lynching reform may also be seen in the church publications. The Christian Advocate, leading organ of the Methodist Church North, illustrated this development. In 1886, a year of 138 lynchings, mostly in the South, it commented on only one in Illinois. By 1893 it recognized that some mob victims might be totally innocent. By 1896 the Advocate recognized that most lynchings were in the South. It then gradually increased its coverage and condemnation of lynching. It was critical of Wilson's 1918 anti-lynching statement on the grounds that it was too little and too late. The Advocate came out for federal anti-lynching legislation in 1918 as a last resort if needed. The intense racial violence of 1919 disturbed the editors of the Christian Advocate to the extent that they moved to a position forthrightly in favor of federal anti-lynching legislation. Its position weakened, however, as the 1919 riots terminated, and by 1926 it had returned to its 1918 position of only lukewarm support for federal anti-lynching legislation.[62]

In addition to attempts to influence the white churches to join the anti-lynching reform, Blacks also tried to influence the church-related organizations such as the International Sunday School Conventions, Christian Endeavor, the Student Volunteer Movement, the YMCA and the YWCA. These efforts, as with those directed at the parent bodies, bore little fruit before World War I. The change in the attitudes of these religious bodies after the War were not due to the churches' recognition that their earlier attitude was un-Christian as much as it was a continuation of the attitudes expressed by the Presbyterians in 1899 when they stated that lynching disturbed the social order and undermined the constituted authorities. The church was functioning in its role of supporting the state rather than the role of supporting universal application of the Golden Rule.

The Christian impulse in the United States expressed itself in many statements of religious solidarity with the persecuted Christians of other lands. Blacks used this contrast to point up the lack of brotherly love here at home. August Straker, Southern-born Black attorney of Detroit, said in 1894:

> If Christian ministers of the white race would regard lynching as much a sin as drunkeness or theft, some change in public sentiment would soon be evident. But I charge Christianity as practiced, as the apologist for Negro persecution, oppression and discrimination. . . . Armenia is nearer to the Christian heart . . . than the Negro in South Carolina, Georgia, or Mississippi.[63]

This interest in the welfare of those in other countries was at such variance with the interest whites showed to Blacks in the United States, that it only served to underline the callousness of whites to the Black condition. John Edward Bruce said, "It is the refinement of cruelty . . . when these Christian clergy and Christian sentiment of America shuts its holy eyes to the festering scab upon its own body and seeks to heal the sores of other nations." William Pickens, future Field Secretary of the NAACP, told the YMCA Conference in 1914 that the test of Christianity was not how many missionaries could be sent abroad, but what could be done for the ten million Blacks in the United States. In this connection, he said that it was the Christian duty of the good whites to keep the bad whites from lynching. Benjamin Mays said, "Many Black people in this country believe that some white missionaries go to foreign lands to evangelize colored people in order to atone for the way in which Black people are brutalized here in the United States." The Christian Advocate said that lynching statistics put foreign missionary efforts to shame.[64]

While Blacks decried the white Christian impulse to work abroad on the grounds that the whites should first Christianize their own land, Blacks had a positive attitude toward the results that could be obtained by Black missionary efforts in Africa. Bishop J. Milton Waldren, even in 1911, was unshaken in his faith in providential history and saw the Black experience in the United States as preparing the way for the salvation of Africa via Black missionaries from the South.[65]

Blacks who were active in anti-lynching work, often saw a direct connection between their efforts in the United States and the struggle to free Africa from colonialism. Bishop Turner went to Africa in 1898 to help the Black churches which had broken away from the British missions, to organize along A. M. E. lines. Eight years later, the Voice of the Negro reported that in certain parts of Africa, "it now seems as if the Ethiopian Church, a branch of the A. M. E. Church in America, is leading the natives to revolt against the impositions of the white man." An independent Africa, it was hoped and believed, would not be like the United States, but would be truly Christian. The Lagos (Nigeria) Weekly Record expressed this idea in 1898, "The Christianity which he [the Black] has been taught in his exile is a deception and a snare. . . . The American Negro will only learn of God in Africa."[66]

It was believed that a Christian Africa would feed back a humanizing influence to whites in the United States and give more prestige and status to Blacks here. This would be a dual addition to the anti-lynching reform because it would make whites more receptive to the Black demands for equal justice, and it would strengthen the force with which the Black demands could be presented. The Pan-African movement which developed in the early twentieth century hoped to achieve both of these ends.

The positive attitudes toward Pan Africanism continued alongside the attitude that energies devoted to African development were diversionary, that they detracted from the struggle against the evils of society here. Some expressed the concern that it would do no good to make Africa independent and Christian before the United States was Christianized, as the whites would then take the continent back from Blacks' control by force and fraud after Africans had developed the continent's resources.[67]

Black interest in non-Christian religions existed at this time. The interest was slight, but it was there. Some knew that the Black Moslems, captured from among the Hausa and other Sudanese peoples, made very unsubmissive slaves, and that in the Bahia area of Brazil, they had revolted nine times between 1807 and the great rising of 1835. The Chicago Broad Ax, among all the Black newspapers in the United States was probably the most sympathetic to Islam. This paper was established in Salt Lake City in 1895 by

Julius Taylor. Taylor moved it to Chicago three years later, and for the next few years would write long front-page editorials comparing the teachings of Jesus and Mahomet. Of the two, Taylor preferred the doctrine of Islam. Taylor scorned the use of prayer alone in the battle against lynching, "for the Gods only favor those who possess the courage and manhood to stand up and fight for justice and liberty."[68]

The Great Migration was a period of increasing influence of the better educated, urban, militant Black ministers. They were strengthened especially by the growing Black middle class whose members were rejected by the white church. The slow response of the white church to fight for justice and liberty for Blacks was one of the factors contributing to the heightened sense of need for self-defense and racial solidarity among Blacks that characterized the period of the Great Migration. The increase in these two closely related attitudes was directly associated with the growing strength of the anti-lynching reform.[69]

The press, the school, and the church were three institutions which contributed greatly to the changing attitudes toward lynching in the United States. In 1883, most of the white newspapers, schools and churches were committed to the maintenance of a caste society and therefore unable to oppose lynching effectively. Portions of the equivalent Black institutions conducted an unceasing battle to influence their white counterparts, other Blacks, and the general society. These efforts resulted in few changes at first, but they did have some effect, and they laid the basis for later developments. As the states became more interdependent and as regional isolation lessened with the development of the general economy, the Black opposition to lynching became better known and as it did, the anti-lynching reform movement grew.

FOOTNOTES--CHAPTER V

[1] New York Freeman, January 16, 1886, p. 2.

[2] August Meier, Negro Thought in America: 1880-1915, Ann Arbor Paperbacks (Ann Arbor: University of Michigan Press, 1963), p. 127; Indianapolis Freeman, March 28, 1891, p. 1; January 9, 1892, p. 4; Chicago Broad Ax, September 3, 1898; p. 1; October 8, 1898, p. 4; for the Southern Afro-American Press Association see also Clarence A. Bacote, "Some Aspects of Negro Life in Georgia, 1800-1908," Journal of Negro History, 43 (July, 1958), 186-213.

[3] New York Freeman, May 29, 1886, pp. 1-2.

[4] Ibid., August 27, 1887, p. 2; September 3, 1887, pp. 1-2; New York Age, October 29, 1887, p. 1; W. Laird Clowes, Black America: A Study of the Ex-slave and His Late Master (London: Cassell & Co., Ltd., 1891), p. 141. For sequel to "the Duke Trouble" see I. Garland Penn, The Afro-American Press and Its Editors (Springfield, Mass.: Wiley & Co., 1891), p. 303. Concerning Atlanta see New York Age, August 24, 1889, p. 2.

[5] Archibald H. Grimke, "The Ballotless Victim of One-Party Governments," American Negro Academy Occasional Papers 1-22. (New York: Arno Press and the New York Times, 1969) 16:6.

[6] Russel B. Nye, Fettered Freedom: Civil Liberties and the Slavery Controversy (East Lansing: Michigan State College Press, 1949), p. 198.

[7] Benjamin Mays, Born to Rebel (New York: Charles Scribner's Sons, 1971), p. 213; Mary Church Terrell, A Colored Woman in a White World (Washington: Ramsdell Publishers, 1940), p. 230; Indianapolis Freeman, December 25, 1897, p. 2; J. W. Hood, "The Enfranchisement of the Negro No Blunder," Independent, August 27, 1903, pp. 2021-24; Indianapolis Freeman, September 11, 1897, p. 1. New York Age, January 5, 1889, p. 1.

[8] New York Age, December 22, 1888, p. 1; Herbert J. Seligmann, The Negro Faces America (New York: Harper & Bros., 1920), p. 298.

[9] Indianapolis Freeman, September 14, 1889, p. 1; Dancy cited in New York Age, August 31, 1889, p. 2; Fortune on Harrison, Age, September 14, 1889, p. 2; Douglass cited Indianapolis Freeman, December 22, 1894, p. 2; Broad Ax, January 2, 1904, p. 1. See also William H. Ferris, The African Abroad (New Haven: Tuttle, Morehouse, and Taylor Press, 1913), 1:411. Black charges against the Associated Press continued, in 1920 it was "More deadly than the White-Caps of old," see Half Century, 8 (February, 1920), 15; ten years later it was "The Biased AP," see Norfolk Journal and Guide, July 26, 1930, p. 10.

[10] Alexander Pope, Epistle ii Line 217.

[11] Indianapolis Freeman, September 7, 1889, p. 4; July 3, 1897, p. 4.

[12] Penn, Afro-American Press, pp. 498-501; Arkansas Methodist cited in Chicago Broad Ax, November 22, 1919, p. 1.

[13] Indianapolis Freeman, April 18, 1896, p. 4; Voice of the Negro, 2 (August, 1905), 528; Messenger, 7 (June, 1924), 173-77.

[14] William Henry Skaggs, The Southern Oligarchy: An Appeal in Behalf of the Silent Masses of Our Country Against the Despotic Rule of the Few (New York: Devin-Adair Co., 1924), 327.

[15] Frenise A. Logan, The Negro in North Carolina: 1876-1894 (Chapel Hill: University of North Carolina Press, 1964), pp. 186-87; 215-16; Vernon Lane Wharton, The Negro in Mississippi, 1965-1890 (Chapel Hill: University of North Carolina Press, 1947), p. 224; George B. Tindall, South Carolina Negroes: 1877-1900 (Columbia: University of South Carolina Press, 1952), pp. 248-54; Norman B. Wood, The White Side of a Black Subject (New York: Negro Universities Press, 1969), p. 383.

[16] For evidence that some whites read the Black writers see Peter Gilbert, ed., The Selected Writings of John Edward Bruce: Militant Black Journalist (New York: Arno Press and the New York Times, 1971), p. vii; Henry Allen Bullock, A History of Negro Education in the South: From 1619 to the Present (New York: Praeger Publishers, 1970), p. 210; After 1910 the press releases on lynching from the NAACP and Tuskegee reached hundreds of white newspapers.

[17] Broad Ax, March 26, 1904; p. 1; for history of Black dailies see Penn, Afro-American Press, p. 128; one discussion of the coverage was in reply to an attack on the Black press by John R. Lynch, see Indianapolis Freeman, October 19, 1889, p. 5.

[18] Edwin S. Redkey, ed., Respect Black: The Writings and Speeches of Henry McNeal Turner (New York: Arno Press and the New York Times, 1971), p. 60; New York Age, November 30, 1889, p. 1.

[19] Indianapolis Freeman, May 30, 1891, p. 6.

[20] In 1920 the Defender claimed a circulation of 283,571 with possibly five readers per copy, see Roi Ottley, The Lonely Warrior: The Life and Times of Robert S. Abbott (Chicago: Henry Regnery Company, 1955), pp. 138-39.

[21] W. E. B. DuBois, "The Freedom to Learn," Midwest Quarterly, 2 (Winter, 1949), 9-11; W. H. Crogman, "Beneficient Effects of Christian Education," in W. H. Crogman, Talks for the Times (Jennings and Pye, 1896), p. 100; J. B. Cranfill, "The Story of a Mob," Independent, January 24, 1901, pp. 213-14.

[22] New York Globe, March 29, 1884, p. 1; Indianapolis Freeman, June 14, 1890, p. 5.

See Daniel W. Crofts, "The Black Response to the Blair Education Bill," *Journal of Southern History*, 37 (February, 1971), 41-65.

[23] Robert L. Factor, *The Black Response to America* (Reading, Mass.: Addison-Wesley, Pub. Co., 1970), p. 263; D. Augustus Straker, *The New South Investigated* (Detroit: Ferguson Printing Co., 1888), p. 215.

[24] Rackham Holt, *Mary McLeod Bethune: A Biography* (Garden City: Doubleday & Co., 1964), p. 24. On planter discouragement of literacy see Charles S. Johnson, *Shadow of the Plantation* (Chicago: Univeristy of Chicago Press, 1934), p. 129.

[25] Indianapolis *Freeman*, October 17, 1891, p. 1. The census accumulated data on literacy from 1870. The percentage of illiteracy among Blacks declined as follows: 1870, 81.4; 1880, 70.0; 1890, 57.1; 1900, 44.5; 1910, 30.4; 1920, 22.9; 1930, 16.3; see U. S. Department of Commerce, Bureau of the Census, *Negroes in the United States* (Washington: Government Printing Office, 1935), pp. 229-31.

[26] Lerone Bennett, *Confrontation: Black and White* (Chicago: Johnson Pub., Co., 1965), p. 108; Redkey, *Respect Black,* p. 159; For the Northern philanthropists' acceptance of the Southern white concepts of proper education for Blacks see Lewis Harlan, "The Southern Education Board and the Race Issue in Public Education," *Journal of Southern History*, 23 (May, 1957), 189-202.

[27] Meier, *Negro Thought*, p. 122.

[28] Indianapolis *Freeman*, November 23, 1889, p. 1; August 30, 1890, p. 1; July 11, 1891, p. 4; New York *Freeman*, May 30, 1885, p. 4.

[29] Meier, *Negro Thought*, p. 127; Indianapolis *Freeman*, December 7, 1891, p. 4; October 21, 1893, p. 1.

[30] Ferris, *African Abroad,* 2:890.

[31] *Messenger,* 2 (October, 1919), 6; *Half Century*, 8, (June, 1920), 17. Shirley Graham Du Bois, *His Day is Marching On: A Memoir of W. E. B. Du Bois* (Philadelphia: J. B. Lippincott Co., 1971), p. 2.

[32] Indianapolis *Freeman*, October 31, 1897, p. 4. Oliver Cromwell Cox, *Caste, Class, and Race* (Garden City: Doubleday & Co., 1948), p. 435.

[33] Carl Degler, *Neither Black nor White: Slavery and Race Relations in Brazil and the United States* (New York: MacMillan, 1971), Chs. 3, 6; for representative accounts of white persecution and lynching of middle-class Blacks see Indianapolis *Freeman*, September 21, 1895, p. 4; *Crisis,* 12 (May, 1916), 41-2; Norfolk Journal and Guide, June 9, 1917, p. 1; Chicago *Defender*, May 3, 1919, p. 1. Such attacks were motivated by a desire to acquire Black owned property and the felt need to remove role models for other Blacks. The fact racial solidarity between classes has not been greater has been discusses by Black sociologists. See W. E. Burghardt Du Bois, *The Philadelphia Negro*:

A Social Study (Boston: Guinn & Col, 1899), pp. 393-93; E. Franklin Frazier, Black Bourgeoisie (Glencoe, Ill.: Free Press, 1957), pp. 235-38.

[34] Chicago Defender, November 9, 1912; Indianapolis Freeman, February 1, 1890, p. 2.

[35] Ferris, African Abroad, 1:365; W. E. B. Du Bois, "Of the Training of Black Men," Atlantic Monthly, 90 (September, 1902), 289-97.

[36] Francis L. Broderick, W. E. B. Du Bois: Negro Leader in a Time of Crisis (Stanford: Stanford University Press, 1959), p. 114; Du Bois, "Training"; Indianapolis Freeman, August 1, 1898, p. 1; Broad Ax, November 14, 1903, p. 1; Voice of the Negro 2 (June, 1905), 381; 3 (March, 1906), 166; Ferris African Abroad, 1:413-14; Eugene P. Link, "The Civil Rights Activities of Three Great Negro Physicians, 1840-1940," Journal of Negro History, 52 (July, 1947), 169-84.

[37] For a typical white view that education increased Negro criminality see John Roach Straton, "Will Education Solve the Race Problem," North American Review, 170 (June, 1900), 14-39. On Vardaman see William Henry Holtzclaw, The Black Man's Burden (New York: Neale Publishing Co., 1915), p. 127; Meier, Negro Thought, p. 135; Booker T. Washington, The Story of the Negro: The Rise of The Race from Slavery (New York: Doubleday, Page, & Co., 1909), 2:357.

[38] Crogman, Talks, p. 160; Crisis, 1 (January, 1910), 10; 29 (April, 1925), 275.

[39] Robert Moats Miller, How Shall They Hear Without a Preacher: Life of Ernest Fremont Tittle (Chapel Hill: University of North Carolina Press, 1971), p. 337, fn 17.

[40] William T. Alexander, The History of the Colored Race in America (New York: Negro Universities Press, 1968), p. 462.

[41] Archibald H. Grimke, "The Ultimate Criminal," in American Negro Academy, Occasional Papers 1-22 (New York: Arno Press and the New York Times, 1969), 17:12. Typical example: Indianapolis Freeman, July 22, 1893, p. 4; W. E. Burghardt Du Bois, The Quest of the Silver Fleece (Chicago: A. C. McClurg & Co., 1911), p. 434.

[42] Cox, Caste, p. 441; Indianapolis Freeman, August 21, 1897, p. 2; Ottley, Lonely Warrior, p. 164.

[43] Silas X. Floyd, The Life of Charles T. Walker (Nashville: National Baptist Publishing Board, 1902), pp. 77-81.

[44] Meier, Negro Thought 221; A study made in 1933 stated that 20 per cent of the urban Black ministers were college graduates as compared to 3 per cent of the rural ministers. See Benjamin Elijah Mays and Joseph William Nicholson, The Negro Church (New York: Negro Universities Press, 1969), p. 239.

⁴⁵Meier, Negro Thought, p. 220; Messenger, 7 (June, 1924), 179.

⁴⁶New York Globe, March 1, 1884, p. 1; Meier, Negro Thought, p. 73; Robert T. Handy, A Christian America: Protestant Hopes and Historical Realities (New York: Oxford University Press, 1971), p. 108; Earl Conrad, The Invention of the Negro (New York: Paul S. Eriksson, Inc., 1966), p. 189.

⁴⁷S. P. Fullinwider, The Mind and Mood of Black America (Hometown, Ill.: Dorsey Press, 1969), p. 33; Lewis D. Easton, "Negro Literature," American Catholic Tribune cited in New York Age, January 4, 1890, p. 1.

⁴⁸Joseph R. Washington, Jr., Black Religion: The Negro and Christianity in the United States (Boston: Beacon Press, 1964), p. 35; James H. Cone, Black Theology and Black Power (New York: Seabury Press, 1969), p. 107; Major J. Jones, Black Awareness: A Theology of Hope (Nashville: Abington Press, 1971), p. 53; Albert B. Cleage, Jr. disagreed, see The Black Messiah (New York: Sheed & Ward, 1968), p. 270.

⁴⁹Hortense Powdermaker, "The Channeling of Negro Aggression by the Cultural Process," in The Making of Black America, ed. by August Meier and Elliott Rudwick (New York: Atheneum, 1969), 2:94-105; Howard W. Odum, Race and Rumors of Race (Chapel Hill: University of North Carolina Press, 1943), p. 160.

⁵⁰The weakening of caste sanctions was very slow and sight must not be lost of the point that the freedman was worth less than a slave to most whites, see Jones, Theology, p. 54. For the point that the Black church became more of a refuge than an instrument of protest than was necessary is made by Cone, Black Theology, pp. 104-06. Southwestern Christian Advocate cited in New York Freeman, July 3, 1886, p. 2; Crummel cited in Redkey, Respect Black, p. 162; Alfreda M. Duster, ed., Crusade for Justice: The Autobiography of Ida B. Wells (Chicago: University of Chicago Press, 1970), p. 155; Mays, Born to Rebel, p. 16.

⁵¹For both the positive and negative effects of Black religious accommodation see Columbus Salley and Ronald Behm, Your God is Too White (Downers Grove, Ill.: Inter-Varsity Press, 1970), p. 35; Robert T. Haney, A Christian America: Protestant Hopes and Historical Realities (New York: Oxford University Press, 1971), p. 178.

⁵²For the traditional view that the white church was "passive," see I. A. Newby, Jim Crow's Defense: Anti-Negro Thought in America, 1900-1930 (Baton Rouge: Louisiana State University Press, 1965), p. 84. John Hope Franklin, "The Great Confrontation: The South and the Problem of Change," Journal of Southern History, 38 (February, 1972), 3-20; New York Globe, September 29, 1883, p. 2; Peter Gilbert, ed., The Selected Writings of John Edward Bruce: Militant Black Journalist (New York: Arno Press and the New York Times, 1971), p. 47; Chicago Broad Ax, January 19, 1901, p. 1; Voice of the Negro, 3 (September, 1906), 651-2.

⁵³Christian Recorder cited in Meier, Negro Thought, p. 72; Indianapolis Freeman, September 28, 1895, p. 2; October 17, 1896, p. 2; Emma Lou Thornbrough, ed., Booker T. Washington (Englewood Cliffs, N. J.: Prentice Hall, 1969), p. 73; Voice of the Negro, 3 (October, 1906), 395.

[54] New York Age, May 10, 1890; John Cardinal Gibbons, "Lynch Law and Its Remedy," North American Review, 181 (October, 1905), 502-09. See also John LaFarge, S. J., The Race Question and the Negro: A Study of the Catholic Doctrine on Interracial Justice (New York: Longmans, Green, 1944).

[55] Rauschenbusch cited in Carl N. Degler, Out of Our Past: The Forces that Shaped Modern America, Colophon Books (Harper & Row, 1970), p. 346; Gladden cited in Handy, A Christian America, p. 179. For rise of the Social Gospel see Henry F. May, Protestant Churches and Industrial America (New York: Harper & Brothers, 1949), pp. 163-203. For the view that Southern church support of caste required rejection of the Social Gospel see Frederick A. Bode, "Religion and Class Hegemony: A Populist Critique in North Carolina," Journal of Southern History, 37 (August, 1971), 417-38.

[56] Duster, Ida B. Wells, p. 193; Torrence, Hope, p. 135. The Presbyterians and Congregationalists also issued their first anti-lynching Pronouncements in 1892. See David M. Reimers, White Protestantism and the Negro (New York: Oxford University Press, 1965), p. 76.

[57] Andrew E. Murray, Presbyterians and the Negro--A History (Philadelphia: Presbyterian Historical Society, 1966), p. 235; Kenneth K. Bailey, Southern White Protestantism in the Twentieth Century (New York: Harper & Row, 1964), pp. 39-40; Wayne Flynt, "Dissent in Zion: Alabama Baptists and Social Issues, 1900-1914," Journal of Southern History, 35 (November, 1969), 523-42. See also Frank S. Loescher, The Protestant Church and the Negro: A Pattern of Segregation (New York: Association Press, 1948).

[58] Chicago Broad Ax, May 9, 1899, p. 1; Leonard Dinnerstein, The Leo Frank Case (New York: Columbia University Press, 1968), p. 157; Charles Flint Kellogg, NAACP: A History of the National Association for the Advancement of Colored People (Baltimore: The Johns Hopkins Press, 1967), p. 125.

[59] Handy, Christian America, p. 181; Crisis, 7 (December, 1913), 62; 11 (February, 1916), 4.

[60] Christian Advocate, October 2, 1919, p. 1265. For record of church pronouncements see Loescher, Protestant Church, pp. 121-43. For a more complete list of those in 1919-1923 period see Robert Moats Miller, "The Protestant Church and Lynching," Journal of Negro History, 42 (April, 1957), 118-131; for the development of interracial commissions and related activities after World War I see Miller, "The Attitudes of American Protestantism Toward the Negro," Journal of Negro History, 41 (July, 1956), 215-40; and his American Protestantism and Social Issues: 1919-1939 (Chapel Hill: University of North Carolina Press, 1958) which equates dueling and lynching as equally evil (p. 10). For the view that the pronouncements meant little see Reimers, White Protestantism, p. 96.

[61] Loescher, Protestant Church, p. 29; Jones, Black Awareness, p. 52.

[62] *Christian Advocate*, August 5, 1886, p. 488; December 14, 1893, p. 802; March 12, 1896, p. 163; August 1, 1918, p. 954; January 23, 1919, pp. 1000-01; April 22, 1926, p. 496.

[63] Indianapolis *Freeman*, December 22, 1894, p. 5.

[64] Gilbert, *Bruce*, p. 48; William Pickens, "Christianity as a Basis of Common Citizenship," in *The New Voice in Race Adjustments*, ed. by A. M. Trawick (New York: Student Volunteer Movement, 1914), p. 35; Mays, *Born to Rebel*, p. 247; *Christian Advocate*, January 7, 1926, pp. 101--5.

[65] *Christian Advocate*, August 31, 1911, p. 1170.

[66] Redkey, *Respect Black*, p. 178; *The Voice of the Negro*, 3 (June, 1906), 400; Indianapolis *Freeman*, May 21, 1898, p. 4.

[67] Indianapolis *Freeman*, December 9, 1893, p. 4.

[68] E. J. Hobsbawm, *The Age of Revolution: 1789-1848* (Cleveland: World Publishing Co., 1962), p. 224; one typical example, "The Religions of the Teachings of Jesus and Mohamet Compared," Chicago *Broad Ax*, October 23, 1903, p. 1.

[69] For the advanced position of the urban ministers see Mays, *Negro Church*, p. 157.

CHAPTER VI

MILITANCY AND MIGRATION

Many Black Americans held the theory that militant resistance to mobs was a positive contribution to the anti-lynching reform. This view was usually limited to the concept of self-defense on the grounds that greater militancy would be counterproductive. Occasionally the theory of self-defense was extended to include concepts of retaliatory violence. Black militancy increased white awareness of lynching, undermined the stereotype of Black docility, and led to increased interracial cooperation which weakened the belief that white society was monolithic in opposition to all Black advances. Lynching was an important factor contributing to the Great Migration. The Migration encouraged a reassessment of the status of Blacks in the South and helped create a climate for the rapid development of the anti-lynching reform. The migrants who settled in the cities were less inclined to accept harassment and more disposed to fight back when attacked.

Despite the militant rhetoric of Black leaders and despite the many instances of armed resistance to persecution by Blacks, the myth of the meek and humble Black continued into the twentieth century. According to this myth, Blacks had not resisted slavery and did not resist the efforts to deprive them of civil and political rights after the Civil War. This myth was very useful in explaining away racial violence by denying that there had been any violence--none was needed because Blacks proved their inferiority by meekly accepting inferior status. Senator Samuel D. McEnery of Louisiana presented a definitive statement of this in the Independent, "What other race would have submitted so many years to slavery without complaint? What other race would have submitted so quietly to disfranchisement?" Some Blacks echoed the myth of docility. Booker T. Washington characterized his people as innately noncombative, and some militants advised Southern Blacks to assume the role of docility because they recognized that white power made the problem of Black resistance difficult. William Ferris, one of the first Blacks to criticize Washington, advised Southern Blacks to "play the humble, submissive lamb for the time being."[1]

Black militancy was the logical development of the fundamental right of self-defense. Whites had long accepted this concept as legitimate for themselves and Ferris was only drawing on white tradition when he concluded his remarks on docile role-playing with Polonius's advice to Laertes: avoid quarrels, but give a good account of oneself when they are unavoidable. White recognition that Blacks shared in the universal right to self-defense was recognized in the Emancipation Proclamation which advised the slaves to "abstain from all violence, unless in necessary self-defense." The impulse to self-defense was strengthened among Blacks by the belief that they were morally right.

The Northern Black editors led in expressing the militant rhetoric of self-defense. T. Thomas Fortune was perhaps the best known of this group but he was only one of several dozen outspoken editors whose militant statements would fill volumes. In 1883, speaking of a riot, Fortune wrote: "There is but one way to put a period to the force and violence of a Bourbon--use more force and violence than he does." The following year he said, "To be murdered by mobs . . . is not to be endured without protest, and if violence must be met with violence, let it be met." In 1885, his advice was: "If the white scamps lynch and shoot you, you have the right to do the same." The militancy of Fortune's admonitions increased in 1889 as he was promoting the organization of the Afro-American League.[2]

Whites feared Black militancy because they did not understand its motivation. Usually Black resistance resulted from individual decisions born of desperation that it was better to go down fighting than stand meekly and be slaughtered. Since whites generally believed that any assertion of manhood by Blacks was the first step in what could become a general revolt which would destroy the entire caste system, they considered it necessary to suppress ruthlessly all assertions. The result was an environment where violence was commonplace. William A. Pledger, Black Georgian Republican leader, described the situation as approximating a state of war. In his address to the Afro-American League in 1890, Pledger maintained, "In many parts of the South, a system of terrorism and guerilla warfare exists to which open war with two contending armies in the field, governed by the usages of Christian nations would be an improvement."[3]

Blacks won a few skirmishes in this guerilla war, and the editors were eager to report the details. Victory was defined by the editors as surviving the skirmish. They included in this category instances where the Black was severely injured or was forced to abandon his property and flee from his home, sometimes forever. The Indianapolis Freeman devoted five columns on the front page of one issue to tell how Nelson Jones fought off a mob near Savannah, Georgia, in 1890 and barely survived numerous gunshot wounds. The case was a victory, because had Jones not fought the mob, he would surely have died by lynching. These victories were not common, but the fact that there were any encouraged militant resistance to white aggression.[4]

To resist arrest was often a suicidal but, paradoxically, a rational action. All Blacks knew that torture and lynching could be the punishment for trivial offenses against white supremacy. At the same time, the white society was inconsistent, and a Black could not know if his alleged transgression would be deemed sufficiently serious to cause the raising of a lynch mob. Even if the Black suspect escaped lynching, he knew that the court system was weighted against him, and that even a short sentence for a minor offense could be in reality a death sentence because of the brutal prison conditions. If a Black suspect was going to resist, he could not delay until he was disarmed and powerless in the hands of the authorities. The lynching statistics all indicate that murder was the main reason for mob action. Many of the murder victims were officials who were killed by Blacks resisting the arrest that so often preceeded lynching or death in a convict camp.[5]

The law of self-preservation that led to the killing of officials, also led Blacks to fight against mobs when they had a chance. One issue of the Indianapolis Freeman cited two cases. In one, the Black escaped. In the other, William Clement, arrested for a felong in Lynchburg, Virginia, was lynched March 14, 1897. He fought the mob that was taking him from the jail so desperately that some of their face masks were ripped off. Although he died, the identity of the mob leaders had been exposed, and warrants were sworn out for their arrest. Although no convictions were obtained, Clement's action had made it impossible to ignore the affair entirely. Three South Carolina whites were killed in 1913 when they found their quarry, according to W. E. B. Du Bois, who concluded, "He knew that it was his life, or the life of those who pursued." In Early County, Georgia, an argument in 1916 over a white man's right to whip a Black youth resulted in a gunfight in which four Blacks were killed and several whites were severely wounded. In the aftermath, two Blacks were burned at the stake.[6]

The idea of self-defense was extended from the intended victim's fighting the mob to retaliation against mob members after a lynching. Washington D. C., attorney Richard Greener said in 1883, "Brute force is only warranted in absence of law and in such case we deem retaliation a positive virtue." In the most militant statement of his career, Black journalist John Edward Bruce told a Washington audience in 1889, "If they kill your wives and children, kill theirs." "Pursue them relentlessly." And the following year Frederick Douglass, speaking at an Emancipation Proclamation celebration, said that it would be "madness" to retaliate, "but oppression will make even a wiseman mad."[7]

The Black press was not the only source of information on retaliation. The Independent in 1901 stated that three of six men who took a Black prisoner from officers and lynched him had suffered for their actions. One lost his store by fire; another had his home shot into; and the child of a third was killed. The editor concluded, "It is known that among the negroes, a policy of relentless following and terrorizing of men who have been prominently connected with lynching affairs is being openly advocated, and in some instances, put into action." In 1906 the New York Times reported that Blacks were arming in the South because they could not get protection from the law and that troops were being called out in Meridian, Mississippi, because Blacks were gathering to avenge the killing of two by whites.[8]

Retaliation against whites for lynching was a fact given credence by even the white press. White fear and guilt led to exaggerations, and rumors would sweep areas in a manner reminiscent of the rumors of slave revolts. When William Cato and Paul Reed were burned alive before a large crowd at Statesboro, Georgia, in August 1904 even though they had been duly convicted and sentenced to death, rumors of "Before-Day Clubs" were widespread. These clubs were supposedly formed by Blacks to avenge any lynching before the following day. The Voice of the Negro attributed these rumors to fantasies invented by whites because they "treat the colored people so cruel and barbarous they feel they [the Blacks] ought to be planning some method of revenge." Often a specific lynching would be followed by rumors of the formation of militant self-defense leagues by Blacks, particularly if the lynching had been characterized by unusual brutality. One such was the lynching of Sam Petty in Leland, Mississippi, on February 24, 1914, which was followed by reports of the formation of vigilante groups of Blacks who would use guns to put an end to Southern lynchings.[9]

There were two ideas basic to Black theories of militancy. One of these was that it was better for the individual to resist aggression than to submit to it. The other was that although the consequences of resistance might be worse for the individual than submission would be, the individual's sacrifice of his life was an offering laid on the altar of race advancement. Militancy was extremely hazardous and those who would accept the mantle of martyrdom were respected by those who acquiesced to discrimination in order to survive.

The militants regretted that there were not more who would act out the thought: if there be trouble, let it be in my day, that my child may have peace.

There were indications in the 1890s that Black resistance to lynching would reduce the willingness of whites to form mobs. The Indianapolis Freeman's comment on a case in 1893 of resistance in Roanoke, where Blacks had fought and killed whites, was "The unlooked for and sudded death of these Virginia whites was necessary to awaken the national heart . . . from criminal indifference." Editor E. E. Cooper maintained that Blacks should have hope, "for in the shed blood of white men is the commencement of his travail's end." That same year the Cleveland Plaindealer concluded, "There seems to be evidence of returning sense in the South. From several different points comes the glad tidings that the Negro has about made up his mind to fight." When whitecappers were active in Arkansas in 1898, one Black leader said, "When the Negroes of Lonoke County kill about twenty-five of these lawless white men, the outrages against the Negro race will stop, and not until then." This show of resistance led to consultations with Governor Daniel W. Jones who offered rewards for information leading to the conviction of the whites. The belief grew that only by making lynching costly to white life and property would any significant progress be made to end the custom. By 1919, the far from militant Half Century magazine carried numerous letters advocating militant self-defense. One from Joseph Dalton of Brewton, Alabama, was typical. "Lynching will stop down here if every time a Negro is chased by white hoodlums he would turn around and get just one."[10]

Some Southern Blacks were critical of the more extreme calls for militance and retaliatory violence that came from the North. Bishop Henry McNeal Turner, at the 1893 Civil Rights Convention, castigated the Northern Blacks that wanted their Southern brethren to stay and fight "until they were neck deep in blood." Turner charged that they took care to stay out of the South. In his address to the convention, Turner had said, "To talk about physical resistance is literal madness. Nobody but an idiot would give it a moment's thought." A letter in 1892 from Helena, Arkansas, commenting on the militant rhetoric in the Black press said:

> The better class of the Colored People in the South pay little or no attention to the riotous resolutions of their Northern brethren, knowing if they did, a race war would be inevitable, the result of which would be the wiping out of the Negro race in the United States.

Ex-Congressman Henry P. Cheatham complained that Ida B. Wells's militant speech to the meeting of the Afro-American Council in 1898 was an example of what made it hard for the Negro in the South.[11]

The possibility that Black militancy would lead to white retaliation and genocide was openly discussed among Blacks. Bishop Turner regarded the possibility of a race war ending in the genocide of Blacks as a very real one. He read a letter from a white to the 1893 Civil Rights Convention which threatened extermination of Blacks. A year earlier, Albion Tourgee, appalled by the increase in lynchings and seeking to shock the white conscience into action, had predicted a race massacre within ten years if things did not change. This line of thought was not acceptable to George Knox, editor of the Indianapolis Freeman. Knox denied that the Northern and Southern whites would ever unite against Blacks. He believed that a renewal of the Civil War was possible but could not accept the possibility of a race war. According to Knox, Tourgee was the type of friend from whom Blacks needed saving.[12]

Whites also discussed Black militancy in relation to the possibility of genocide. Raymond Patterson, Yale classmate of William Howard Taft, argued that the Indians were wiped out because they resisted, and "the salvation of the Negro lies in the fact that he is of a weak race." Many of the New South's spokesmen threatened genocide if Blacks resisted the imposition of the caste strictures. Frank Tannenbaum's discussion of the possibility of a general massacre of Blacks concluded, "But fortunately for the white race, the negroes are learning to fight." "Fortunately," Tannenbaum thought, because it would not be good for whites if whites became mass murderers.[13]

Among the Blacks who openly discussed genocide were Frederick Douglass, Charles W. Chesnutt, and W. E. B. Du Bois. However, just as militancy reduced lynching, so did it reduce the possibility of genocide. As Blacks increased their ability to "take one with them," the necessity for such extreme action diminished.[14]

Other techniques for militant opposition to lynching which did not involve killing whites were advanced. The Reverend A. M. Middlebrooks of Pine Bluff, Arkansas, hired an attorney and forced the court to set bond for Blacks in danger of lynching. He then put up the bond and encouraged them to escape from the state. The Indianapolis Freeman called it "the most heroic act any man had done for his race against mobism." Daniel Murray, a Black who was Assistant Librarian for Congress and later in the Niagara Movement, suggested a strike in 1904. If all the Blacks in the South went on a ten-day strike at the next lynching and lived on one-half rations and spent their time praying, "there would not be a second lynching in any county in the South," Murray said. J. Max Barber thought it a good suggestion. "Do it," he advised. "Negroes! Starve and to your knees." The Voice of the Negro received more letters to the editor on Murray's suggestion than any other item it had printed. John W. Hubert of Tuskegee wrote, "We must work out, not strike out, our salvation." Others did not approve a sanction that would be equally hard to all whites, but most joined Bishop Turner in approving the idea.[15]

In World War I, when Black labor was not surplus, the reaction to many lynchings was in effect a strike against the lynch-minded persons and areas. In late August 1917, A. N. Page was lynched by white farmers in Heathville, Virginia, and although wages were doubled, the Norfolk Journal and Guide predicted that another lynching there would depopulate the county as already all Blacks refused to work on the farm of a mob leader. In another type of strike, 16,000 Negro policyholders of a white Florida life insurance company withdrew their patronage from the company when its agents led a lynch mob in Jacksonville in 1920. Even though the agents started addressing their clients as "Mr." and "Mrs." and took their hats off when coming into the homes to call, they were unable to get the business back. As a last resort the company hired Black agents, but Blacks organized the People's Industrial Insurance Company and took over the business lost by the white-owned company.[16]

The Black consensus fell between the extremes of retaliatory violence and quiet acceptance. The acceptance of Booker T. Washington's views did not mean an acquiescence to lynching. Washington, despite the statements of some of his critics, rarely condoned lynching and frequently protested against it. He never believed that his Gospel of Wealth led to any goal other than acceptance of Blacks by whites. Judge James Dean, identified by Fortune as "one of the braniest of our younger man," in a speech in 1891 in Key West, Florida, said that "wealth, education, self-respect and assertion go hand-in-hand," and that property accumulation meant less cringing. At the same time, the acceptance of Washington's philosophy tended to disarm Blacks and led to acquiescence to wrongs which should have been resisted. When this happened, the militants would reproach Washington's followers with charges of lack of manhood. Some of those accused by the militants responded by denying the existence, or at least the degree, of the existing evils and defended their position by pointing out that the society was not as oppressive as the militants charged. As proof, they cited the advances that had been made in the South. An example of this dialogue between militant and conservative was in an exchange of letters published in the summer of 1894 in the Indianapolis <u>Freeman</u>. The first was from a militant charging that the South was despotic and that those who did not fight vigorously for change were cowards. The reply, from J. A. Jones, Principal of the Turner Normal College of Shelbyville, Tennessee, stated that to agree the South was despotic "is to acknowledge ourselves the most pusillanimous wretches the world has ever produced." Jones then minimized Southern despotism by citing the advances in education for Blacks.[17]

In the 1890s there was general agreement that individual Blacks would sometimes find themselves in situations where militant self-defense was called for, and such martyrs were to be admired, but the race as a whole should avoid major confrontations. Looking back from a later time, moderate leaders such as Mary Church Terrell wondered "how self-respecting colored people can patiently endure such treatment year in and year out without getting desperate is difficult to understand." Yet there were many reasons that militant resistance to oppression was not greater. E. A. Johnson, a Black historian, summed up the reasons he saw in 1904: Blacks did not resist lynching more effectively because they were overawed by white numbers and resources; they believed the slave rebellions had failed; and the heritage of slavery made it difficult to organize effectively. Sociologist John Dollard credited the displacement aggression impulse of whites with limiting self-defense. Dollard stated:

> One of the most effective checks on acts of violence by Negroes against whites is the reprisals which may follow against the family of the Negro man. If the man, himself, gets away, it has been known to happen that the white crowds will go to his home, perhaps rape the women and shoot the women and children, perhaps burn down the house or loot it and destroy the furniture.

Another reason limiting the ability of indivudual Blacks to resist their own lynching was that they could not be certain of their ultimate fate until it was too late and they were disarmed and helpless. In addition it should be noted that some of the more effective Black leaders in the South had been driven out or bought off.[18]

After 1883, as Blacks gradually increased their stake in society by the acquisition of wealth, property, education and status, they found they had to defend these gains from whites. The great majority of Blacks were employed in agriculture where the points of friction were the annual settlements, the trespassing of white-owned stock on the land and crops of Black farmers, the Black ownership of land which resulted in the withdrawal of the proprietor from the labor market and his land from white control, and the right of the Black tenant to move to another place. Black tenants believed that landlords had become better about making fair settlements after some of the landlords had been shot at by Black tenants who could not get settlements.[19]

Blacks would sometimes have to defend themselves against whites who resented their status. R. R. Church, wealthy Black Republican leader of Tennessee, shot at whites who were throwing rock-centered snowballs at him in Memphis. His daughter, Mary Church Terrell, remarked that this action was "a desperate thing." When the Ku Klux Klan burned a cross at Tuskegee, a symbol of Black status, armed Blacks came in from the surrounding areas to join the Cadet Corps in guarding the institution.[20]

The double sexual standard was a source of much tension, led to many lynchings, and was bitterly resented and often militantly resisted. White assaults on Black women could not be openly defended by any segment of the racists ideology, and such assaults so violated the professed view of proper race relations that this was one of the first areas in which whites could accept the Black perspective and join in the anti-lynching reform. In a case in 1915 which Du Bois said "brings even the New York Times to its feet," a Georgia mob lynched a father, his son, and two married daughters who were charged with "resisting arrest for murderous assault." The trouble started when a white police officer struck one of the Black women. World War I increased the Black sense of injustice, and even the more conservative Black publications, such as the Competitor, spoke of Blacks "driven reluctantly to retaliation" by the humiliation of Black women, lynching, and unequal justice.[21]

The unwillingness of Blacks after the war to continue to accept the old double standard was expressed in increasingly militant terms. Dr. M. A. Majors, a New York physician who often wrote editorials for the Chicago Broad Ax, wrote in 1922,

> Whenever it becomes as dangerous for a white to consort with a Negro woman as a Negro with white, things will change all around in the South. What we want will come to pass but it will take fighting, a deal of dying, throats cut, heads cracked, a few mysterious white hangings and a general striking back at the enemy all along the line.

Because of this increased militancy, and because a growing number of whites accepted the idea that it was wrong to lynch Blacks for protecting Black women, it became more difficult to raise a mob whenever it happened. In the 1920s and early 1930s, press reports of successful defenses by Black men of Black women increased, and the prewar certainty that mob action would follow was no longer true. In one Southern town, whites had been going into the Black section for women and planned to attack the Black men who had indicated their resentment. The Blacks armed themselves, got reinforcements from nearby towns, and demonstrated that they were ready to die in battle if need be. The white community was divided and unprepared to pay the price for continuation of the old pattern of sexual relations, so peace was re-established on Black terms.[22]

Black militancy tended to strengthen whites who had any commitment to racial justice, and Black acquiescence to injustice tended to reduce the white contribution to the anti-lynching reform. Theodore Roosevelt said that he would have been more willing to attempt to enforce the Fourteenth and Fifteenth Amendments in 1904 if Blacks in the South would have found some way to protest disfranchisement more vigorously. Almost all the Black leaders believed that more militancy would strengthen, not weaken, the anti-lynching reform. Booker T. Washington, though he did much to discourage militancy, did occasionally regret that it was not greater. Alexander Walters, widely known Bishop of the A. M. E. Zion Church, in a Boston speech attacking the Atlanta Compromise, said that one of the reasons leading to the Northern abandonment of Blacks in the South was lack of Black militancy.[23]

Determined to resist, but so circumscribed in the South that any dissent could be suicide, many Blacks expressed their militancy by pulling up stakes and leaving the South. Most went North, but "any place but here" was the real destination, and any improvement in status and any mitigation of repression was the goal. Escape from the threat of the lynch mob was one of the things uppermost in the minds of the Black migrants.

It was only natural that many Blacks would wish to leave the South. Other parts of the United States, other countries in the Americas, and Africa were considered as new homes. As information drifted back from these other places that life there was no bed of roses either, the realization grew that most Blacks would remain in the South. This knowledge contributed to a determination to improve conditions there. At the same time, those who did leave also contributed by pointing up the criticism that Blacks were making of the South, and by forcing whites to make concessions to those who remained in order to slow the migration.

The Northern migration of Blacks has a long history. The Underground Railway was a device to escape the violence of slavery. After the war, the increased freedom to move about, to look for a better place, culminated in the Exodus of 1879 led by "Pap" Singleton. Southern Democrats could not accept the fact that the Exodus was a protest movement, so they charged that it was a political plot to tighten the hold of the Republican party in those areas to which Blacks were moving. Booker T. Washington said that there was no truth to this Democratic charge, and he criticized Congress for spending money to investigate the Exodus only to find out what every schoolboy knew: "Negroes were leaving the South because of systematic robbery and political cruelties." The migrants were quoted as saying, "We might as well starve or freeze to death in Kansas as to be shot-gunned here."[24]

The Exodusters suffered great hardships and failed to escape from the terror of lynching, for the number of lynchings per thousand Blacks in Kansas during the 1890s was practically the same as in Mississippi. Because Southern oppression remained unchanged and migration was based on the hope of a better life, the difficulties of the migrants were never sufficient to shut the movement off completely. The New York _Freeman_ reported in 1887 that Southern agricultural labor was moving West because of unjust crop lien laws, land sharks, and company stores. These were among the basic complaints of the Exodusters and in 1879 and of those in the Great Migration a generation later.[25]

Blacks believed that migration out of the South would reduce lynching in two ways. There was the hope of the migrants to find a new home where the threat of lynching would not hang over them. There was also the valid belief that migration was the single most important anti-lynching weapon in the Black arsenal because it would encourage the whites who profited from Black labor in the South to oppose lynching in order to stem the migrations.

Planters were quick to realize the connection between lynching and the desire of Blacks to leave. Near the end of Reconstruction, when terrorist white gangs were killing Blacks for voting, white planters would sometimes intervene, even to the extent of killing some of the terrorists in order to avoid losing Black labor from migration. This contributed to the paternalistic tradition that a white protector was the best defense against the lynch mob. This tradition continued into the 1930s as occasional planters protected their tenants from lynching in order to prevent a labor exodus at harvest time.[26]

The initial reaction of the planters and capitalist entrepreneurs was not to ameliorate conditions for Blacks. Obstacles were thrown in the paths of labor agents in the form of legal restrictions and extra-legal intimidation. One of the reasons the practice of payment in scrip was developed was so that Blacks would never have cash for traveling expenses. Caesar A. A. Taylor, Black political leader, toured the South in 1889 and protested this practice. Douglass suggested that one of the campaigns the Afro-American League might mount should be directed against the use of scrip. An 1892 report from Arkansas stated, "Whenever the Afro-Americans begin to emigrate, there is a great commotion among the whites stopping them, passing resolutions to pay the darkies in scrip for fear if they get ahold of money they will leave." The fraudulent annual settlements also functioned to keep the tenants penniless, in part to prevent them from leaving. The long range effect of oppression was to stimulate the migrations, but some of the proscriptions made it more difficult for Blacks to pull up stakes and leave.[27]

The white South was divided on the issue of Blacks' leaving. The whites who profited from Black labor desired that they remain. The poorer whites who competed with Blacks for jobs and land were glad to see them go. It was from this division among whites that the idea arose that lynch mobs were composed primarily of the poorer whites. The corollary belief that the "best people" deplored lynching also comes from this. The idea was a myth, for when Blacks competed with the white bourgeoisie or challenged local planter hegemony, these "best people" did not oppose the mobs and they frequently participated in lynchings.[28]

After 1883, when criticism of lynching started coming from the North, one of the responses of the South was to propose emigration schemes, the implication being that the Blacks were a burden that the South would willingly do without. At the same time, of course, the proposers of these plans worked actively to erect obstacles to Black migration. Part of the motivation behind the emigration plans was the idea that this seeming nonchalance about whether the Black stayed or went would indicate to the Black and the Northern white critics of lynching that they were wasting their time, that pressure for change in the South would not be strengthened by any fears of losing the Black worker.[29]

The Black press generally encouraged the migrations. T. Thomas Fortune summed up the reasons in 1886 which were valid for the subsequent decades.

> Denied any voice in the making or enforcement of the laws; denied all civil rights, and supplied with inadequate school facilities; and given a pittance as wages for labor and robbed of the greater portion of this by contractors, shopkeepers, and others with whom they have money dealings-- why should this people be restless.

Blacks used the threat and promise of exodus to protest conditions in the South and to agitate for change. The Reverend W. J. White, editor of the Georgia Baptist, told the South in 1885 that if it would treat the Black as a man, then all thoughts of exodus would end. John Edward Bruce, a few years later in an article entitled, "Negro Depopulation or Extermination," appealed to the South's conservatism by emphasizing the lack of radicalism among Blacks as compared to imported labor. Speaking of Black labor, he said: "He stands as a barrier between us and the hordes of anarchists, socialists, Communists, and activists who are flooding the Northern and Western states and menacing their welfare and perpetuity." Bad as the race conflict in the South was, Bruce submitted that it was not as bad as the conflict culminating in the Haymarket affair.[30]

The migrations led to the view that lynching was a national problem. When the spokesmen for the New South said that lynching was a national problem, they meant that the South had no monopoly on the practice, and they tried to develop the belief that there was as much lynching in other parts of the nation as there was in the South. When Blacks said that lynching was a national problem, they meant that the South would never come up with a regional solution, and to end lynching it would be necessary for the entire nation to address itself to the problem. This meant, in the Black view, that pressure from the whole nation expressed as Federal action would be required. A significant segment of the white North also saw lynching as a national problem, but meant by this that the continuation of lynching in the South would increase the flow of Blacks to the North and thereby bring to the Northern white supremacists the same problems that their Southern compatriots had. This Northern white view had been important in the past. The South had increased Northern interest in the annexation of Texas with the argument that it would prevent the North from being flooded with Blacks. Part of the motivation for Radical Reconstruction was predicted on the belief that the status of Blacks in the South should be improved so that they would stay there.[31]

These views were important to the anti-lynching reform which received reinforcement from those Northerners who wished Blacks would stay in the South and from the Southern employers of Black labor who shared this attitude. The promises of the Bourbons, made in the period 1875-1877, to protect the rights of Blacks were motivated by the apprehension that Blacks might leave as well as by the need of white leaders to disarm Republican opposition to fraudulently acquired Democratic control of the South. Daniel Murray explained one reason why these Bourbon promises were not kept in an address to the Washington, D. C., 1903 Sociological Conference on the Race Question. Murray said that although the 1879 Exodus had modified the deteriorating race relations in the South:

> Then followed ten years of comparative peace, or until it was seen that no amount of harsh treatment would drive the Negro away, and when this fact became apparent, that lelment of the population who had been, through self interest, in a large measure his defense against outrage, gave up all further concern about him, and then began the enactment of the series of laws which today oppress him and deny him justice.[32]

Hearings on a House of Representatives Representatives bill to establish a commission to study the race question in 1892 reflected the Northern white concern that Blacks would come North. The Committee on Labor sought answers to such questions as "Why are there 90,000 Blacks in Washington, D. C. ?" and made recommendations on how to keep Blacks content in Southern agriculture. Key testimony was given by William A. Pledger on the oppression of peonage and lynchings as the most important factors leading to urbanization of Blacks who would first go to the Southern cities and then go North. Lynching continued to be a motivation for migration. A study published in 1906 stated that nearly every large Northern city contained many exiles from the South who left to save their lives and their daughters' virtue.[33]

When reports started coming back from the North that life there also had its problems for Blacks, impetus was given to the idea of emigration to Africa. Though a large part of this thought was based on the desire to help Africa, either by Christianizing it or helping it to throw off colonialism, or both, a significant element of the desire to go there was based on the wish to escape the terror of the South. The best known advocate of emigration to Africa in the late neneteenth century was Bishop Henry McNeal Turner, who strengthened his missionary and anti-colonial position with a constant barrage of statements which indicated he believed that whites would never open the door to full equality for Blacks in the United States. He frequently cited lynchings as proof for this contention. He had copies of the Supreme Court's Civil Rights decision of 1883 printed and distributed as proof of the need to go to Africa. Although he was never able to win much support for this idea, he did enjoy the support of many Blacks because of his passionate advocacy of civil rights and his constant agitation against lynchings.

Bishop Turner returned from a trip to Africa in February 1892 in time to learn of the recent arrival in New York of a penniless group of 300 Blacks from Arkansas and Oklahoma expecting the white American Colonization Society to transport them to Africa. This colonization society could only handle fifty and told the rest to return to the homes from which they had fled. Blacks in New York City under the leadership of T. Thomas Fortune, T. McCants Stewart, and Theodore Gould held a mass meeting to raise funds to help the stranded refugees to go back home. Turner was incensed. The refugees were "trying to escape from the jaws of slaughter and death," Turner said. "May God hurl thunderbolts at the head of every Negro who would advise those people to return, is my sincere prayer." Turner protested that the mass meeting's sponsors should have found them jobs and not have tried to return them to the South "where they lynch you, shoot you and murder you at will and pleasure of the mob."[34]

The idea of helping to create a strong and independent Africa was energizing and increased militancy, but at the same time African emigration diverted funds and energy from the anti-lynching struggle. Turner's greatest single contribution to the anti-lynching reform came in 1893 when he temporarily subordinated his interest in Africa to organize the Civil Rights Convention.

Reports came back from Africa, as they had come back from other places, that life there was difficult at best. When twenty South Carolina Blacks returned from Liberia in 1891, it was reported that "they were thankful to get back alive, and with a few rags on their back." Edward Wilmont Blyden, the scholarly president of Liberia College in Sierra Leone and longtime promoter of the idea of African colonization, was attacked in 1890 in the New York Age as a "spy hireling and firebrand; dangerous, a treacherous man. We warn people everywhere to steer clear of him." A week later Blyden was accused of sending a few dupes to Africa every year where they promptly died of fever. In 1894, the Indianapolis

Freeman, in a departure from routine, devoted the entire front page to Mrs. Celeste H. McCoy, widow of a Minister-Resident and Consul-General to Liberia, who had spent two years there with her husband. She strongly condemned emigration to Africa. As the realization grew that emigration to Africa was no immediate solution, the problem of improving the condition of Blacks in the United States received an even higher priority.[35]

Despite adverse publicity, interest in African emigration continued. Bishop Turner assisted in the organization of the Colored National Emigration Association in 1900 to finance the purchase of a ship to aid emigration. By 1903, only twenty per cent of the needed funds were collected and the organization collapsed. Turner continued to cite lynching mobs as proof of the need to go to Africa, giving as one reason that Blacks lacked the manhood to make the sacrifices that effective protest required.[36]

In addition to Africa and other parts of the United States, other American countries were the goals of migrants fleeing Southern oppression and lynching. These efforts were usually disappointing, and in one instance, President Cleveland asked Congress for funds to return a destitute colony of Blacks from Mexico to Alabama in 1895. In Texas, promoters of Brazilian colonization were opposed by whites in 1888 on the grounds that Blacks should stay and defend their interests where they were. The colonists did not bother to answer the white critics but engaged in a dialogue with the League. After the Cuban-Spanish-American War, there was an interest in Black colonization of the Philippines which had some white support.[37]

Migration from the South was thought to hold the solution to the lynching problem because it reduced the percentage of Blacks there. Other ideas, current at the time, indicated that the solution might lie in increasing the ratio of Blacks in the South. Conclusions derived from inaccurate and misinterpreted census returns led some to believe that Blacks would eventually outnumber whites in the South to such an extent that they would inherit the region. This was seen as one possible solution to the lynching problem. Bishop Turner speculated in the early 1880s that if the Black population kept increasing at the rate of the preceeding decade, it would "put the Southern States in the hands of the Negro in 1900." Some whites came to the same conclusion. Professor C. A. Gardiner predicted in 1883 that Blacks would take over the South in thirty years. Dr. R. H. Allen, Secretary of the Standing Committee on Freemen of the General Assembly of the Presbyterian Church, said in 1885 that the Black population doubled every twenty years, while the white population doubled in thirty-five years. From this he concluded that in one hundred years there would be 192 million Blacks and only 96 million whites. Senator George F. Hoar told the Senate in 1890 that there would be 50 million Blacks in the United States by 1930. Dr. Joseph Cook, the Boston lecturer, agreed with these demographic estimates and suggested that perhaps the solution would be for the whites to leave the South. The Reverend Bryan, Black editor of the Selma (Alabama) _Independent,_ was entranced by the prospect of the whites' leaving. "Were you [the whites] to leave this Southland, in twenty years it would be one of the grandest sections of the globe. . . . You would never see convicts, or lynching." In 1890 the Afro-American League passed a sarcastic resolution offering to help the whites leave.[38]

One white view was that if anyone was going to leave, it would not be the whites. William B. Smith, in his widely-read book, The Color Line: A Brief in Behalf of the

Unborn, concluded that nature had doomed the Negro to amalgamation or extinction and that the whites would not permit the former. Blacks were aware of such threats of genocide. The Reverend Bryan said in 1889, "We will have our war, and we hope, as God intends, that we will be strong enough to wipe you out of existence." W. H. Crogman was also concerned by statements in the Southern white press such as, "The Negro knows his place. It will be woe to him the day he forgets it. He will be exterminated like the Indian."[39]

One reason Turner thought the Supreme Court anti-civil rights decision of 1883 was so important was that he believed that if Blacks were set aside by increasing Jim Crow and discrimination, all the white racism and belief in Black inferiority would be reinforced and the arguments of those who sought extreme solutions would be strengthened. While Turner said, "Prepare to return to Africa or get ready for extermination," he also said to Daniel A. Payne, senior bishop in the A. M. E. Church, and to Frederick Douglass, "Tell them they [Blacks] must have social contact or go to the wall. . . . Whoever this white race does not consort with, they will crush out; that social equality is as necessary to our existence in this land as air to breathe and water to drink."[40]

All of the movements of Blacks out of the South between 1883 and World War I were slight compared to the later migrations. Perhaps 40,000 were involved in the 1879 Exodus. Far fewer went abroad, and the steady and gradual movement of Blacks to the North was not enough to raise that section's percentage of the total Black population above 10 per cent before 1910.

The Great Migration that began in 1915 was an acceleration of a century-long movement. It came at this time because opportunities for survival in the North increased as the war in Europe closed off foreign immigration and many foreign nationals returned to their European homes. This reduction in the supply of cheap unskilled white labor came at a time when industrial expansion stimulated by the European war increased the demand for labor of all types. Northern industries endeavored to meet their labor needs by an active recruitment campaign aimed at Blacks which included sending agents to the South to publicize the opportunities.

The period was one of great demographic change. In 1910 about one million Blacks, or 11 percent of the United States' total Black population, lived outside the South. By 1920 this number increased 50 per cent to more than 1,500,000, or 15 per cent of the total Black population. Most of this increase came in the second half of the decade. The movement peaked, in 1923, and by 1930 there were more than 2,500,000 Blacks living outside the South, comprising 21 per cent of the total Black population. Preceding and accompanying this movement North was the urbanization of the Black population in the South. These demographic changes were of vital importance in the development of the anti-lynching reform.[41]

The generalized knowledge that any Black could be lynched at any time on any excuse spurred many to migrate who may not have been immediately menaced by a mob. R. R. Wright, Sr., President of the Georgia State Industrial College for Negroes in Savannah, explained to whites that though Blacks had ties in the South, unfair and cruel treatment was driving them away. Wright stated in 1917:

There is scarcely a negro mother in the country who does not live in dread and fear that her husband or son may come in unfriendly contact with some white person so as to bring the lynchers or the arresting officers to her door, which may result in the wiping out of her entire family.

Two years later, Robert Moton, Washington's successor at Tuskegee, stated, "I am of the opinion that lynching is the chief cause of unrest among Negroes. . . . It was the cause most often given as a reason for wanting to migrate North." The Chicago Defender actively promoted the migration, not by picturing the North as a paradise, but by publicizing the lynchings in the South while offering the North as a refuge from the mob. Many lynchings were followed immediately by an exodus of Blacks from the immediate area of the lynching. The fact that this did not always happen led some observers to minimize lynching as a cause of migration and to disagree with Herbert Seligmann, publicity director of the NAACP, who wrote in 1920 that "the migration was least from the districts in which there was no lynching and mobbism."[42]

The white South was aware of the fact that lynching contributed to the migration. Howard Snyder, a Mississippian, wrote in the North American Review for January 1924 that the many burnings at the stake were the cause of the migration then. The Southern press also recognized the relationship between lynching and the migration. A Georgia newspaper stated that "the heaviest migration of negroes has been from those counties in which there have been the worst outbreaks against negroes." The newspaper considered significant the fact that there had been no migration from one county which had never had a lynching.[43]

Black Sociologist Charles S. Johnson stated that the migration of Blacks was "motivated more by the desire to improve their economic status than by fear of being manhandled by unfriendly whites." He wished to show that the migration was not motivated by "fugitive, uncourageous opportunism." Johnson cited as evidence for his thesis that the Black population increased in some counties which also had high lynching frequencies. The fact remains that Blacks wished to live in a society that was not symbolized by the lynching tree. Johnson stated that persecution "plays its part---a considerable one, but when the whole of Southern Negroes is considered, this part seems limited." Many have taken this one statement out of context, ignoring the great body of evidence to the contrary, and have concluded that lynching was little related to the migration.[44]

Emmett J. Scott, one of the historians of the Migration, contributed to the misunderstanding by stating:

> Both whites and negroes in mentioning the reasons for the movement generally give lynching as one of the most important causes and state that fear of the mob had greatly accelerated the exodus. . . . A careful study of the movement, however, shows that bad treatment by representatives of the law caused almost as many negroes to leave the South as lynchings.

Statements such as these by Charles Johnson and Emmett Scott neglect the vital point that the other conditions Blacks fled from such as "bad treatment by representatives of the law," systematic robbery of the fruits of their labor, poor schools and public services, were all ultimately enforced by the mob. Lynching was the symbol of this society and the migration was a positive and rational effort to seek a solution.[45]

The migration affected the anti-lynching reform in several ways. Urbanization stimulated the development of a heightened group consciousness among Blacks. This led to greater militancy, thereby increasing the cost of lynching. The loss of much needed labor caused the power structure of the white South to reassess its treatment of Blacks and to rein in mob action somewhat. The movement of Blacks into Northern areas where they could vote modified the attitude of both the major political parties toward Blacks. The increased political influence made the specter of federal legislation more real to the South, which then moderated its behaviour just enough to avoid such legislation. The above factors, working together and reinforcing each other, led to an increase in the level of interracial activity.

One reason the migration changed things was because the Southern economy was adversely affected by the departure of a significant portion of the labor force. For example, when J. W. Tucker of the Jackson, Mississippi, Board of Trade, stated in 1920 that the labor shortage had become a serious menace to the business interests of the city and state, he was reflecting a view that found continuous expression. Five years later, Congressman Thomas Bell of Georgia wrote to Coolidge that the exodus had caused financial ruin to many planters. The Black press made certain that Blacks knew that whites viewed the migration as an economic threat. Blacks hoped that whites who had not listened to pleas for justice based on moral principles might heed economic self-interest. J. Max Barber said the exodus was "like a gigantic strike against intolerable conditions." The Defender repeatedly noted, "The South is in dire straits for help, large productive fields are abandoned, cotton gins and mills are limited in their output and on every hand can be seen signs of depression."[46]

The first reaction of the white South was to ignore the movement or to congratulate themselves on getting rid of some of the people they had been long blaming for the backwardness of the region. As the flow North increased, the second reaction was to increase the repression. As Herbert Seligmann said, "It is not much good being a superior race if the inferior race moves away." Labor agents were harassed, fined, and jailed. In many localities they were charged prohibitive license fees. In some instances legislation was passed to prevent or limit workers from leaving the state. Efforts were made to exaggerate the hardships which Blacks would endure in the North, and planters even spread stories that medical students and body snatchers in the Northern cities would capture Blacks for vivisection. In extreme cases individual Blacks who had declared their intention to leave were lynched as an object lesson for other Blacks. All of these efforts failed. When an earlier lynching of a Black for challenging the bookkeeping at the company store might have discouraged others from questioning their accounts, the lynchings after 1914 only encouraged and increased the migration.[47]

As the migration continued in the face of repression, some whites turned to the tactics of conciliation. Many communities had their first interracial meeting, and to the surprise of whites, Blacks used them to press for a variety of goals including an end to lynching, peonage, and discrimination. Chambers of Commerce and white service clubs such as the Lions and Rotary began to pass anti-lynching resolutions and even to call for the conviction of lynchers.[48]

The pressures of the migration caused some Southern state and local governments to take a stronger stand against lynchings, and in 1921, for the first time, the number of lynchings prevented exceeded the number carried through to completion. Georgia, responding to the needs of her developing war industries and an articulate Black leadership centered in Atlanta, showed the greatest official concern. Governor Hugh M. Dorsey, in an effort to direct public opinion, issued a statement on April 22, 1921, which detailed 135 cases of lynching, peonage, and other outrages against Blacks. In addition, twenty-two lynchers were indicted and four were actually sentenced while Dorsey was governor. In all the preceding history of Georgia, there had been only one conviction for this crime. Many of the affidavits on which the governor's statement was based were obtained by prominent Black leaders who contended that incidents such as the burning of Lee Eberhardt, a Black charged with murder, had accelerated the exodus earlier in 1921. Dorsey gave the lynching problem much publicity, although the Messenger charged that Dorsey's action was an opportunistic eleventh hour conversion which would help him in the New York City law practice to which he was moving.[49]

White Georgia was far from united behind Dorsey's efforts to reduce lynching. "The Guardians of Liberty" sponsored a mass meeting in Atlanta which called for Dorsey's impeachment and resolved that "Georgia--our mother--is being defiled before the world." Governor-elect Thomas W. Hardwick said that the Dorsey statement was untrue and a slander on the fair name of the state. The severe losses to the South resulting from the migration were not enough to end lynching, for there were still too many whites benefitting from the caste system and profiting from the exploitation of Blacks. The interracial movement was not yet sufficiently strong to have a decisive impact. Another ingredient was needed.[50]

The additional force which propelled the anti-lynching reform forward was provided by the increased militancy of Blacks. The new spirit of militancy had been growing for years. The Amsterdam News, heretofore a relatively conservative paper, began to speak in new tones early in 1915 when it said, "Lynching would cease in short order if the Colored people of this country resented the lawless murdering of friends, relatives and compatriots as they should--with rifles and sword." When an angry white speaker shook his fist at the Black audience in a bond-selling rally in Baltimore during the summer of 1917, he was hissed. By the end of the war, many whites were also aware of what the Messenger in 1919 named "the New Negro."[51]

The more reactionary South was deeply concerned about the New Negro, a concern which it attributed mainly to the foreign experiences of the Black troops. Senator James K. Vardaman, who had opposed the war and was defeated in the Mississippi primaries in 1918, partly because of Wilson's influence, represented the extreme racist Southerner who feared the old order would not be secure after the war. His newspaper constantly warned against the "Frendh-woman-ruined Negro soldiers." He said that there was a need for twenty-five or thirty armed whites in every community, operating outside the law and court system to "regulate" the returning troops. The urban riots made him frantic as the news spread that Blacks were shooting back as never before, and he increased the pitch of his appeals to whites to wake up to the danger of the New Negro. Vardaman was not alone in this fear. The South generally was apprehensive about the returning Negro soldiers, and there was much other evidence to indicate that lynching was to be the openly sanctioned instrument to suppress the new spirit.[52]

The "New Negro" was an urban phenomenon. There was nothing new about Blacks' sharing the universal willingness to fight and die, if need be, for what they believed were just causes. The urbanization accompanying the Great Migration increased the size of Black enclaves in both Northern and Southern cities. This enhanced the feelings of racial unity and group consciousness, and it increased the levels of sophistication and understanding among Blacks. In the cities, white racism was more subtle and less crude and blatant. Because role models of successful Blacks were more common, it was easier for Blacks to reject the image of inferiority. The urban Blacks read newspapers more and had greater opportunities to be aware of the larger world. This world was full of the democratic rhetoric that was used to unify the country behind the war effort. The urban Black ministers were more likely to be well-educated, more conscious of the gap between democratic theory and practice, and more free to inform their congregations of this gap. Urban Blacks also had a longer history of organization for self-help and enlightenment. These organizations had been contributing to the protest tradition for generations. For example, the Bethel Literary Society was at the peak of its influence as early as 1883. For generations, individual Blacks had shot back at mobs and officers who would turn them over to mobs, but the increased security and consciousness of the urban Blacks meant that militant self-defense would play a greater role in the urban setting. Also, as social anthropologist Hortense Powdermaker has explained, there were psychological changes attendant upon urbanization that would tend to increase militancy. The more secular atmosphere of the city encouraged securing the goals of this world by competition and aggressive struggle rather than the otherworldly goals of the Southern rural Blacks which were attained by meek endurance and suffering. Some of the more other-worldly leaders were left behind in the South.[53]

The tradition of self-defense among urban Blacks has a long history. James Weldon Johnson was impressed by the Blacks in a Florida town who organized to prevent a lynching in the 1890s when he was a child in Jacksonville. Blacks armed in the aftermath of the New York City riot in 1900. Following the burning at the stake of George White in Wilmington, Delaware, in 1903 one of the lynchers was arrested. A white mob demanded his release and attacked the Black section of Wilmington after they had been successful in freeing the prisoner. A number of Blacks then armed themselves and marched through the town "in an ugly mood." Four persons were wounded in the fighting. The Nation concluded that Blacks were learning that the way to secure their rights "was to arm themselves and strike terror in every heart." In 1904 a white mob in Springfield, Ohio, lynched Richard Dixon and attacked and burned part of the Black section, after which, troops were called in. The Voice of the Negro stated that the reason for the presence of the troops was not to protect the Blacks from further attacks but to prevent Black retaliation. A Black response to the Atlanta riot of 1906 was the collection of arms and the killing of some of the white attackers. Walter White recalls that the most memorable experience of his youth was crouching at an upstairs window with a loaded gun beside his father who was determined to shoot the first white who set foot on their property during this riot. A few perceptive whites realized that self-defense by Blacks and even retaliatory violence would reduce, not increase, the total amount of violence in society.[54]

The experiences of the Black soldiers in World War I also contributed to the increased inclination and capacity for self-defense. This heightened determination to resist brutal treatment was foreshadowed by the Houston riot of August 23, 1917. As indicative of the atmosphere in Texas at this time, a coroner's jury returned a verdict of "suicide" for a Black shot by a sheriff's deputy. Northern Black troops arrived on August 20 and immediately faced the full array of Southern Jim Crow, gratuitous insult and harassment. When the police beat up two Black military police who were performing their duties, 150 of the Black troops marched into town where they were joined by Black civilians. One white policeman and one army officer were killed, the latter by mistake. The press converted this militant response to police brutality into a great riot. Sixty-three Black soldiers were court-martialed. Of these, thirteen were hanged immediately without any opportunity to appeal; forty-one received life imprisonment; four got long prison terms; and five were slated for later execution. A second court-martial sentenced eleven others to death. For the next eight years the issue of the legal lynching of the Houston soldiers was second only to illegal lynching on the list of Black grievances. [55]

The racist basis of the Houston court-martials was emphasized by the contrasting treatment accorded the white troops who participated in the East St. Louis riot six weeks earlier. Archibald Grimke, militant Black attorney, submitted a moving poem to the Atlantic Monthly protesting the treatment of Black soldiers. It was rejected, according to the editor, because "we hate to believe the soldiers would not have been hanged had they been white." In East St. Louis the troops had joined the mob in killing dozens of Blacks, but a court-martial of the white troops was not even considered. [56]

All lynchings and riots generated protests from Blacks, but during World War I the volume of the protests dramatically increased. By 1919 the new level of Black determination to resist was demonstrated in the twenty-six riots of that "Red Summer." Most of these disturbances were in the urban centers where the Blacks were less inclined to accept the old patterns of accommodation and many of them involved retaliatory violence. The pattern started in Charleston, South Carolina, in May when the Blacks fought with the white sailors who attacked them. Riots planned by whites in Memphis and Montgomery were cancelled when it became known that Blacks were armed and prepared to go down fighting. In Longview, Texas, Dr. C. P. Davis had organized a Black Business League for cooperative cotton marketing and supply purchasing. Whites took out their frustration at the prospect of losing economic control of Blacks by nearly killing Samuel L. Jones, a Black school teacher who was accused of writing the Chicago Defender in protest to an earlier Texas lynching. Jones took refuge in Davis's home where the Business League members had assembled. When the Davis home was attacked, the Blacks opened fire on the mob and killed eleven whites who were trying to storm the house. The Messenger concluded, "50 Negroes can defeat a mob of 1,000 lynchers because whites don't want to get killed."[57]

The riot in Washington, D. C., in July, 1919 was described in the Messenger as the time "when Negroes shot a lynching bee into perdition" by killing two whites for each Black who died in the affair. John E. Bruce wrote in the Kansas City Call, "Let the white man bent on murder ponder this African slogan: 'If we go foreward we die; if we go backward, we die. Better go forward and die.' We are going forward." Some Blacks, such as District of Columbia Judge Robert H. Terrell and Emmett J. Scott, Special Assistant to the Secretary of War, deplored this retaliatory violence in Washington, but most of it did not occur until the third day of the riot, and many Blacks were delighted to have at last found a way to limit white aggression. Blacks from Baltimore came to reinforce those in the Capital. Both cities had NAACP branches which were perhaps more militant than the national office. The Baltimore Blacks had developed strong feelings of racial solidarity from fighting housing discrimination from 1908. The subject had become a political issue there earlier than in other cities because Baltimore was a terminus of earlier migrations. The Washington, D. C., branch was strengthened by the concentration of the Talented Tenth who were employed in business, government, and public education. Dunbar was probably the best Black high school in the United States and Howard University had long been developing Black leaders. The Washington Blacks' militancy had been growing since 1913 when the implications of the Wilson Administration's employment discrimination and officially-sanctioned Jim Crow became apparent. An even more severe riot broke out in Chicago less than a week after the Washington riot ended. Hundreds were injured, and fifteen whites and twenty-three Blacks were killed.[58]

The riot at Omaha on September 28, 1919, contributed to the anti-lynching reform in a somewhat different way. The mayor was almost lynched when he refused to turn William Brown over to the mob. The mob placed a rope around his neck, and the mayor was unconscious when rescued. Federal troops arrived and arrested fifty-nine after the mob had lynched Brown. This white attack on an elected official and subsequent looting and arson by the white mob did much to strengthen that segment of the anti-lynching movement which was motivated by a desire to resist anarchy. The Omaha riot also contributed to the understanding that the migration had made the problem more national in scope. Omaha, like Chicago and the other Northern urban centers, not only had many recent Black arrivals from the South, but also had experienced a large influx of white Southerners. The _Defender_ blamed the Omaha riot on the 20,000 Southern whites who had come there since 1915.[59]

The anti-lynching reform received another type of support from the last of the 1919 cataclysms. Events in Phillips County, Arkansas, exposed to many the knowledge that Southern planters used terror and manipulation of the courts to maintain peonage. Some of the Black farmers met in a little church at Hoop Spur to organize a cooperative league, "The Progressive Farmers and Household Union," which would help them to get a fairer price for their cotton and escape the usurious interest and inflated prices charged at the plantation stores. The planters in the area had a history of lynching those who challenged these practices, so the Blacks were forced to keep their plans secret. The meeting was fired on by county and Missouri Pacific Railroad officials. The Blacks returned the fire and a deputy sheriff was killed. James Weldon Johnson, the Field Secretary of the NAACP, said: "A reign of terror followed. Between two and three hundred Negroes were hunted down in the fields and swamps to which they had fled, and were shot down like animals. Many of them had no idea what the trouble was about." To disguise what was actually happening, stories of Black uprising, conspiracies and murder plots were hatched. Blacks who were arrested were tortured into confessing things they had never dreamed of doing, and the confessions were entered as evidence in a trial which was dominated by the mob. Twelve Blacks were sentenced to death and sixty-seven others were given long prison sentences in a trial lasting less than one hour.[60]

Part of the defense of the Elaine farmers was conducted in the press in an effort to educate the public on the nature of the systematic robbery of the Black agricultural worker. The migration had already introduced the topic to public discussion. By proving that the Elaine cooperative union was both non-violent and legitimate, it was hoped that a ground swell of opinion in support of the Elaine defendants would be created which could be used to condemn all lynchings of those protesting peonage.[61]

As the United States entered the 1920s, the increasing militancy of Blacks had accomplished several things. It has inspired more Blacks to protest lynchings directly either by moving away from areas where lynching was common or by fighting back when attacked and sometimes even by use of retaliatory violence. The militancy had led some whites to try to understand the new Black attitudes if only to determine how few concessions needed to be made to restore as nearly as possible the earlier relationship. Other whites saw in the new militancy the assurance that pre-World War conditions could never be restored. Some of these became active in working with Blacks to further the anti-lynching reform. A larger group of whites perceived a threat in the militancy. The millions who joined the Ku Klux Klan in the 1920s were in part motivated by the desire to put the Blacks in "their place."

The clock was not to be turned back. Most of the migrants remained in the North; their numbers swelled by large additions in the early 1920s. As Blacks became a more significant political force, the anti-lynching reform entered a more political phase than would have been possible without the Great Migration.

FOOTNOTES--CHAPTER VI

[1] McErney cited in Charles W. Chesnutt, "Disfranchisement of the Negro," in The Negro Problem (New York: James Pott & Company, 1903), p. 111; William H. Ferris, The African Abroad: Or His Evolution in Western Civilization, I (New Haven, Conn.: Tuttle, Morehouse, and Taylor Press, 1913), pp. 413; 102. For a typical statement of the myth of docility, see Kirk H. Porter, A History of Suffrage in the United States (Chicago: University of Chicago Press, 1918), p. 206-207, or I. A. Newby, Jim Crow's Defense: Anti-Negro Thought in America: 1900-1930 (Baton Rouge: Louisiana State University Press, 1965), p. 149.

[2] New York Globe, November 10, 1883, p. 2; January 12, 1884, p. 2; New York Freeman, July 18, 1885, p. 2; For a collection of militant statements by Black editors, see Martin E. Dann, The Black Press 1827-1890: The Quest for National Identity (New York: G. P. Putnam's Sons, 1971), p. 107. See also Donald E. Drake, II, "Militancy in Fortune's New York Age, Journal of Negro History, 55 (October, 1970), 307-322.

[3] Indianapolis Freeman, February 1, 1890, p. 2. This warfare was of long standing, the official history of the A. M. E. Church notes that in the 1870s "where the trail of the Ku Klux Klan became known, it was ambushed by colored men, and the horses of numberless Ku Klux went home without riders." See Charles Spencer Smith, A History of the African Methodist Episcopal Church (New York: Johnson Reprint Corp., 1968), p. 70.

[4] Indianapolis Freeman, February 8, 1890, p. 1. For similar accounts, see Indianapolis Freeman, May 30, 1896, p. 4; January 15, 1898, p. 6; Bradford Chambers, Chronicles of Negro Protest (New York: Parents Magazine Press, 1968), pp. 181-3; Chicago Broad Ax, November 26, 1898, p. 4.

[5] For examples of Blacks' killing officials rather than submit to arrest, see Crisis, 11 (April, 1916), 303; 2 (July, 1911), 99; 4 (September, 1912), 221; Norfolk Journal and Guide, December 2, 1922, p. 2.

[6] Indianapolis Freeman, April 4, 1896, p. 4; Chicago Broad Ax, March 27, 1897, p. 1; Crisis, 6 (June, 1913), 77; 6 (July, 1913), 120; 11 (February, 1916), 168.

[7] New York Globe, June 2, 1883, p. 2; Peter Gilbert, ed., The Selected Writings of John Edward Bruce: Militant Black Journalist (New York: Arno Press and the New York Times, 1971), p. 32; New York Freeman, July 18, 1885, p. 2.

[8] "Not by Violence," Independent, April 4, 1901, pp. 496-97; New York Times, December 3, 1906 (4-4); December 25, 1906 (1-5); December 26, 1906 (1-7).

[9] Voice of the Negro, 1 (October, 1904), 445; 1 (November, 1904), 563-65; I (December, 1904), 618-19: "The Lynching of Sam Petty," Crisis, 8 (May, 1914), 20; Leslie H. Fishel,

Jr., and Benjamin Quarles, *The Negro American: A Documentary History* (Glenview, Ill.: Scott, Foresman and Co., 1967), p. 374.

[10] Indianapolis *Freeman*, October 7, 1893, p. 1; Cleveland *Plaindealer* cited in Indianapolis *Freeman*, September 30, 1893, p. 4; Indianapolis *Freeman*, February 5, 1898, p. 4; *Half Century,* 7 (October, 1919), p. 21. For other positive effects of retaliatory violence see Lewis Hylan, *Blackways of Kent* (Chapel Hill: University of North Carolina Press,1955), pp. 186-90, 278.

[11] Edwin S. Redkey, ed., *Respect Black: The Writings and Speeches of Henry McNeal Turner* (New York: Arno Press and the New York Times, 1971), pp. 156-60; Indianapolis *Freeman*, January 13, 1894, p. 1; May 21, 1892, p. 1; August Meier, *Negro Thought in America: 1880-1915,* Ann Arbor Paperbacks (Ann Arbor: University of Michigan Press, 1963), p. 172.

[12] Redkey, *Respect Black,* p. 156; Indianapolis *Freeman*, June 25, 1892, p. 4.

[13] Raymond Patterson, *The Negro and His Needs* (New York: Fleming H. Revell Co., 1911), p. 151; Frank Tannenbaum, *Darker Phases of the South* (New York: G. P. Putman's Sons, 1924), pp. 156-57.

[14] W. E. B. Du Bois wrote a short story on the subject of genocide and how it might be accomplished. See "A Mild Suggestion," in *The Seventh Son: The Thought and Writings of W. E. B. Du Bois,* ed. by Julius Lester, Vintage Books (New York: Random House, 1971), 2:29-32.

[15] Indianapolis *Freeman*, November 12, 1898, p. 7; *Voice of the Negro,* 1 (October, 1904), 489-90; 1 (November, 1904), 548; James Weldon Johnson suggested a general strike of Southern Blacks in 1919, see Arthur Waskow, *From Race Riot to Sit-in, 1919 and the 1960s* (Garden City, N. Y.: Doubleday & Co., 1966), p. 211.

[16] Norfolk *Journal and Guide*, October 6, 1917, p. 1; Chicago *Defender*, January 24, 1920, p. 1; *Messenger*, 2 (March, 1920), 7; *Half Century*, 8 (March, 1920), 17.

[17] New York *Age,* March 7, 1891, p. 6; Indianapolis *Freeman*, August 8, 1894, p. 3.

[18] In a typical expression of this view, J. M. Henderson, a newspaper columnist said, "Isolated Negroes must defend themselves but the race must march on and up and not get involved in minor skirmishes," Indianapolis Freeman, December 10, 1898, p. 1; Mary Church Terrell, *A Colored Woman in a White World* (Washington: Ramsdell Publishers, 1940), p. 307; E. A. Johnson, *Light Ahead for the Negro* (New York: Grafton Press, 1904), p. 43; John Dollard, *Caste and Class in a Southern Town* (New Haven: Yale University Press, 1937), p. 333; Martin E. Dann, *The Black Press 1827-1890: The Quest for National Identity* (New York: G. P. Putman's Sons, 1971), p. 116; Carter G. Woodson, *A Century of Negro Migration* (Washington: Association for the Study of Negro Life and History, 1918), pp. 165-66.

[19] Dollard, *Caste and Class*, p. 292; Allison Davis, Burleigh B. and Mary R. Gardner,

Deep South: A Social Anthropoligical Study of Caste and Class (University of Chicago Press, 1941), p. 373.

[20] Terrell, Colored Woman, pp. 7-8; Pete Daniel, "Black Power in the 1920s: The Case of the Tuskegee Veterans Hospital," Journal of Southern History, 36 (August, 1970), 368-388.

[21] Crisis, 9 (March, 1915), 225; Competitor, 1 (June, 1920), 31. For typical accounts of Black men being lynched for resisting attacks on Black women see Chicago Broad Ax, September 8, 1906, p. 1; December 21, 1907, p. 1; Crisis, 2 (July, 1911), 99; William H. Ferris, The African Abroad: Or His Evolution in Western Civilization (New Haven: Tuttle Morehouse and Taylor Press, 1913), 1:441.

[22] Chicago Broad Ax, December 2, 1922, p. 2; Dollard, Caste and Class, pp. 154-55. For examples of white failure to retaliate against Black men who attached and killed white men interested in Black women see the Broad Ax, March 10, 1923, p. 1; Arthur F. Raper, The Tragedy of Lynching (Chapel Hill: University of North Carolina Press, 1933), pp. 203, 210; Dollard, Caste and Class, p. 290.

[23] George Sinkler, Racial Attitudes of the American Presidents: From Abraham Lincoln to Theodore Roosevelt (Garden City: Doubleday, & Co., 1971), p. 348; Ferris, African Abroad, 1:379-80.

[24] Booker T. Washington, N. B. Wood, and Fannie Barrier Williams, A New Negro for a New Century (New York: Arno Press and the New York Times, 1968), pp. 288-91; For the 1879 Exodus see U. S., Congress, Senate, The Removal of the Negroes From the Southern States to the Northern States, S. Rept. 693, 46th Cong., 2d sess., 1880, 3 vols; Frederick Doublass, "The Negro Exodus from the Gulf States," American Journal of Social Science, 11 (May, 1880), 1-22; R. T. Greener, "The Emigration of Colored Citizens from the Southern States," American Journal of Social Science, 11 (May, 1880), 22-35; George W. Williams, History of the Negro Race in America: From 1819 to 1880 (New York: G. P. Putman's Sons, 1882), pp. 529-43; Norman B. Wood, The White Side of a Black Subject (New York: Negro Universities Press, 1969), pp. 268-82; Woodson, Century of Negro Migration, pp. 126-46; John G. Van Deusen, "The Exodus of 1879," Journal of Negro History, 21 (January, 1936), 111-29.

[25] For hard times in Kansas see vol. 3, S. Rept. 693 (1880), esp. p. 215; New York Freeman, January 22, 1887, p. 1.

[26] Davis, Deep South, pp. 292-93; Guion Griffis Johnson, "Southern Paternalism Toward Negroes After Emancipation," Journal of Southern History, 23 (November, 1957), 483-509.

[27] New York Freeman, January 16, 1886, p. 1; April 2, 1887, p. 1; New York Age, March 23, 1889, p. 2; Indianapolis Freeman, May 21, 1892, p. 1; May 14, 1892, p. 1.

[28] Woodson, Century of Negro Migration, p. 176, ch. 8; W. T. B. Williams, "The Negro Exodus from the South," in Negro Migration in 1916-17 by R. H. Leavell, et al (Washington: Government Printing Office, 1919), p. 96.

[29] Rayford W. Logan, The Negro in American Life and Thought: The Nadir 1877-1901 (New York: Dial Press, 1954), pp. 188-89.

[30] New York Freeman, January 23, 1886, p. 4; April 18, 1885, p. 1; Gilbert Bruce, p. 31; for Black and white Southern attitudes toward foreign immigration see Roland T. Berthoff, "Southern Attitudes Toward Immigration, 1865-1914," Journal of Southern History, 17 (August, 1951), 328-360; Ferris African Abroad, 1:388; Wilfred H. Smith, "The Negro and the Law," in The Negro Problem (New York: James Pott & Co., 1903), p. 155.

[31] Louis Filler, The Crusade Against Slavery Harper Torchbooks (New York: Harper & Row, 1960), 1. 178; V. Jacque Voegeli, Free but not Equal: The Midwest and the Negro During the Civil War (Chicago: University of Chicago Press, 1967), pp. 173-77.

[32] Vernon Lane Wharton, The Negro in Mississippi, 1865-1890 (Chapel Hill: University of North Carolina Press, 1947), p. 195.

[33] U. S., Congress, House, Committee on Labor, Freeman's Inquiry Commission, H. Rept. 2194 to accompany H. R. 12940, 57th Cong., 1st sess., 1902. R. R. Wright, Jr., "Migration of Negroes to the North," American Academy of Political and Social Science Annals, 27 (January-June, 1906), 571.

[34] Indianapolis Freeman, March 12, 1892, p. 4; April 2, 1892, p. 1; Redkey Respect Black, pp. 135-36.

[35] Indianapolis Freeman, May 2, 1891, p. 2; December 22, 1894, p. 1; New York Age, January 11, 1890, p. 1.

[36] Redkey, Respect Black, pp. 194-95.

[37] For colonization efforts in Mexico see U. S., Congress, House, Congressional Record, 54th Cong., 1st sess., 1895, 28 pt. 2:1017, 1052; U. S., Congress, House, Failure of Negro Colonization in Mexico, H. Doc. 169, 54th Cong., 1st sess., 1895. For Brazilian and Philippine migration see New York Age, March 17, 1888, p. 2; Chicago Broad Ax, April 25, 1899, p. 1.

[38] Redkey, Respect Black, p. 56; Gardiner cited in William B. Smith, The Color Line: A Brief in Behalf of the Unborn (New York: McClure, Phillips & Co., 1905), p. 197; Allen cited in New York Freeman, June 6, 1885, p. 1; U. S., Congress, Senate, Congressional Record, 51st Cong., 1st sess., 1890, 21 pt. 1:630; Cook cited in New York Freeman, March 14, 1885, p. 1; Independent cited in W. Laird Clowes, Black America: A Study of the Ex-slave and His Late Master (London: Cassell & Co., Ltd., 1891), p. 138.

[39] Clowes, Black America, pp. 138-39; W. H. Crogman, Talks for the Times, p. 263.

[40] Redkey, Respect Black, pp. 56, 74.

[41] Charles E. Hall, Negroes in the United States 1920-32 (New York: Arno Press and

the New York Times, 1939), p. 5.

[42] The Black press published many letters from migrants citing lynching as the main reason for moving, for typical example see Half Century, 8 (April, 1920), 17; Wright cited in Emmet J. Scott, Negro Migration During the War (New York: Oxford University Press, 1920), p. 172; Robert Russa Moton, "The South and the Lynching Evil," South Atlantic Quarterly, 18 (July, 1919), p. 191-96; Chicago Defender, May 24, 1919, p. 1; Herbert J. Seligmann, The Negro Faces America (New York: Harper & Bros., 1920), p. 150.

[43] Howard Snyder, "Negro Migration and the Cotton Crop," North American Review, 219 (January, 1924), 21-29.

[44] Charles S. Johnson, "How Much is the Migration a Flight from Persecution," Opportunity, 1 (September, 1923), pp. 272-73.

[45] Scott, Negro Migration, p. 72. Among those who believed Southern Oppression was of major importance were Benjamin Mays and Joseph Nicholson, The Negro's Church (New York: Negro Universities Press, 1969), p. 95; Woodson, Century of Migration, pp. 169, 177; Williams, "The Negro Exodus from the South," pp. 107, 111.

[46] Chicago Defender, June 26, 1920; November 21, 1925; Barber cited in Opportunity, 1 (August, 1923), 254; Defender, April 3, 1920. Many Black newspapers carried frequent stories of how lynching was bad for business, for example see Norfolk Journal and Guide, December 2, 1921, p. 4. See also Williams "Negro Exodus," pp. 98-99.

[47] Seligmann, Negro, p. 93; Chicago Defender, May 10, 1924, p. 2; for vivisection rumors see Gladys-Marie Fry, "The Night Riders: A Study in the Social Control of the Negro" (unpublished Ph.D. dissertation, Indiana University, 1967), p. 205. For examples of lynching to prevent migration see Chicago Defender, May 24, 1919, p. 1; December 3, 1921, p. 1; July 28, 1923, p. 1.

[48] Williams, "Negro Exodus," p. 96; Scott, Negro Migration, pp. 79-83; Half Century, 6 (May 1919), 10; 9 (July, 1920), 10; 14 (May-June, 1923), 9; Chicago Defender November 5, 1921; June 17, 1922, p. 1

[49] For table listing lynchings prevented, by years, see Arthur F. Raper, The Tragedy of Lynching (Chapel Hill: University of North Carolina Press, 1933), p. 484; for Dorsey see George B. Tindall, The Emergence of the New South: 1913-1945 (Baton Rouge: Louisiana State University Press, 1967), p. 181; Gustavus Myers, History of Bigotry in the United States (New York: Random House, 1943), p. 229; Norfolk Journal and Guide, January 22, 1921, p. 1; February 26, 1921, p. 1; Messenger, 3 (July, 1921), 210.

[50] Nation, May 25, 1921, p. 727; Norfolk Journal and Guide, May 21, 1921, p. 1; Atlanta Constitution, May 22, 1921, p. 3A.

[51] Crisis, 9 (April, 1915), 280-81; Terrell, Colored Woman, p. 368; Messenger, 2 (July, 1919), p. 32.

[52]Tindall, Emergence, p. 64; Vardaman's Weekly, May 15, 22, 1919; August 21, 1919; for the generalized white apprehension see St. Clair Drake and Horace R. Clayton, Black Metropolis: A Study of Negro Life in a Northern City (New York: Harcourt, Brace, and Co., 1945), p. 65; for white expressions of the need to put Blacks back in "their place" by lynching some, see Competitor, 2 (October, November, 1920), 192; Robert Brisbane, The Black Vanguard: Origins of the Negro Social Revolution 1900-1960 (Valley Forge, Pa.: Judosn Press, 1970), p. 75.

[53]John W. Cromwell, The Negro in American History: Men and Women Eminent in the Evolution of the American of African Descent (Washington: American Negro Academy, 1914), pp. 171-78; Hortense Powdermaker, "The Channeling of Negro Aggression by the Cultural Process," in The Making of Black America, ed. by August Meier and Elliot Rudwick (New York: Atheneum, 1969), 2:104; Williams, "Negro Exodus," p. 95.

[54]James Weldon Johnson, Along This Way (New York: Viking Press, 1933), pp. 131-32; Gilbert Osofsky, Harlem: The Making of a Ghetto (New York: Harper & Row, 1963), p. 49; "Anarchy in Delaware," Outlook, July 4, 1903, pp. 543-46; Nation, July 2, 1903; p. 4; Voice of the Negro, 1 (April, 1904), 126-27; John Hope Franklin, From Slavery to Freedom: A History of Negro Americans (New York: Alfred A, Knopf, 1967), p. 441; Walter White, A Man Called White: The Autobiography of Walter White (New York: Viking Press, 1948), p. 12. See also August Meier and Elliott Rudwick, "Negro Retaliatory Violence in the Twentieth Century," New Politics, 5 (Winter, 1966), 41-51; for the idea that Black militancy would reduce the total violence see John Spencer Bassett, "String up Race Antipathy," South Atlantic Quarterly, 2 (October, 1903), 304.

[55]Mary Frances Berry, Black Resistance/White Law (New York: Meredith Corp., 1971), p. 141; Charles Flint Kellogg, NAACP: A History of the National Association for the Advancement of Colored People (Baltimore: Johns Hopkins Press, 1967), pp. 260-61; Edgar A. Schuler, "The Houston Race Riot of 1917" Journal of Negro History, 29 (July, 1944), 301-38; Stephen R. Fox, The Guardian of Boston: William Monroe Trotter (New York: Atheneum, 1970), p. 245.

[56]Messenger, 2 (October, 1919), pp. 8, 25-26.

[57]Berry, Black Resistance, pp. 143-44; Allen D. Grimshaw, "Lawlessness and Violence in America and Their Special Manifestations in Changing Negro-white Relationships," Journal of Negro History, 44 (January, 1959), 52-72; Seligmann, Negro, 147-49; Brisbane, Black Vanguard, p. 77; Messenger, 2 (August, 1919), p. 9. Police action in siding with the white mob was frequently the precipitating event for Black retaliatory violence in 1919, see Waskow, Race Riot, pp. 209-10.

[58]Messenger, 2 (September, 1919), pp. 28-29, 7, 13; Gilbert, Bruce, pp. 149-50; for the Chicago riot see The Chicago Commission on Race Relations, The Negro in Chicago: A Study of Race Relations and a Race Riot (Chicago: University of Chicago Press, 1922), William M. Tuttle, Jr., Race Riot: Chicago in the Red Summer of 1919 (New York: Atheneum, 1970); Alfreda M. Duster, ed., Crusade for Justice: The Autobiography of Ida B. Wells (Chicago: University of Chicago Press, 1970), pp. 405-10.

[59] Chicago Defender, October 4, 1919.

[60] Kellogg, NAACP, p. 245; Chicago Defender, November 1, 1919; February 28, 1920; Johnson, Along This Way, p. 342; Franklin, Slavery to Freedom, p. 483.

[61] Williams, "Negro Exodus," pp. 103-06; Kellogg, NAACP, pp. 270-71; Chicago Defender, June 19, 1920; Robert T. Kerlin, "Open Letter to the Governor of Arkansas," Nation, June 15, 1921, p. 847.

CHAPTER VII

AFTER WORLD WAR I

The anti-lynching reform grew stronger in the 1920s. The base of the reform movement was broadened by the inclusion of many more Blacks and both Northern and Southern whites. The Blacks became involved by supporting their own and interracial organizations. Whites became involved as their realization grew that violence to maintain caste was not only antithetical to the nation's professed ideals but could be counterproductive and lead to social disruption and a more radical attack on white supremacy. Some of the Black and much of the white support for the reform was motivated by a growing fear that unless the polarization which produced the Red Summer of 1919 was reversed, the ensuing chaos and turmoil might weaken the entire social structure. The reform grew in both the North and the South. Although the two segments sometimes worked together, their programs differed because Blacks had much more influence on the Northern-based segment.

Southern Progress

The Southern anti-lynching reform among whites got its start when the Southern Sociological Congress was founded in Nashville in May, 1912 in response to a call issued by Tennessee Governor Ben W. Hooper at the urging of Kate Barnard, the Jane Addams of Oklahoma. The Congress attracted the social justice wing of the Southern progressives, "social workers associated with churches and private charities, social-minded ministers, education leaders, and a scattering of urban reformers and clubwomen." This group spearheaded the penetration of the South by the social gospel and obtained Walter Rauschenbush, its outstanding protagonist, to speak at the 1913 meeting. The session in 1912 was all-white, but Blacks were invited to listen to, but not to present, papers at the meeting in 1913. Clarence Poe, apostle of rural segregation and editor of the Progressive Farmer, resigned from the Southern Sociological Congress because Blacks were present at this meeting. By 1915, some of the papers were delivered by Blacks, and the Crisis thought the attitude of the white speakers was encouragingly sympathetic. In 1916, the Congress recommended that sheriffs who lost prisoners to mobs should automatically resign. With the added pressure of the wartime exodus of the Blacks, Professor Edwin Mims of Vanderbilt University told the 1919 Congress that lynching was never justified, that it brought economic peril, and was a political mistake and a sin. The Congress was reorganized as the Southern Cooperative League and tried to get all thirteen Southern states to agree on a model state anti-lynching law as an effort to forestall federal legislation. Its functions were taken over by the Commission on Interracial Cooperation, organized in 1919, and the Congress faded away.[1]

The University Commission on Southern Race Questions was formed as an auxilliary of the Southern Sociological Congress in 1912. YMCA worker Willis D. Weatherford, James H. Dillard, Director of the Jeanes and Slater Funds, and Mrs. John D. Hammond, wife of the president of Paine College, were its guiding hands. The Commission, consisting of one faculty representative from each of eleven Southern state universities, was formed to stimulate discussion. The University Commission was primarily interested in education but set aside some time to consider other problems. No Blacks were invited to attend the first four conferences, but the all-white group invited Booker T. Washington to attend in 1915 and thereafter listened to an increasing number of Black views. John Hope, president of Morehouse College, advised the 1917 session that the migration from the South would increase if whites continued to ignore the problems of Blacks. Lynching had been discussed in earlier sessions, and in 1916 the Commission began an annual practice of sending open letters to the South's college men, appealing to them as society's leaders to take the lead in the "crusade" against mob violence because "the wrong that it does to the wretched victims is almost as nothing compared to the injury it does to the lynchers themselves, to the community, and to society at large."[2]

These groups paved the way for postwar organizations and contributed to the anti-lynching reform by giving liberal whites a prestigious and respectable forum to use in undercutting the more virulent demagogues such as James K. Vardaman and Cole Blease. The University Commission's statements encouraged the more liberal currents, especially in the press and pulpit. Their activities had to continue for decades before the myth that the "best people" did not support lynching acquired any real substance.

Southern liberals were particularly cognizant of the need to influence the Southern press which too often carried stories of mobs under such headlines as, "The Good Work of Judge Lynch." In March, 1918, William English Walling, the first chairman of the executive committee of the NAACP, wrote about the need for a Southern anti-lynching initiative to James H. Dillard, founder of the University Commission on the Southern Race Question. Walling told Dillard that he was depending on him to hire a newspaper man to distribute NAACP publicity to the white press of the South and to find someone to contact the Southern preachers. Dillard obtained the services of Mrs. John D. Hammond, a Southern-born white, to head up a new organization, the Southern Publicity Committee. This committee was supported by the Phelps-Stokes Fund, in its efforts to gather and disseminate news about Black achievements. It enlisted the sympathies and support of the preeminent Southern editors, including Marse Henry Watterson of the Louisville Courier-Journal, Clark Howell of the Atlanta Constitution, and C. P. J. Mooney of the Columbus Enquirer-Sun. Mrs. Hammond had long given thought to the race problem and had written a book published in 1914 on the growing social conscience of the South. Although Dillard did not notify Walling of this action, when Walling learned of it two months later, he discussed with fellow NAACP official Mary White Ovington ways by which the NAACP could cooperate with the new Publicity Committee and concluded, "Of course I regret that we were not told about it in advance."[3]

This reluctance of the white Southern liberals to work more closely with the NAACP continued throughout the 1920s and 1930s and reflected Southern inability to accept the more fundamental program of the NAACP. The two groups, however, did find much common ground and opportunities for cooperation in specific anti-lynching work. This was one more example of the fact that whites would work with Blacks to oppose lynching when they would not engage in inter-racial activities for other goals.

After World War I the white liberals in the South were particularly disturbed by the violence against Blacks which followed the armistice. They had believed that the improvements in race relations which accompanied the war period would be continued. They had observed and participated in the interracial conferences which had been created in an effort to stem the Great Migration, and they believed that the white society would continue to move in the direction of greater tolerance and continue to make small concessions to Blacks. The racial moderates also were aware of the Black contribution to the war effort through service in the military, labors on the home front, and enthusiastic work in behalf of the various government drives to conserve resources and raise funds. These signs all indicated that the white ruling majority was willing to permit Blacks to make gains which might eventually result in some sort of "Junior Partnership." Therefore, when the war ended and white aggression was intensified in an effort to nullify the small wartime gains of Blacks, the racial moderates were impelled to act.

In the 1920s, the most important channel through which the progressive Southerners worked was the Commission on Interracial Cooperation (CIC). The CIC, organized in Atlanta in 1919, adopted a program for improving race relations which included attacks on lynching, peonage, police brutality, and the inadequacy of educational and public services to Blacks. The CIC accepted the Black view that lynching was the touchstone of race relations, and it gradually concentrated its resources on the lynching problem. However, the CIC did not accept the Black view that only the complete elimination of the caste system would end lynching, and therefore, the CIC did little to increase the ability of Blacks to fight their own battles. It, instead, continued the tradition of Southern white paternalism to give Blacks that which whites thought they deserved.

The CIC followed the path blazed by earlier organizations. It built upon the foundations laid by the interracial committee which had been formed in 1906 as a result of the Atlanta riot, by the YMCA interracial efforts developed under the leadership of Willis Duke Weatherford, and by the War Work Councils promoted by the government to strengthen the domestic economy during the war. The University Commission on Southern Race Questions, the Southern Sociological Congress, and the several Law and Order Leagues, the most significant of which was formed in Tennessee in 1918, also helped to prepare the way for the new organization. The leaders of these groups, particularly those in Georgia, recognized that rapidly deteriorating race relations in 1919 called for an immediate response. Concerned by the nineteen lynchings of Blacks in Georgia in 1918, which were more than in any previous year of the twentieth century and almost three times the 1917 total, Atlanta whites met to discuss the ominous situation in January 1919, and as a consequence the Committee on Interracial Cooperation was launched a few months later. The organization grew quickly and within a year had established 500 state, county, and local interracial councils. By 1921, the number had grown to 800, although many existed on paper only. Will W. Alexander was the executive director of the CIC throughout its twenty-five years of life. Alexander had been a Methodist minister in Nashville and had been active in YMCA work among Blacks during the war.[4]

Black participation in the CIC was never great and tended to decline after the first few years because the dominating white leaders did not develop beyond their original 1919 positions. The Blacks most closely associated with the CIC were already known by the white South. The first, Robert Moton and Bishop Robert E. Jones, were invited to join the CIC in March 1920. Moton had inherited Booker T. Washington's position at Tuskegee and wore his predecessor's mantle with little discomfort. Bishop Jones edited the <u>Southwestern Christian Advocate</u> and was the only Black bishop in the Methodist Eqiscopal Church at that time. Will Alexander thought Jones was particularly well qualified to work with the CIC because his work in the church had accustomed him to the compromises of well-meaning whites. Although the Commission was paternalistic, it did adopt some of the concepts for social improvement which Blacks had suggested forty years earlier.[5]

The CIC's direct anti-lynching work was in many ways very similar to the work of the NAACP. The Commission relied heavily on publicity, making many efforts to obtain the endorsement of prominent officials and to influence governors and legislators. It developed a women's auxiliary, opposed police brutality, exposed the fact that rape was not even alleged in most lynchings, and that some whites put on burnt cork to escape detection while committing criminal acts. Like the NAACP, the Commission supported state legislation and pinned medals on brave sheriffs for protecting prisoners. It differed from the NAACP primarily in that Black thought had less influence in determining its policies and consequently it did not support federal anti-lynching legislation in the 1920s, despite NAACP requests.[6]

The activities of the Commission were primarily educational and were aimed at broadening the base of the anti-lynching reform movement in the South. The Committee on Publicity directed by Mrs. John D. Hammond was reorganized as the Education Department of the CIC in 1922 under the direction of Robert B. Eleazer, Jr. By the early 1930s the press service was distributing material to newspapers and journals with a combined circulation of over twenty million. The CIC published a periodical, the <u>Southern Frontier</u>, and a number of small pamphlets designed for mass distribution. One of these pamphlets, "Burnt Cork and Crime," listed some twenty-five cases where whites had blackened their faces and committed crimes for which Blacks were initially accused.[7]

The Commission on Interracial Cooperation developed a program for education in other areas also. It was critical of the biased and unfair portrayal of the Black's role in the United States in school textbooks. The Commission encouraged collegiate forums to discuss lynching and race relations and was helpful in the establishment of college level courses on the subject. By 1930 there were thirty-nine courses on the Negro and Race Relations in Southern white colleges. This activity was a direct continuation of the work of the Southern Sociological Congress and that of Willis Duke Weatherford who had written a textbook, <u>Negro Life in the South,</u> in 1915.[8]

The CIC had a strong religious orientation. Its executive director, Will W. Alexander, was a Methodist minister, as was its president, the Reverend E. Blackwell. White church leaders of Atlanta were the initiators of the original plans for the Commission in 1919. Much of the publicity of the CIC was presented in the form of sermonettes on love, peace, and brotherhood, which appealed to the Christian conscience in order to foster more church involvement in the movement. A founder of the National Urban League, Black sociologist George E. Haynes, secretary of the Commission on the Church and Race Relations of the Federal Council of Churches, told the National Baptist Convention in 1924: "During the past three years the campaign to array the churches against the lynching evil has been one of several important forces in reducing the number. . . . Another year or two will see this black blot wiped off our entire land." Although Hayes was overly optimistic, the

Commission's encouragement of interracial cooperation at the pastoral level did lead to some erosion of the stereotyped conceptions of Blacks held by whites and exposed whites to broader and more liberal views on race relations than those held originally by the CIC. Blacks welcomed this contact as they had long noted the lack of contact between the Talented Tenth and the white establishment had been a great obstacle to the erosion of the stereotype concepts of whites.[9]

Although the Commission conducted an intensive anti-lynching campaign, it did so within the "states' rights" framework and refused to accept the Black view that federal legislation was necessary. In justification of its failure to support the NAACP's efforts to obtain federal legislation, the CIC issued a press release in January, 1923 which declared that state actions would be sufficient to continue the decline of lynching "to the vanishing point." The state measures especially recommended by the CIC would reduce the influence of courthouse rings by placing the state constabulary under the control of the governor and would remove officers who surrendered prisoners to the mob. Neither of these measures could influence the suddenly-formed mob which completed its work before the victim had been arrested, because such measures did not provide any means for the punishment of the actual lynchers. The NAACP-backed Dyer bill provided for removal, fines, and even imprisonment of derelict officials. By virtue of great effort the NAACP had forced the Dyer bill to a successful vote in the House of Representatives on January 26, 1922. The Senate delayed consideration until December, 1922 at which time a combination of Republican apathy and a filibuster by Southern Democrats prevented the measure from coming to a vote. The CIC position reinforced both the Northern apathy and the Southern intransigence and contributed to the failure of Congress to give further serious consideration to federal anti-lynching measures in the 1920s.[10]

Some of the Commission's opposition to the Dyer bill was directed toward its provision for fines against the county in which the lynching occurred, with some of the fine money to be used to provide indemnities for the dependents of the mob's victim. Opponents to this provision stated that the indemnities would encourage Blacks to provide for their families by committing heinous crimes which would inciet the mob to lynch them. While the CIC did not encourage such illogical opposition to the Dyer bill, its members did argue that innocent taxpayers would have to pay for the acts of the guilty. However, the Commission in 1926 encouraged and applauded the raising of a fund of $10,000 by Blacks of Lexington, Kentucky, for the benefit of a white woman who had been widowed by the murder of her husband by a Black.[11]

In an effort to give credibility to the Southern argument that the Dyer bill was unnecessary, the CIC urged state action for anti-lynching reform. The CIC's endeavor to influence the states included appeals to governors, legislators, and local law enforcement officials. The governors of Arkansas, Kentucky, and North Carolina sponsored state committees of the Commission. The governors of Oklahoma and Georgia called state conferences to discuss lynching. Governor Hugh M. Dorsey of Georgia was responding in part to pressure put on him by the Commission when he issued his statement in 1921 of 135 postwar atrocities against Blacks. The governors of Mississippi, Virginia, and South Carolina expressed support for the Commission. Part of this favorable response by the governors followed their receipt of an anti-lynching petition prepared by the Commission and signed by forty-three college presidents and twenty-four professors of Southern colleges. In his inaugural address Governor Henry L. Whitfield of Mississippi acknowledged CIC influence when he called for the courts and law enforcement officials to end lynching.[12]

The Commission encouraged local officials to resist mobs and defend their prisoners. Starting in 1925, the Commission by 1932 had awarded medals to fifteen sheriffs, one constable, and one jailer in eight states for "particular bravery or intelligence, or both in outwitting mobs or defending prisoners." These presentations encouraged the use of force against mobs and directly helped reduce the number of lynchings. By 1932, 80 per cent of the mobs were thwarted; four years later the figure had risen to 90 per cent. This white determination helped to increase the level of interracial activity as Blacks saw that some whites would defend them. When a Madisonville, Kentucky, mob planned to burn out the Black community following the killing of a popular sheriff by a "drug-crazed" Black in 1922, the Commission intervened and prevented the pogrom, whereupon Blacks helped to apprehend the murderer, who was duly tried and executed. At Corbin, Kentucky, later in the same year, the Commission was unable to prevent an attack on the Black community, but it did help send the leaders of the mob to prison.[13]

One of the most significant aspects of the work of the Commission on Interracial Cooperation was the development of its women's auxiliary. The CIC's religious orientation, its emphasis on slow reform, and its reliance on the academic techniques of study and publication, all combined to make its work respectable in the South and to make it possible for white women to support its anti-lynching activities. By opposing lynching, the white women had traditionally regretted. The white women's opposition to lynching was an indirect attack on the double sex standard which was limiting only to white women and Black men. The Southern white women were not asking for the freedom which their men had; they were asking instead that white men be restricted.

The women's auxiliary developed when the CIC and the women of the Methodist Church arranged for nine fraternal delegates to attend the 1920 meeting of the National Congress of Colored Women's Clubs at Tuskegee. At Tuskegee the Methodist women learned that they shared common hopes and problems with Black women. The Tuskegee conferees gave the Methodist women a seven-point agenda which included the prevention of lynching. The Methodist women then arranged a meeting to be held in Memphis in October, 1920. There 103 white women leaders heard Black women present a statement of wrongs which was headed by lynching. The Black representatives included Mrs. Booker T. Washington, Mary McLeod Bethune, founder of Bethune-Cookman College, and Charlotte Hawkins Brown, a Wellesley graduate and also a founder of a Black school. This meeting laid the foundation for the Commission's Department of Women's Work headed by Mrs. Luke G. Johnson of Atlanta. The women took the revolutionary position that lynching did not promote their security. This contributed to the process of discrediting the time-worn myth that lynching protected the virtue of white women and the admission was an important step forward in the anti-lynching reform because it forced whites to consider the true causes of lynching. The women's argument was reiterated in the many publications of the Commission, picked up in the Black press and the white liberal press, and repeated in many Southern newspapers and some pulpits. This publicity, by reversing the process by which the New South had built up the rape myths, began to erode the popular misconceptions about lynching. The statement of the women's branch of the South Carolina Commission was typical:

> There is no crime more dangerous than that which strikes at the root of constitutional authority, breaks all restraint of civilization and substitutes mob violence and masked irresponsibility for established justice. There is no greater fallacy than that which holds up the shield of Southern womanhood in defense of the crime of lynching, and burning of human beings, claiming that such acts are the outcome of Southern Chivalry.[14]

The white women attacked the white male prerogative in another indirect way by defending the honor and virtue of Black women. The white women in the past had contributed greatly to the myth and stereotype that no Black woman was virtuous. Dr. A. M. Moore, the president of the North Carolina Mutual Life Insurance Company, one of several successful Black insurance companies founded in the nineteenth century, explained the origin of this myth to the 1921 session of the North Carolina Sociological Congress. The Black woman, he said,

> Became the victim of the passions of her white overlord. . . . This so enraged the white mistress . . . that she thrust from her, and from her heart, the dishonored mother, and from that day she came to hold in light regard the virtue of Negro women.[15]

The idea of white women's active participation in the anti-lynching reform spread almost as rapidly as that of the parent interracial Commission. The state and local organizations all refuted the myths that lynching was necessary to protect white women and that Black women were immoral. When the white women of Little Rock, Arkansas, organized in early 1922, they adopted a statement deploring the lack of respect shown Black women and asked that the full protection of the law be extended to them. This last point was a fundamental attack on the double sexual standard in that it implied that a Black woman should be able to win court-ordered support for her child even if the father was white.[16]

The CIC found confirmation of its belief that state action was sufficient to bring an end to lynching in the continuation of the long-term decline in the number of lynchings. The CIC's efforts to justify resistance to federal legislation had contributed to an all-time low of sixteen in 1924. The number jumped to thirty in 1926 but dropped back to sixteen the following year. By 1929 a new low of ten lynchings was established. However, stresses induced by the depression contributed to an increase which more than doubled the lynching frequency in 1930. This increase sparked a new growth of the entire anti-lynching reform movement and gave birth to a number of new organizations in both the North and the South.

One of the Southern responses was the formation of the Association of Southern Women for the Prevention of Lynching (ASWPL) in 1930. This organization absorbed and expanded the Women's Work Department of the CIC. Under the direction of its executive director, Mrs. Jessie Daniel Ames, the ASWPL grew rapidly. Two years after its founding, it had 7,000 members. By 1935, it had 35,000 members and continued to add 1,000 members a year for the next five years. The members of the ASWPL carried the message back to other groups to which they belonged. These other groups had a combined membership of over two million. Mrs. Ames had been active in the suffrage movement and in Democratic politics, and like many who were deeply involved in the anti-lynching reform, she had been influenced as a child by personal knowledge of a lynching.[17]

The ASWPL developed a three-point program: repudiation of the idea that lynching was necessary for the protection of Southern womanhood; recognition that lynching undermined the Constitution; and the admission that lynching detracted from the credibility of foreign missionary efforts. Implementation of the program led to active lobbying in state capitals, visits and letters to county sheriffs, and an active "letters to the editor" campaign. The ASWPL set up a card file of every women in every county who could be depended upon to go out and confront mobs, and a telephone system was set up to alert the women volunteers to these emergencies. Although ridiculed and even threatened, the women persevered, and some of their work had the additional benefit of increasing the contact between the races. Benjamin Mays, president of Morehouse College, believed that it was this organization, not the Southern churches, which provided the main voice of the South against lynching.[18]

By 1934, although the Southern Methodist women were endorsing the Costigan-Wagner anti-lynching bill, the NAACP-backed measure of that year, the ASWPL pointedly did not, and instead, they asked President Roosevelt to take action to federate the efforts of federal, state and local officers "to stamp out lynching." As Roger Baldwin, head of the American Civil Liberties Union said, the ASWPL and the CIC were not yet quite convinced that federal legislation was necessary. The ASWPL would not support federal anti-lynching legislation, but it did undercut some of the arguments used by the Southern legislators who were the most extreme opponents of such measure. When the Costigan-Wagner bill was being debated in 1935, Mrs. Ames wrote Senator Henry F. Ashurst of Arizona to warn him that the women of the South would repudiate any argument that the bill should be defeated in order to protect Southern women.

> We feel strongly that our honor cannot be used to add a halo of chivalry to acts which grow out of conflicts between men without reference to women.
> It would be embarrassing to Senators who should be moved to resort to such false arguments in defense of lynching to have women of their own states repudiate them and it would be unpleasant to the women to be forced to do this. . . . There are many sound arguments against the bill, but the defense of Southern women is not one of them.

In 1937 the ASWPL lobbied against the penalty-laden Gavagan anti-lynching bill, which was patterned after the earlier Dyer bill, by supporting a watered-down version which the Senate Judiciary Committee voted to substitute. Mrs. Ames stated of the weaker Senate bill, "This substitute Bill is free from threats and gratuitous insults. The difference between the Bills are so great that you will want to have the material which I am sending you."[19]

The continuing faith in education of the Commission on Interracial Cooperation was indicated by its formation of the Southern Commission on the Study of Lynching in 1930 with George Fort Milton, editor of the Chattanooga News, as chairman. Dr. Arthur Raper, a white sociologist, became research director, and together with his assistant, prepared three important studies on lynching. Walter Chivers, Raper's assistant, was a Black sociologist with degrees from Columbia University and the New York School of Social

Work who was teaching sociology at Morehouse College in Atlanta at this time. In 1931, Lynchings and What They Mean was published. This work contunued the battle to change public opinion and chided the opinion makers for too little effort. The following year, The Mob Murder of S. S. Mincey, and in 1933, The Tragedy of Lynching were published.[20]

Lynchings and What They Mean was so well-received that the Southern Commission on the Study of Lynching developed a twenty-three page methodological guide for field investigators. The field studies included sociological surveys of the communities in which the lynchings occurred, investigations of the facts of the lynching--including the alleged crime, and information on the mob members. The response of the community, legal action against lynchers, if any, press reactions, and the reactions of the local Blacks were also studied. The investigations concluded that young Blacks tended to leave the community and the older ones were noticeably disturbed, and "as the planters say, 'stubborn'." When bodies were left hanging, only whites viewed them. Black landowners would sometimes ask to drop down to sharecropper status because this would reduce their likelihood of being a mob target. Whites feared Black retaliation, and Black boycotts of white stores were common. The "collective guilt" of the white community protected the actual lynchers.[21]

George Fort Milton's position on federal anti-lynching legislation was ahead of that of Will W. Alexander or Jessie Daniel Ames. In 1930 he thought that the defeat of Cole Blease, "and some of his like," meant that such legislation could then be passed. In "Reflections on the Vanishing Mob," Milton drew several conclusions: lynching led to fewer sales for merchants, fewer patients for doctors, and fewer worshippers for ministers; the local press might oppose a specific lynching at first, but as the community was attacked for permitting a mob to function, the local editor would become defensive; the opponents of lynching were usually threatened and Black leaders were compromised and ruined by the white community if they protested; some Blacks would tell whites that the whites wanted to hear, namely, that the specific lynching was necessary.[22]

Jessie Daniel Ames and Will Alexander were representative of many liberal Southerners who were willing to spend time promoting the anti-lynching reform but were unable to promote the societal changes needed to prevent the formation of lynch mobs. This would have required a more fundamental attack on the myth of race than the Southern liberals were willing to undertake. Benjamin Mays stated that the Commission had no choice; that it was as radical as the South would tolerate at that time; and that had it moved against segregation, the bulk of the white population would have permitted the Ku Klux Klan to wipe it out in the early 1920s. As it was, the attitude represented by the Klan was sufficiently pervasive to force the Commission to use conspiratorial tactics. Mays observed that the Commission members had to "sneak and hide" when they held meetings in their churches. Even in the 1930s, Mrs. Ames was frequently threatened.[23]

At the same time the Commission on Interracial Cooperation was daringly fighting the Klan spirit, it was covertly reinforcing certain aspects of Southern society which made the Klan possible. Will Alexander wrote in 1928 that it was fortunate that Blacks were not employed in the Southern cotton mills because the jobs were not desirable, and he praised the race relations of the Tennessee Coal and Iron Company in statements which could only support segregation in industry and encourage the racism of the poor whites. In 1923 Alexander advised Mays to drop his suit against the Pullman Company for permitting him to be ejected from the accommodations for which he had paid. Mays went to court anyway, and won the suit.[24]

In education, the Commission leaders did not advance beyond the Southern white liberal position of 1900 that lynching would cease when the whites became educated. They argued that educational funds should continue to be unequally divided because Blacks would profit in the long run if white children advanced two steps for every one step Black children were allowed to advance. Jessie Daniel Ames was particularly enamoured by the "one-step, two-step" plan. Willis Duke Weatherford, in connection with his interracial YMCA work, had written a pamphlet against lynching in 1915 in which he indicated acceptance of the New South's myth that lynching had started after Reconstruction because Blacks raped white women. In response, Du Bois stated that Weatherford's analysis was untrue. Twenty years later, Will Alexander clung to the equally mistaken view that "lynching is almost galloping into extinction." This position was one consistently taken by Southern white liberals to head off federal anti-lynching legislation because the precedent of federal interference, once established, could lead to attacks on the basic discriminations of segregation.[25]

The Commission was a combination of paternalism and the progressive urge for social justice. In the early 1920s when the Klan threat was uppermost, the Commission's position was quite progressive for that period, but as society continued to change, the Commission became relatively conservative because it did not advance to new positions. In the late 1920s and throughout the 1930s it came to be regarded by the great majority of Blacks as being too conservative. Even such an extreme conservative on the racial question as Herbert Hoover praised the Commission in 1929. Edwin Embree of the Rosenwald Foundation suggested in the 1930s that the Commission should merge with the NAACP and the National Urban League. Had this suggestion been followed, the degree of white control of the latter two segments would have been increased and the new organization would have been a less effective influence for change than the sum of the efforts of the three separate organizations had been. At this time the Commission was reaching out to other groups, seeking a broader coalition of forces to attack lynching. This effort had its greatest success in Maryland where a coalition of thirty-two groups formed which forced a special session of the state legislature to consider an anti-lynching bill. The bill failed to pass. A similar coalition was formed early in 1931 in North Carolina when that state's nine-year record of no lynchings was broken.[26]

The Commission was born and enjoyed its early rapid growth in a South which was fundamentally disturbed by the migration of Blacks. It helped to focus and organize the concessions which whites were willing to make to stem the migration, but it could not force the issue of a more fundamental discussion of genuine equality for Blacks, because the white leaders of the Commission did not believe in racial equality. The Commission viewed the NAACP as Booker T. Washington had earlier viewed the Niagara Movement as too radical, an organization which demanded the impossible. In the final analysis, neither Jessie Ames and the ASWPL nor Will Alexander and the Commission on Interracial Cooperation would advocate the enforcement of the Constitution for Blacks.

Not all of the Southern women agreed with even the program and goals of ASWPL. The Women's National Association for the Preservation of the White Race was formed in 1931 with Mrs. J. E. Andrews of Atlanta, Georgia, as national president. Although it quickly passed from the scene, it was an example of the South's ability to set up organizations representing an attitude on racial matters which had not advanced beyong the "New South" of Henry Grady. This organization attacked George Fort Milton, chairman of the Southern Commission on Lynching, for questioning the guilt of mob victims and for leaguing with Tammany liquor interests and the "increadibly wealthy" NAACP in order to promote the ruin of the pure white race. Mrs. Andrews protested to President Hoover because he had met with Milton in 1931. She wrote a four-page pamphlet published by her organization in which she expressed regret that there was no white equivalent of the African Blood Brotherhood, a militant Black fraternal organization active in the early 1920s, to defend the white race and concluded, "All we need to do is to insist that the Negro get back in line." One study stated that this opposition to the anti-lynching reform was limited to the mimeograph and the printing press.[27]

Progress in the North

The Northern response to the increased racial violence and lynching associated with the immediate postwar period differed from the Southern in that it was primarily Black-led, and it made far more sweeping demands. It was also more fragmented and was composed of a greater variety of organizations. The largest of the new Black organizations was the Universal Negro Improvement Association (UNIA) founded by Marcus Garvey in Jamaica in 1914. Although the UNIA was created before the effects of the war were felt in the United States, it did not become important until Garvey moved the headquarters to New York City in 1917. By that time the war-associated events stimulating the development of anti-lynching forces in the United States were well underway.[28]

The UNIA expressed attitudes on lynching similar to those which Bishop Henry McNeal Turner had held. Turner and Garvey both believed that white society in the United States would never open up equal opportunities for Blacks but would continue to be a place where lynching would be tolerated. Turner laid more emphasis on the need for Blacks to oppose injustice by fighting against it in the United States and believed that integration was a desirable, if unattainable, goal. Both believed that the development of Africa under Black leadership would help secure the rights of Blacks around the world, but Garvey emphasized this point more than Bishop Turner had.

The UNIA, like other organizations, built on foundations constructed by earlier anti-lynching activities. It was a logical development of a segment of the Black protest which had been manifested in the growth of the cultural societies and discussion forums of the preceding generation. These organizations had reached for Black power by exploring the African past for knowledge that would offset the white myth of racial inferiotity, and they had improved the Black self-image in order to resist lynching more effectively. The UNIA's original nucleus in New York City was in the membership of a history club. William Sherill, president of the UNIA after Garvey's death, was already a contributor to anti-lynching campaigns when he first met Garvey in 1919. Dr. Leroy Bundy, another UNIA leader, had lived through the East St. Louis riot. Lynching and urban racial violence were recognized by the UNIA as evidence of the correctness of its theories. The second item under the heading "We Complain," in the Preamble of "The Declaration of Rights of the Negro Peoples of the World" which was adopted at the 1920 UNIA Convention, concerned lynching as did three of the fifty-four rights demanded in the body of this document. Garvey frequently condemned lynching in his speeches. His statement, "Negroes are determined to be liberated from mob rule," made at the 1921 International Congress of the UNIA, was typical. Methods to combat lynching were discussed extensively at the Convention of 1922. Some of the delegates who had witnessed lynchings and race riots related their experiences and gave their opinions on the best way to cope with these white attacks. The ideas expressed varied from support for federal legislation, through self-defense, to retaliation--"lynch the lynchers."[29]

In 1922 there were about 100 divisions of the UNIA in the South. They avoided racial confrontation and the lynch mob by emphasizing their distaste for integration. When Garvey endorsed President Harding, he said, "All true Negroes are against Social Equality." The white supremacists equated this separatism with a reluctance to fight racism and concluded that the UNIA was not as great a menace as the NAACP or William Monroe Trotter's Boston-based National Equal Rights League. Garvey saw that one of the results of lynching was an increased determination of Blacks to resist oppression, and he said on more than one occasion that Blacks should be glad that whites had "lynched race pride into the Negro." This was not an original idea with Garvey, for it had been used by anti-lynching reformers a generation earlier. However, his enemies distorted Garvey's meaning and falsely charged that he encouraged lynching. Garvey always opposed lynching and consistently argued that the development of a strong Black national state in Africa would be the best insurance against future lynchings. He pointed to the official concern of the federal governments' protests were the only reason for this official concern. By extension, Garvey argued that the most effective deterrent to the lynching of Blacks in the United States would be the existence of their own national state in Africa.[30]

Although the UNIA had maintained a low profile in the South, the Ku Klux Klan began to harass it. Garvey went to Atlanta in the summer of 1922 to explain the UNIA to the Klan. This caused the ranks of his enemies to swell, since the UNIA appeared to be compromising with the Klan instead of stoutly opposing lynching and discrimination. Carter G. Woodson, editor of the Journal of Negro History, stopped contributing to the Negro World, the UNIA organ; William Pickens, field secretary of the NAACP, refused UNIA honors; and some who had previously opposed Garvey for other reasons increased their attacks in 1922. W. E. B. Du Bois, Cyril Briggs of the African Blood Brotherhood, and A. Philip Randolph and Chandler Owens of the Messenger, were in this group. Garvey countered that those who favored integration and "social equality" were fomenting race trouble. "Unity" between the UNIA and the Klan never existed. Garvey's Atlanta trip was misconstrued and led to such extravagant statements as that of William Pickens who accused Garvey of being "the wrongest man who ever attempted to lead Negroes anywhere." A Messenger editorial that summer joined in the misrepresentation by charging that Garvey was in a league with lynchers. The 1924 UNIA Convention debates further confused observers as to the UNIA's real position on the Klan.[31]

Garvey did not cooperate with the Black organizations working to end lynching for two reasons. He recognized that the NAACP and most other groups opposing lynching were integrationist and opposed to the principles of the UNIA, and he believed that such efforts as those supporting the Dyer bill were diversionary and doomed to failure.[32]

No organization dependent upon Black resources could long survive in the United States if it created any impression that it upheld lynching. Garvey's contact with the Klan gave to those who competed with him for Black support the weapon they needed to undermine his influence. Although Garvey tried to clarify his position after being attacked for his Atlanta trip in 1922, he could not dispel the idea that he did not wholeheartedly oppose lynching. The UNIA convention in 1924 went on record "to protest against the brutalities and atrocities" of the Klan, but the concensus of the convention was that attacks on the Klan would divert the UNIA from its main program redeeming Africa. Garvey, however, declined to put anti-lynching reform sufficiently high on his order of priorities when this would have been the one theme most calculated to make him immune to attacks from other Blacks.[33]

Although the UNIA was the largest segment of the Black protest movement immediately after World War I, the conditions which caused its rise also produced other new organizations. The African Blood Brotherhood and the Friends of Negro Freedom were two which further diversified, complicated, and added to the anti-lynching reform movement.

The Friends of Negro Freedom was organized by A. Philip Randolph, Chandler Owen, and Nevel Thomas in early 1920. The organization's initial convention was held in Washington, D. C., on May 25. It was a Black-led interracial organization concerned with urban problems with a higher degree of class consciousness than the Urban League. It hoped to organize urban Blacks to oppose strikebreaking, to promote trade unions, tenants' leagues, and cooperative businesses, and to boycott discriminatory businesses. The new organization attracted numerous intellectuals, some of whom already belonged to the NAACP but chafed at the degree of white leadership in it. Archibald Grimke, longtime militant Black intellectual, and Carter G. Woodson, were among the charter members. New York City and Philadelphia had the most active branches. The Friends of Negro Freedom met regularly and had nationally prominent guest speakers such as Boise Penrose, Republican Senate leader, and Robert LaFollette, Wisconsin Progressive, and Congressman Dyer. Anti-lynching resolutions were frequently passed at their meetings. By the spring of 1922 it reported having twenty-five councils in thirteen cities and anticipated rapid growth.[34]

The African Blood Brotherhood, founded by Cyril V. Briggs in 1919 in New York City, also shared the anti-lynching impulse. Theodore G. Vincent's study, Black Power and the Garvey Movement stated that the Brotherhood was the first left wing Black nationalist movement. Never intended as a mass organization, its strength lay in a few urban centers, although at one time, Cyril V. Briggs claimed 150 branches and 50,000 members. Like several other organizations, it denounced lynching and denied that the United States had any right to interfere with other countries under the guise of promoting democracy as long as there was so little democracy for Blacks in the United States. The Crusader, organ of the Brotherhood, had announced a few weeks before the Tulsa riot of 1921 that force would be used by Blacks to oppose any lynching. It was the Brotherhood which organized the armed Blacks who came to guard the Tulsa jail when a mob was threatening to lynch one of the prisoners. This Black militancy touched off the worst riot of the year. When the mob forced the armed Blacks to retreat, a defense perimeter was established around "Little Africa," the Black ghetto in Tulsa. The state militia overran the Black defense line and disarmed the Blacks. The mob then descended, looting and destroying over 1,000 Black homes. Twenty-one Blacks and ten whites died in this battle.[35]

The new organizations which were created shortly before and after the end of World War I augmented the anti-lynching work being done by the older organizations of which the NAACP and the National Equal Rights League (NERL) were the most significant in the North. The NERL developed out of the Negro American Political League which was formed in 1908. It, in turn, had developed out of the various suffrage leagues and protest forums which had sprung up, principally in New England, around the turn of the century to protest the declining status of Blacks in the United States and Booker T. Washington's apparent acquiescence to this decline. As these groups began to take their ideological lead from the Boston Guardian, its editor and publisher, William Monroe Trotter, rose in prominence as the leader of the anti-Washington militants. The NERL underwent several reorganizations in its early years with Trotter remaining as corresponding secretary throughout. Trotter was a consistent militant with a world view which included opposition to discrimination everywhere and on all remaining fronts. His biographer, Stephen R. Fox, stated that Trotter's contribution to the civil rights struggle in the United States chiefly consisted of the role he played up to the founding of the NAACP, but Trotter was active and played a significant role for a long time after that. The role of the Equal Rights League was obscured by the NAACP which worked to keep the NERL in the NAACP's shadow. One reflection of this rivalry was the tendency of the Crisis to ignore the work of the NERL.[36]

Anti-lynching activity was always high, if not first, on the NERL's program. Several of its officers had personal knowledge of lynching. The Reverend Byron Gunner, a Presbyterian minister for six years national president of the NERL, talked his way out of the clutches of mobs five different times in Mississippi. N. S. Taylor was driven penniless from his Greenville, Mississippi, home because he became president of a local branch of the NERL in 1919. The NERL promoted many forums, lectures, and debates which publicized the lynching problem. In 1917 the Tenth Annual Meeting of the National Equal Rights League took the form of a broad Race Congress at the Mother Zion Church in New York attended by 200 delegates. At the time the Norfolk Journal and Guide thought that the NERL was a more important organization than the NAACP. This Race Congress reaffirmed the long-established program of the NERL which emphasized support for federal anti-lynching legislation and opposition to peonage, disfranchisement, and segregation.[37]

Trotter overcame government opposition and went to Paris in 1919, in an effort to focus world public opinion on lynching and the status of Blacks in the United States. When he returned, he testified before a congressional committee, "We are stopped in the fight we more reasonably could be engaged about, to secure equality of rights, by having to fight for the basic right of life itself." This was a recognition of the old point that until lynching was overcome, all other advances would be blocked.[38]

Ida B. Wells, longtime anti-lynching crusader, worked more closely with the NERL than she did with the NAACP. She attended the 1917 Race Congress and in 1921 was the publicity director for the NERL when she recommended placing anti-lynching first and fighting the Ku Klux Klan second on a nine-point program of action for the League. Also included were plans for a Defense Bureau to cooperate with law enforcement officials.[39]

Trotter had always chafed at the lack of consideration shown Black voters by the political parties, but he never ceased to try to influence them. The formation of the Negro-American Political League in 1908 was motivated by his opposition to William Howard Taft. Trotter supported the Democrats in 1912, but his disillusionment with President Wilson was complete when Wilson told Trotter never to come back to the White House while he was President. Wilson objected to Trotter's protesting segregation in government agencies too earnestly in 1914. In 1920 Trotter again tried to influence political events. The NERL sent a delegation to the Republican Convention in Chicago in 1920 which managed to intercept Warren G. Harding in his hotel corridor. Harding responded to the delegation by saying, "I am for Democracy in its fullness," and was then pushed into his private room by his managers.[40]

In addition to the NERL, the NAACP, the Friends of Negro Freedom, and the African Blood Brotherhood, Blacks worked to promote the anti-lynching reform through other organizations, among them being the fraternal orders. E. H. Morris, leader of the Odd Fellows, the largest Black fraternal organization at the time, was an ally of W. E. B. Du Bois and Ida B. Wells in their 1904 efforts to force Booker T. Washington into a more militant stance. Grand Master Tinsley of the California Prince Hall of Masons bitterly protested the government's treatment of the Brownsville soldiers. In an address, "The Race Question," delivered in 1907, Tinsley said that lynching was the repayment Blacks received for their loyalty. This speech was circulated through the lodges in other states because the Masons believed that Masonry had a major role to play in the defense of Black liberties. In the 1908 presidential campaign, The Reformer, journal of the True Reformers, took a strong position against lynching and the treatment of Black troops. Some fraternal orders supported the various NAACP fund drives during the war. In 1918, the Grand Master of the Prince Hall Masons of Texas noted that making the world safe for democracy included ending mob violence against Blacks. Some of the fraternal orders heeded the call of the Messenger in 1919 to vote funds for the defense of Blacks accused of rioting during the Red Summer.[41]

White supremacists recognized the role of the Black fraternal organizations in contributing to Black power. Cole Blease called for their suppression in 1912 on the grounds that they promoted racial solidarity and self-help. In 1919 other Southern whites called for the Southern sheriffs to take legal jurisdiction over the Black lodges as they were "hotbeds of Bolshevism."[42]

Fraternal leaders continued to play a role in the 1920s. They joined with the NAACP in lobbying for the Dyer bill and sent numerous petitions and memorials to Congress protesting lynching. H. P. Slaughter, editor of the Odd Fellows Journal, was a member of the NERL delegation that called on President Warren G. Harding in 1922 to protest racial injustice. Others were with Trotter when he headed a protest delegation calling on President Calvin Coolidge.[43]

None of these efforts completely eliminated lynching. In the first four postwar years, 90 per cent of the 265 lynching victims were Black. The racist nature of lynching was becoming increasingly obvious. The number of lynchings had been considerably higher a quarter of a century earlier, but in that period less than 70 per cent of the victims had been Black. These facts, combined with the recognition that none of the tactics pursued by the individual Black and Black-influenced organizations was producing a result commensurate with the efforts expended, led to a search for a new vehicle for Black protest. This search led to a revival of the convention movement in the form of a race congress, the Negro Sanhedrin, which met in Chicago in 1924.

The Sanhedrin was originally seen as an organization through which all Blacks could speak out in one great united voice of protest, and lynching was originally at the top of the list of grievances. M. A. N. Shaw, president of the NERL, wrote President Morefield Storey and Secretary James Weldon Johnson of the NAACP in December, 1922, proposing a great civil rights congress with anti-lynching as the number one point on the agenda. Johnson replied to Shaw that the NAACP was already working on such a project. Early in 1923, Monroe Trotter proposed that the four major Black civil rights groups meet to deal with the question of lynching. This coincided with Du Bois's belief, stated in the January, 1923 Crisis, that the defeat of the Dyer bill illustrated the need for a national race congress. The idea was in the air and crystallized when Kelly Miller called a "Preliminary United Front Conference," to meet in March, 1923. Miller, Dean of the Howard University College of Liberal Arts, was well known for his extensive literary output which was primarily in the field of popular sociology. He was an ambitious moderate who saw himself as an ideal compromise leader standing between the radicals and the conservatives. In addition to the NAACP, the NERL, the African Blood Brotherhood, and the Friends of Negro Freedom, two additional organizations attended this conference, the National Race Congress and the International Uplift League. The Brotherhood particularly tried to point the conference down the road of more militant protest. They got some support from the NAACP and the NERL, but the idea of militant protest was lost under Kelly Miller's leadership, and this March meeting ended in a shouting match between the moderates and the radicals. After the meeting, the Brotherhood continued to press Miller for a more militant Sanhedrin agenda. Cyril Briggs wrote Kelly Miller in July on the need to focus on race prejudice, discrimination, economic exploitation, "Ku Kluxism," and lynching among other things. Briggs wrote James Weldon Johnson in June of 1923 criticizing Miller's leadership. Briggs asked if Miller was going to shunt the important questions such as lynching into the background. Benjamin J. Davis, Sr., Black Republican leader and editor of the Atlanta Independent, also objected to Miller's preeminence in the upcoming Sanhedrin. Davis said that Miller was a member of the same old gang that had been misrepresenting the race for twenty-five years.[44]

Kelly Miller successfully fought off the attacks on his leadership and issued a call for the Sanhedrin to meet the week of Frederick Douglass's and Abraham Lincoln's birthdays. Fifty-seven of the sixty-one Black organizations which had been invited sent representatives. Among these were many of the Black fraternal groups. The Call stated that the need for racial unity was more important than the specifics of a program or movement in any speical direction. The conservative forces under Miller won control of the Sanhedrin meeting. They allocated only one forty-minute session of the five-day conference to the militants. This was a panel session on "The Function of Agitation in Race Betterment," chaired by Trotter. Panel members were James Weldon Johnson, representing the NAACP, and the Reverend T. J. Moppin, new president of the Equal Rights League, who had replaced M. A. N. Shaw on the latter's death. The rest of the conference dissolved into a swamp of generalizations about race betterment. George Schuyler, acrid and derisive columnist for the Messenger, said that the entire Sanhedrin was only an effort of Miller to obtain the presidency of Howard University.[45]

The Sanhedrin's attempt to unite all Blacks failed. It dissolved into a generalized discussion of race problems that tended to shift the onus for the condition of Blacks from white oppression to the failure of Blacks to work sufficiently hard at self-improvement. It did not carry the protest movement forward by the adoption of an agenda that the rank and file Black could rally around. Specifically, it failed to utilize the lynching issue which was still the one item upon which most Blacks could agree.

The organization which had grown strong by protesting lynching first, last, and always, was the NAACP. Unlike the earlier organizations such as The Afro-American League, the NAACP did not quickly forget the reason for its birth or get idverted into other activities, but retained the opposition to lynching as its main activity. As a result, instead of being strongest at the instant of organization, it started to grow and did not reach a peak membership for decades. One factor contributing to its growth and its appeal to a diverse membership was that the NAACP defined anti-lynching activities broadly to include all attacks on the caste system. The NAACP also differed from earlier organizations in that it was the first interracial group willing to place anti-lynching reform at the top of its agenda, and its members submerged their political differences and did not permit partisan politics to distract them unduly from the goal.

The NAACP's first effort was in defense of Pink Franklin, a South Carolina tenant farmer who killed an officer who burst into his bedroom in the dead of night to serve a warrant for violating the "false pretense" law. This law, which made it a crime for a farm worker to leave his employer after receiving an advance on his wages, had already been declared unconstitutional by the South Carolina Supreme Court. Franklin had no way of knowing this nor did he know the officer, but he did know that many lynchings began with whites bursting into homes at night. Franklin's response was in the pattern of the many who chose to resist arrest rather than face the lynch mob or possible death in prison.[46]

The Franklin case contrasted sharply with the first cases undertaken by previous civil rights groups. It involved peonage, police brutality, enforcement of unconstitutional laws, and violation of the simple courtesy of knocking before entering. The Afro-American League's first case involved the right of T. Thomas Fortune to have a glass of beer in a hotel bar in New York City. The first action of Bishop Turner's Equal Rights Council of 1893 involved attacks on "separate car" laws. Neither of these issues affected the daily lives of most Blacks. It was this consistent policy of attacking the most obvious injustices, the ones affecting the most people, which was one of the differences between the NAACP and earlier organizations.

Part of the effectiveness of the NAACP was due to white support, especially in the early years. Some whites had matured in the Progressive Era to the realization that industrialization and urbanization created new problems which could not be solved by the paternalism that organized solutions to the problems of the earlier agricultural society. These white progressives were few in number but they knew of the Black critique of society through their reading of the Black press and contacts with Blacks in religious, educational, settlement house social work, and political organizations.

The Blacks were influential in the NAACP and their influence grew as the organization developed. Many of them had personal experiences with mob violence. Dr. William A. Sinclair, a member of the original executive committee, had lost his father, a South Carolina Reconstruction legislator, to a lynch mob.[47]

Much of the success of the NAACP must be attributed to its policy of putting anti-lynching activities at the top of its agenda. Although some of the formal policy statements and the informal lists of demands and goals that appeared in the Crisis and elsewhere may not always have placed the elimination of lynching in the number one position, there is no doubt that anti-lynching was the single most important impulse energizing the Association. Charles Flint Kellogg's history of the early NAACP discussed the entire spectrum of the Association's activities and stated, "Calling public attention to the shamefulness of mob violence in modern society was the foremost task of the NAACP." William English Walling's "A Minimum Program of Negro Advancement," which appeared in the May, 1913 Crisis had the suppression of lynching as the number one point. Du Bois's editorial of September, 1917 placed "To stop lynching and mob violence," first of the seven things necessary to make the United States a democracy. In 1925, the elimination of lynching was the first of five aims of the Association. James Weldon Johnson wrote President Hoover in 1929 requesting a statement which could be read at the upcoming annual conference and stated that discussion of anti-lynching activity was the first concern. Anti-lynching reform remained the number one point until the 1930s.[48]

The NAACP grew as local groups joined, became active, and raised money. This rank and file response increased the effectiveness of the national organization's efforts, which in turn reacted on the local organizations to further stimulate their development. Earlier organizations, such as the Afro-American League and the Equal Rights Council, broke such a cycle (of mutually reinforcing feedback) at the national level when their leaders failed to concentrate on anti-lynching activity, the original motivation for the formation of the local branches of their organizations. Du Bois noted that lynching stimulated a response that no other issue did and wrote in 1912 of the many letters Blacks were writing to editors on this subject as examples of the first creative writing they had ever done.[49]

Opposition to lynching was also a much more effective tool for fund raising than defense of the right to drink beer in a downtown New York City hotel or the right to ride in a Pullman. The Afro-American League was able to raise fifty-six dollars to help Fortune conduct his case in 1890, whereas the NAACP's defense of the Elaine, Arkansas, tenant farmers resulted in contributions of $50,000. The Elaine case dramatically represented the type of injustice which oppressed the largest number of Blacks. The treatment received by the Elaine farmers constituted a far more shocking contrast to the average person's sense of justice than did the discrimination to which Fortune was subjected.[50]

The NAACP's consistent policy of giving anti-lynching its number one priority meant that all local groups had the most vital issue as a unifying concept. This tapped a great source of leadership in the Black communities which greatly strengthened the Association. Illustrative of this leadership-developing process was a letter to the national office in August, 1911 signed by R. W. Bagnall of Detroit requesting affiliation with the NAACP for the Detroit Society for the Prevention of Unjust Race Discrimination. Bagnall later became the astute and effective director of branches for the National Association.[51]

The Crisis played a significant role in the Association's activity because it was widely read and financially successful, thus giving its editor, W. E. B. Du Bois, a measure of independence from the predominantly white executive committee in the early years. Du Bois was able to keep the Crisis attuned to Black needs and resist the efforts of Oswald Garrison Villard to take the edge of the anti-lynching message. Du Bois had had considerable experience as a writer and editor. He had written several books and many articles before 1910; he had authored and supervised the production of the fourteen volumes of the series, Atlanta University Studies on the American Negro; he had edited the Moon while at Fisk University; and he was still editing the Horizon: A Journal of the Color Line when the NAACP was formed. It was Du Bois's recognition of the need for a Black-controlled journal that led to the establishment of the Horizon in 1907 to fill the void left by J. Max Barber's Voice of the Negro which had to suspend publication shortly after Barber had been driven out of Atlanta for exposing the white role in the riot of 1906.[52]

The Crisis grew rapidly in circulation and influence. One thousand copies of the first issue were printed. Ten years later the circulation passed 100,000. Although Du Bois was an able editor, he had to fight to keep control of the Crisis. Oswald Garrison Villard, Chairman of the Association's Board of Directors from January, 1911 to January, 1914, tended to be patronizing toward Blacks and resented Du Bois's failure to take orders from him. A major clash which led to Villard's resignation as chairman occurred in 1913 when Du Bois refused to publicize crimes committed by Blacks as he did those committed against Blacks.[53]

The contribution to the anti-lynching reform made by the NAACP did not consist of any new ingredient or formula, but in the fact that it brought more force and consistency to bear in applying the older techniques of lobbying, investigation, agitation, and publicity. The NAACP worked for federal and state anti-lynching legislation; it investigated lynchings and publicized the findings. Its speakers were readily available and constantly pointed out the idealistic and materialistic reasons for opposing lynching. The Association's campaign plan was "the old, well-worn path," according to Du Bois, which included publicity, better administration of existing laws, new laws, court action, and federal interference. "We frankly placed our greatest reliance on publicity," he concluded. The publicity appeared in some strange places. Vardaman's Weekly cited the NAACP program of 1916 "with some concern" as proof that there was indeed a race problem and white supremacists should not be complacent.[54]

Du Bois's belief in the value of publicity and protest was widely shared in the Association. Many specific outrages were publicized and protested. This led to further interest in anti-lynching reform and the continued growth of the Association. The "silent parade" of 10,000 in New York City on July 28, 1917 protesting the East St. Louis riot was organized by a non-partisan citizen's movement which then merged into the NAACP. This riot stimulated a membership campaign throughout the nation and brought contributions to the NAACP for the first time from the Black fraternal organizations. This important development broadened the rank and file base of the NAACP.[55]

The conservative and reactionary Southern response to the NAACP was very similar to the New South's response to earlier criticism of lynching. Du Bois summed it up under these headings: The North lynches also; the North is responsible for Southern lynchings because they are a result of Reconstruction; any anti-lynching campaign will injure Blacks; the NAACP is only interested in Southern crime; and lawlessness is everywhere.[56]

As the racial violence increased after World War I, so did the intensity of the NAACP anti-lynching campaign. In 1919 the Association sponsored over 2,000 public meetings against mob violence. This great increase in the level of open, public discussion of the subject was a reflection of some of the changes which had occurred since the formation of the NAACP. More prominent people were willing to speak out against lynching after the war than when the NAACP was organized a decade earlier. By 1916 an anti-lynching fund of over $10,000 was raised. In addition to the many forums, the Association held a national conference in New York City. During 1919 it spent $14,555 on investigations and publicity, and launched a campaign for 100,000 members. In many localities where lynchings had taken place, branches of the Association were formed. This indicated to some white supremacists that lynching, which had long been unnecessary because state laws were effectively maintaining caste, had become counterproductive. Naked terror did not intimidate after the war as it had earlier. In 1919 the NAACP membership in Texas went from 872 to over 5,000; Georgia increased its members sixfold; and the first branches were formed in Alabama.[57]

This great growth in the NAACP, indicated by the circulation of the <u>Crisis,</u> the growth of the branches, the development of Black leadership at both the national and local levels of the Association, its ability to raise funds because of its greater membership and ties to white sources of capital, as well as the increasing willingness of whites to discuss lynching, set the stage for a serious effort to obtain federal anti-lynching legislation in 1922. The campaign centered around an attempt to pass the Dyer bill, and although the NAACP failed in this objective, the drive did contribute to the anti-lynching reform. The effort to pass the Dyer bill also increased the strength and influence of the NAACP. Other Black organizations competed with it for preeminence in the defense of civil rights immediately after the war, but by 1923 the Association stood out unmistakeably as the leader of Black protest because it had become known as the most effective opponent of lynching. The cumulative effect of the frequent references to the NAACP anti-lynching campaign in the press, pulpit, and the many forums, debates and meetings where the rank and file Blacks had an opportunity to contribute funds, sign petitions and pass resolutions, was to give the NAACP the support and prestige among Blacks that no other protest organization had ever obtained.[58]

After World War I, lynching was viewed as a problem by more people. Many of them, taking the democratic rhetoric of the war's supporters seriously, believed that the custom of lynching was so antithetical to the professed aims of the society that they must act to bring an end to such barbarism. This feeling was intensified by the increase in racial violence in 1919 and led to the formation of a number of new organizations to oppose lynching as well as to the growth of some of the older organizations involved in the earlier anti-lynching reform movement.

Many of these organizations were ephemeral and became overshadowed by the NAACP which became the main organizer of the Black protest movement after the Universal Negro Improvement Association began to decline in the early 1920s. The single most important activity that placed the NAACP in its preeminent position was its sponsorship of the drive for federal anti-lynching legislation.

FOOTNOTES--CHAPTER VII

[1] Wilma Dykeman and James Stokely, Seeds of Southern Change: The Life of Will Alexander (Chicago: University of Chicago Press, 1962), p. 39; George B. Tindall, The Emergence of the New South: 1913-1945 (Baton Rouge: Louisiana State University Press, 1967), p. 7.

[2] University Commission on Southern Race Questions, Minutes (n.p.: University Commission on Southern Race Questions, n.d.).

[3] Letter, W. E. Walling to J. H. Dillard, March 6, 1918, Library of Congress, NAACP papers, Admin. File, C-205; Lily Hammond, In Black and White: An Interpretation of Southern Life (New York: Fleming H. Revell Co., 1944); Tindall, Emergence, pp. 175-77; Letter, W. E. Walling to M. W. Ovington, NAACP papers, Admin. File, C-205. See also Dykeman, Seeds, p. 58, Half Century, 4 (April, 1918), 9.

[4] On origin of the CIC see R. B. Eleazer, "Origin of the Interracial Committee," Chicago Broad Ax, February 23, 1924, p. 2; Will W. Alexander, "The Negro in the New South," American Academy of Political and Social Science Annals, 90 (November, 1928), 145-52; Dykeman, Seeds, pp. 177-79. For significance of Tennessee Law and Order League see letter Southern Sociological Congress to Henry Watterson, March 12, 1918, NAACP papers, Admin. file, C-205. For rapid growth of the CIC see R. B. Eleazer, "Interracial Committee Methods," Chicago Broad Ax, March 1, 1924, p. 2.

[5] Dykeman, Seeds, p. 71; Chicago Defender, October 13, 1923; Benjamin Mays, Born to Rebel (New York: Charles Scribner's Sons, 1971), p. 72.

[6] Charles Flint Kellogg, NAACP: A History of the National Association for the Advancement of Colored People (Baltimore: Johns Hopkins Press, 1967), p. 210.

[7] Tindall, Emergence, p. 182.

[8] Crisis, 30 (August, 1925), 194; Tindall, Emergence, p. 183; Willis Duke Weatherford, Negro Life in the South: Present Conditions and Needs (Miami: Mnemosyne Pub., 1969).

[9] Haynes cited in Chicago Defender, September 27, 1924, p. 15.

[10] Commission on Interracial Cooperation, "Eradication of Lynching Seen," press release dated January, 1923 located in NAACP papers, Admin. file, C-310.

[11] Letter Josephus Daniels to James Weldon Johnson, January 13, 1923, NAACP papers, Admin. file, C-63; CIC Press Release, February, 1926, NAACP papers, Admin. file, C-310.

[12] Tindall, Emergence, p. 181; Chicago Broad Ax, May 5, 1923.

[13] On awards to sheriffs see Tindall Emergence, p. 180; Chicago Broad Ax, July 16, 1927, p. 3; Norfolk Journal and Guide, June 6, 1931, p. 1; Dykeman, Seeds, p. 141; State Interracial Committee of Tennessee, "They Shall Not Pass," press release located in Library of Congress, George Fort Milton Papers, Box 88. On increase of mobs thwarted see Arthur F. Raper, The Tragedy of Lynching (Chapel Hill: The University of North Carolina Press, 1933), p. 484; Dykeman, Seeds, p. 152.

[14] Dykeman, Seeds, pp. 89-96. Nation, September 28, 1921, p. 337; Women's Branch of the Interracial Commission of South Carolina, "Women of South Carolina are Opposed to Lynching," Norfolk Journal and Guide, February 25, 1922.

[15] A. M. Moore, "Brotherly Love Must Abide Throughout the Land," Competitor, 3 (April, 1921), 9.

[16] St. Louis Argus, May 26, 1922, p. 7.

[17] On the number of women working in the ASWPL see Association of Southern Women for the Prevention of Lynching, Bulletin no. 7, "Lynching is Wholesale Murder," February, 1937, Milton papers, Box 88; Atlanta Constitution, November 20, 1932; Dykeman, Seeds, p. 145.

[18] Jessie Daniel Ames, Association of Southern Women for the Prevention of Lynching: Beginning of the Movement (Atlanta: Commission on Interracial Cooperation, 1932); Dykeman, Seeds, pp. 147-52; Mays, Born to Rebel, p. 243.

[19] Letter, J. D. Ames to H. F. Ashurst, April 25, 1935, National Archives, Record Group 46, S. 1978, 73d Cong.; Letter Roger Baldwin to Roy Wilkins, March 28, 1934, NAACP Admin. file C-205; Letter, J. D. Ames to Council Members of the ASWPL, July 1, 1937, Milton Papers, Box 88.

[20] Dykeman, Seeds, p. 137; In his review of Arthur F. Raper's The Tragedy of Lynching, Rayford W. Logan stated that it was "one of the most notable contributions to the literature about America's greatest shame." Journal of Negro History, 18 (January, 1933), 486.

[21] Milton papers, Box 88.

[22] George Fort Milton, "Editorial," New York Telegram located in NAACP papers, Admin. file, C-204; George Fort Milton, "Reflections on the Vanishing Mob," unpublished mms., Milton papers, Box 88.

[23] Mays, Born to Rebel, p. 72; Dykeman, Seeds, p. 149. For the view that the hostility directed against the CIC was mild compared to that directed against the NAACP in the South see Henry Allen Bullock, A History of Negro Education in the South (New York: Praeger Publishers, 1970), p. 213.

[24] Alexander, "The Negro in the New South,"; Mays, Born to Rebel, p. 96.

[25] Mays, Born to Rebel, p. 102; Crisis, 12 (June, 1916), 72; Norfolk Journal and Guide, January 5, 1935, p. 18.

[26] Tindall, Emergence, p. 175; Howard W. Odum, Race and Rumors of Race (Chapel Hill: University of North Carolina Press, 1943), p. 184; letter Herbert Hoover to Robert Moton, December 3, 1929, Hoover Presidential papers, Pers., Commission on Interracial Cooperation; Norfolk Journal and Guide, January 20, 1934.

[27] Telegram J. E. Andrews to Herbert Hoover, November 30, 1931; letter, Andrews to Hoover, December 4, 1931, Hoover Presidential Papers, Colored Question; J. E. Andrews, "First Message from Our President: God Must be the Father and the White Race the Sire of Civilization," (Atlanta: Women's National Association for the Preservation of the White Race, n.d.), Hoover Presidential Papers, Colored Question.

[28] Theodore G. Vincent, Black Power and the Garvey Movement, (Berkeley: Ramparts Press, 1971), p. 41.

[29] Claude McKay, Harlem: Negro Metropolis (New York: E. P. Dutton & Co., 1940, p. 147; Vincent, Black Power, pp. 153-55; "The Declaration of Rights of the Negro Peoples of the World," cited in Vincent, Black Power, pp. 257-65; Garvey's 1921 speech cited in Opportunity, 1 (August, 1923), 233; for 1922 convention see Vincent, Black Power, pp. 197-98.

[30] Vincent, Black Power, pp. 165-70; McKay, Harlem, p. 157; Under the headline, "Lynching good for my people," the Chicago Defender, November 11, 1922, p. 2, quoted Garvey, "I thank the Southern white man for giving the Negro race consciousness. Sometimes it has required beating, sometimes lynching, but he has it."; Amy Jacques-Garvey, Philosophy and Opinions of Marcus Garvey (New York: Arno Press and the New York Times, 1968), 1:52-53.

[31] Vincent, Black Power, pp. 190-92; Messenger, 4 (August, 1922), 472.

[32] Marcus Garvey, "An Expose of the Caste System Among Negroes," in Amy Jacques-Garvey, Philosophy, 2:61.

[33] Vincent, Black Power, pp. 205-06; Mary Frances Berry, Black Resistance/White Law (New York: Meredith Corp., 1971), p. 159.

[34] Messenger, 2 (April-May, 1920), 3-4; 2 (August, 1920), 63; 2 (September, 1920), 88-90; 2 (November, 1921), 274; 4 (June, 1922), 429; 4 (July, 1922), 449; 4 (October, 1922) 508.

[35] Vincent, Black Power, pp. 74-75, 80; New York Times, June 4, 5, 20, 1921; R. Halliburton, Jr., "The Tulsa Race War of 1921," Journal of Black Studies, 2 (March, 1972), 333-58; Walter White, "I Investigate Lynchings," American Mercury, 16 (January, 1929), 77-84.

[36] For history of the National Equal Rights League see Stephen R. Fox, The Guardian of Boston: William Monroe Trotter (New York: Atheneum, 1970), pp. 112, 140; for Du Bois failure to recognize Trotter's contribution see Kellogg, NAACP, p. 97; Crisis, 7 (February, 1914), 171; 10 (May, 1915), 10; 10 (September, 1915), 228-9; 11 (November, 1915), 9; 12 (July, 1916), 117; The attitude was continued by the new NAACP leadership in the 1920s and later. Walter White declined to attend a two-day anti-lynching conference Trotter called in 1930. See letter, White to Trotter, November 5, 1930, NAACP papers, Admin. file C-204.

[37] Chicago Defender, December 13, 1919; February 18, 1922; Norfolk Journal and Guide, September 29, 1917, p. 1; Half Century, 2 (November, 1917), 8.

[38] U. S., Congress, House, Judiciary Committee, Anti-Lynching Hearings on H. R. 259, 4123, 11873, 66th Cong., 1st sess., January 29, 1920, p. 38.

[39] Chicago Defender, August 16, 1921, p. 2.

[40] Ibid., June 18, 1920.

[41] Edward Peeks, The Long Struggle for Black Power (New York: Charles Scribner's Sons, 1971), p. 146; William Muraskin, "The Social Foundations of the Black Community: The Fraternities--The California Masons as a Test Case," Midcontinent American Studies Journal 11 (Fall, 1970), 12-35. Chicago Broad Ax, July 25, 1908; Kellogg, NAACP, p. 225; Messenger, 2 (September, 1919), 4.

[42] Crisis, 3 (February, 1912), 141; St. Louis Argus, May 16, 1919, p. 1.

[43] Chicago Defender, November 11, 1922; October 13, 1923.

[44] Letter, M. A. N. Shaw to Storey and Johnson, December 29, 1922; Johnson to Shaw, January 1, 1923, NAACP papers, admin. file C-232; Fox, Trotter, pp. 243-44; St Louis Argus, March 30, 1922, p. 1; letter, Cyril V. Briggs to James Weldon Johnson, July 18, 1923, "One wonders whether the dean and his 'advisers' have mentally abolished such questions as lynching. . . ." NAACP papers, admin. file C-232; Vincent, Black Power, p. 84; letter Briggs to Miller, July 25, 1923, C-232; Atlanta Independent, June 28, 1923; August Meier, Negro Thought in America 1880-1915, Ann Arbor Paperbacks (Ann Arbor: University of Michigan Press, 1963), p. 230.

[45] Kelly Miller, "The Negro Sanhedrin: A Call to Conference" in Black Nationalism in America, ed. by John H. Bracey, Jr., August Meier, and Elliott Rudwick (Indianapolis: Bobbs-Merrill Co., 1970), pp. 249-65. Sanhedrin Program, n.d., NAACP papers, admin. file C-232; Messenger (November, 1923).

[46] Kellogg, NAACP, p. 58.

[47] Mary White Ovington, The Walls Came Tumbling Down (New York: Arno Press and the New York Times, 1969), p. 130.

[48] Kellogg, NAACP, p. 209; Crisis, 6 (May, 1913), 31-33; (September, 1917), 216; 30 (August, 1925), 182; Letter, Johnson to Hoover, May 5, 1925, Hoover Presidential Papers, Secy. file, National Association, 1929. See also W. E. B. Du Bois, Black Folk Then and Now: An Essay in the History and Sociology of the Negro Race (New York: Henry Holt & Co., 1939), p. 215. A retrospective editorial on past accomplishments indicates the primacy of anti-lynching activities in this period, see Crisis, 79 (May, 1972), 175.

[49] Crisis, 3 (January, 1912), p. 112.

[50] Ovington, Walls, 154-64; Kellogg, NAACP, p. 243.

[51] Crisis, 6 (October, 1911), 241-42.

[52] Elliott M. Rudwick, "W. E. B. Du Bois: in the role of Crisis Editor," Journal of Negro History, 43 (July, 1958), 214-240; Paul G. Partington, "The Moon Illustrated Weekly--The Precursor of the Crisis," Journal of Negro History, 48 (July, 1963), 206-16; For the Du Bois-Villard split see Kellogg, NAACP, p. 103; for bibliography of Du Bois see Ernest Kaiser "A Selected Bibliography of the Published Writings of W. E. B. Du Bois," in Black Titan: W. E. B. Du Bois, ed. by John Henrik Clarke, et al. (Boston: Beacon Press, 1970), pp. 309-330; Julius Lester, ed., The Seventh Son: The Thought and Writings of W. E. B. Du Bois Vintage Books (New York: Random House, 1971), 2:740-67. A more complete bibliography on Du Bois is Herbert Aptheker, Annotated Bibliography of the Published Writings of W. E. B. Du Bois, (Millwood, N. Y.: Kraus-Thomson, 1973).

[53] Kellogg, NAACP, p. 94; W. E. B. Du Bois, The Autobiography of W. E. B. Du Bois: A Soliloquy on Viewing My Life from the Last Decade of Its First Century (New York: International Publishers, 1968), pp. 256-57; Ovington, Walls, p. 108.

[54] Crisis, 13 (December, 1916), 61; Vardaman's Weekly, May 15, 1916, p. 7.

[55] Kellogg, NAACP, p. 226; Peeks, Black Power, pp. 174-75.

[56] Crisis, 3 (January, 1912), 105. Mary White Ovington, "The National Association for the Advancement of Colored People," Journal of Negro History, 9 (April, 1924), 112.

[57] Robert H. Brisbane, The Black Vanguard: Origins of the Negro Social Revolution 1900-1960 (Valley Forge, Pa.: Judson Press, 1970), p. 61; Ovington, Walls, p. 112; Kellogg, NAACP, pp. 216-17; Albert E. Pillsbury was very critical of the "Address to the Nation" that the national conference on lynching produced. He wanted it to say the function of lynching was "to terrorize negro labor into a properly servile state of subjection." Instead, he said it "roars as gentle as any sucking dove." Letter A. E. Pillsbury to J. R. Shillady, June 25, 1919, NAACP papers, admin. file C-205; St. Louis Argus, May 23, 1919, p. 1.

[58] For the best account of the drive of the NAACP for passage of federal anti-lynching legislation see Robert Lewis Zangrando, "The Efforts of the National Association for the Advancement of Colored People to Secure the Passage of a Federal Anti-lynching Law, 1920-1940" (unpublished Ph.D. dissertation, University of Pennsylvania, 1963).

CHAPTER VIII

THE DEVELOPMENT OF THE ANTI-LYNCHING

REFORM MOVEMENT, 1922-1932

The epidemic of racial violence that characterized the year 1919 subsided in the early 1920s, but the momentum which it had given the anti-lynching reform continued with sufficient strength to make the passage of federal anti-lynching legislation a possibility. Under the leadership of the NAACP much of the energies of the more militant Northern segment of the reform was channeled into a lobbying effort in behalf of the Dyer bill. When this failed, Black disillusionment with the Republican party was more complete than ever before. The reformers continued to advocate both federal and state action but returned to the older tactics of investigation, publicity, and education to create a climate of opinion wherein the lyncher would become a pariah. When the historic decline in the frequency of lynchings was reversed with the advent of the depression, the reform was revitalized. Economic problems and the rise of fascism did much to broaden further the base of the reform.

When the NAACP made the decision to concentrate on supporting the Dyer bill, it sought to build a coalition of all who would support this one goal. In order to mobilize women, a new organization was created, the Anti-lynching Crusaders. This ad hoc group was headed by Mary B. Talbert, president of the National Association of Colored Women which had worked with Congressman L. C. Dyer for anti-lynching legislation before the NAACP had. Mrs. Talbert had been active during the war promoting the sale of war bonds. In this connection she had traveled throughout the country extensively and was consequently not only well-known among Black clubwomen but to many outside the club movement. The Crusaders were mostly Black women, but they had some 200 white members. Zona Gale, the novelist, and Florence Kelly of the National Consumer's League, were active volunteers in this group.[1]

One of the motivations of the anti-lynching reform had always been religious. The Southern white women working with the Commission on Interracial Cooperation channeled some of their religious fervor into their anti-lynching campaign. The Black women in the Crusaders emphasized the religious reasons for supporting the Dyer bill and printed on their letterhead, "To your knees and don't stop praying."

The Crusaders were organized on July 15, 1922, in response to Congressman Dyer's statement made to the 1922 Annual Conference of the NAACP at Newark, New Jersey. There Dyer stated that if one million people were united behind this bill, it would pass. The Crusaders sought this goal and hoped for a one dollar contribution from each of the members. The NAACP furnished an initial capital of $500, continuing advice, and help with the publicity. The agreement between the two organizations was that the Crusaders would endeavor to raise $1 million for the Dyer bill promotion and then would disband on

December 31, 1922.[2]

The Anti-lynching Crusaders were primarily a fund-raising and publicity-generating organization. The women donated their time; there was no paid staff because the overhead was provided from other funds so that the Crusaders could assure contributors that every cent of their contributions would go directly to support the Dyer bill. The Crusaders became a broader-based organization than the NAACP because its members only needed to unite on the one point of advocating federal anti-lynching legislation. Acceptance and understanding of the rest of the NAACP program was not necessary for membership. The million-dollar goal was a huge sum when compared to the annual NAACP budget which never exceeded $15,000 before 1918 and was under $50,000 even after the great membership increase of 1919. The funds were to be spent in a variety of ways. Newspaper advertsisements were to be placed "until not a single person who reads the daily papers shall be ignorant of the fact that we are the only country that burns human beings at the stake." The goal included $25,000 to publicize the need for voters to write Congress. A similar amount would be used to support state legislation. The Crusaders hoped to raise $500,000 to be used to help the federal government prosecute lynchers after the Dyer bill became law. The women had ambitious plans and, had they succeeded, the chances of passage of the proposed legislation would have been greater.[3]

The Crusaders had difficulties. It was easier to claim enrollment of one million members than it was to produce one million dollars. There were totally unfounded rumors of graft in the organization which stated that the Crusaders were self-seeking. Mary Talbert lacked the political sophistication that comes with long years of struggle in the public arena. Less than three months after the organization was founded, James Weldon Johnson had to ask that one of Mary Talbert's publicity releases be withdrawn. The release inferred that the Dyer bill would make it easier to prosecute the union members who participated in the "Herrin Massacre" in Williamson County, Illinois, in June 1922. This affair grew out of a strike of union mine workers that had racial overtones. Johnson wrote Talbert that unions would oppose the Dyer bill if they thought the federal government would use it against strikers who might become involved in a riot.[4]

The Anti-lynching Crusaders failed in their main goals, but they did obtain additional publicity and helped to raise $70,000 for the anti-lynching reform. Robert R. Moton of Tuskegee said that he heard of the movement while he was in Europe. Articles were sent to the fifteen leading periodicals for women and the wire services gave national distribution to some of the Crusader's press releases. In December, 1922, when it appeared that the Senate would not follow the House in passing the Dyer bill, Mary Talbert notified the state leaders that the organization would disband on schedule, but, like the suffrageists, their work would go on to final victory. She urged one last effort to raise $100,000 immediately for the NAACP's 1923 anti-lynching work.[5]

When the NAACP permitted the Anti-lynching Crusaders to pass from existence, it lost a good ally and perhaps made a mistake. Nevertheless, the involvement of women in the anti-lynching movement continued. Anti-lynching committees became more common in the local clubs of both Black and white women and the flow of protests and petitions to various divisions of government remained high. The contacts made with white women increased their understanding of the problems of Blacks. The Colored Women's Clubs of

Michigan prepared material for the 1924 election to defeat congressmen who voted against the Dyer bill. The Illinois Federation of Colored Women's Clubs sent Ida B. Wells to Washington in 1926 to testify in behalf of the McKinley bill, the Senate version of the Dyer bill current at that time. When the anti-lynching forces were revitalized in the 1930s, many who had been involved in the Anti-lynching Crusaders became active again.[6]

One of the principal beneficial beneficiaries of the NAACP activities was Leonidas Carstarphen Dyer. Dyer represented the Twelfth Congressional District of Missouri which included a majority of the Blacks of St. Louis. He was elected as a Republican to the House of Representatives in 1910 for the first of eleven terms. Usually a party regular, he opposed the national policies of the Republican party on only the one issue of federal anti-lynching legislation.[7]

Dyer introduced his first anti-lynching bill in 1911. Although it was ignored as all earlier efforts had been, he continued to drop an anti-lynching bill into the hopper in almost every session of Congress until he was retired in the Democratic sweep of 1934. In 1911 it was not necessary for Republicans to do anything positive for Blacks in order to obtain the support of most Black voters. Therefore, Robert Zangrando's assessment of Dyer's motivation as being basically humanitarian has much validity. The riot in East St. Louis in 1917 shocked Dyer much as the riot in Springfield, Illinois, in 1908, had shocked William English Walling, by bringing home the fact of white brutality and deteriorating race relations. Dyer testified before a congressional committee investigating the riot that the local police and the state militia had been extremely barbaric and his estimate of over 500 people killed is the highest appearing in any comments on the riot. The riot not only offended Dyer's humanitarian sensibilities, but it changed the character of his district by increasing the number of Blacks he represented. Many of the refugees from East St. Louis settled in safer St. Louis, Missouri, which had indicated its attitude by letting the refugees from the riot stream across the Mississippi River bridge while blocking the pursuing whites from entering Missouri territory.[8]

In opposition to Zangrando's assessment of Dyer is the theory that Dyer's primary motivation for sponsoring anti-lynching legislation was the belief that the struggle for Black advances had to be controlled by whites. Many of Dyer's actions can be seen in the light of the urban political boss who campaigns on national issues to obscure the fact that he is doing little or nothing about local issues. In general, Dyer's relations to his Black constituency were paternalistic. He would obtain jobs in Washington, D. C., for students from St. Louis who were attending Howard University in Washington and use his political patronage to see that a few Blacks got jobs in St. Louis, but he resisted any Black efforts toward independence and opposed those who ran for elective offices. He did not want any Black leaders who were responsible directly to the Black voters. He only encouraged those who were responsible to white officials.[9]

Dyer's principal contact in the NAACP in the early 1920s was with James Weldon Johnson, the executive secretary. Harold Cruse, in <u>Crisis of the Negro Intellectual</u>, contends that Johnson was content with white paternalism and was therefore unable to develop the correct strategies that would lead to effective changes in the Black status. Under Johnson's direction, the major portion of the efforts of the NAACP were directed into the campaign to obtain federal legislation by passage of the Dyer bill, and much of the tremendous energy accumulated during the Great Migration was expended in lobbying Congress.[10]

In St. Louis, Dyer stood in the way of the Black community which was trying to repeat the experience of white immigrant groups who developed political power by first being loyal voters and receiving their rewards in the form of patronage appointments to minor offices and then running for elective offices which developed power for the ethnic community. Dyer consistently opposed this last step. The effect of his support of anti-lynching legislation was to disarm his St. Louis opposition and insure that no Black would replace him in Congress.

Dyer's attitude toward Black political power was important nationally. St. Louis was viewed by the National Negro Congressional Campaign Committee, organized in the fall of 1919 in Washington D. C., as the place where there was the most realistic opportunity to elect the first Black congressman since George H. White left Congress in 1901. The Committee thought the second most viable opportunity to elect a Black congressman was in Chicago. Dyer thwarted this possibility in St. Louis, and eight more years passed before Chicago Blacks had an opportunity to be represented by Oscar DePriest.[11]

Dyer's sponsorship of the anti-lynching bill was enough to insure him the support of Black voters and the sponsorship functioned to advance Dyer's political ambitions much as Republican rhetoric in support of Black rights had overcome Black opposition to Republican deeds in the past. Dyer defeated George L. Vaughn for the Twelfth Congressional District Republican nomination in 1920. Vaughn, the most prominent Black attorney in St. Louis, was executive secretary of the St. Louis NAACP and well-known as a civil rights advocate. In the general election of 1920, Dyer defeated Robert N. Owen, another Black attorney of St. Louis, who was running on the Farmer-Labor ticket. Dyer did nothing for anti-lynching legislation that a Black congressman could not have done. The fact that the Dyer bill passed the House of Representatives in 1922 was due to the great lobbying campaign organized by the NAACP, not to any special political magic supplied by Dyer. Dyer traveled extensively and spoke to many Black audiences in behalf of his bill but did little to influence white opinion. A Black congressman probably would have been no more able than Dyer to force the Senate to vote on the bill which was defeated by a combination of Republican indifference and Southern Democratic hostility. The prophecy of Missouri's ex-Senator James Reed was fulfilled. Reed had said that the bill was never intended to pass, that it was never intended to do more than disarm Black discontent with the Republican party.[12]

After a filibuster in the Senate killed the Dyer bill in 1922, the NAACP changed the emphasis of its anti-lynching struggle to the investigation of individual lynchings and a campaign for state anti-lynching legislation. Congressman Dyer continued to introduce his bill periodically, and the NAACP continued to support it but not to the exclusion of other matters.

The lynching issue, which was playing an ever-increasing role in national politics, also affected the balance of power within the NAACP. Until the depression, the NAACP leader most influential among Blacks was the one who was most clearly perceived as the leader of the anti-lynching struggle. This position was occupied by W. E. B. Du Bois, the editor of the Crisis, during the first decade of the Association. With the change in emphasis that the lobbying effort in behalf of the Dyer bill brought about, the leadership of the anti-lynching reform gradually slipped into the hands of the administrators and organizers skilled in human relations. Although Du Bois played a large part in the Dyer bill campaign through the Crisis and by extended speaking tours, he was eclipsed in the popular mind by James Weldon Johnson.

Johnson became field secretary of the NAACP in 1916 and moved up to the position of executive secretary in 1920 when John R. Shillady resigned. In 1919 Johnson had initiated the first steps of the Association toward securing federal anti-lynching legislation. As the interest of the Association became centered on efforts to pass the Dyer bill, Johnson became the Black most closely associated with the anti-lynching reform. It was Johnson's name and activities that were in most of the press releases. His movements and conversations with the nation's leaders were well known to Blacks who heeded his calls for greater efforts. The person who shared the limelight with Johnson that the open battle for the Dyer bill required was not Du Bois but a relative newcomer to the Association, Walter White.[13]

Walter White joined the NAACP in 1918 as assistant secretary. Because of his light complexion, blue eyes, and Caucasian features, he was able to pass as white almost any time he wished. The Association took advantage of this and assigned him the role of chief investigator. His first case received much publicity and catapulted him into prominence among Blacks. This case was the sensationally brutal lynching of eleven Blacks in Georgia, one of whom was Mary Turner, the pregnant wife of one of the other victims. White personally investigated forty-one lynchings and eight race riots. These important investigations received wide publicity in both the Black and the white press. He was an able writer and journalist whose works were welcomed by publishers. In 1924 he published a novel, Fire in the Flint, in which lynching was a very important part of the plot. This work aroused wide comment and sharp controversy and brought attacks on him by white supremacists which only increased his stature among Blacks. When the Dyer bill was defeated in 1922, the NAACP shifted its emphasis from the lobbying, in which James Weldon Johnson had played the major role, to investigations, in which Walter White played the major role. White increased his stature as the leading Black spokesman against lynching in 1929 with the publication of an important book, Rope and Faggot: A Biography of Judge Lynch.[14]

Other milestones in Walter White's career were the Sweet case in 1925 and the defeat of Supreme Court nominee John J. Parker in 1930. The Parker case involved lobbying Congress on a massive scale reminiscent of the 1922 effort in behalf of the Dyer bill. White moved up to acting executive secretary in 1930 while James Weldon Johnson was on leave. He became permanent executive secretary in 1931 when Johnson had to resign for reasons of health. These events thrust White to the forefront and he became the adknowledged leader of the anti-lynching reform movement in the United States. This gave him so much prestige that when Du Bois opposed White on other issues later, it was Du Bois who had to leave the NAACP, not White.[15]

The lynching issue played a part in the presidential campaign of 1928. Al Smith wanted Walter White to direct the Democratic campaign among Blacks. White declined, but not because of any admiration for Hoover or faith in Republican promises. As Secretary of Commerce, Hoover was in charge of the relief and reconstruction work following the flood in the Mississippi Valley in 1927. White investigated the reports of mistreatment of Blacks by the authorities and found that the National Guard was impressing Black workers into peonage. White reported the facts and Hoover never forgave him. White, however, refused to work for Smith who had rejected White's advice to issue a strong statement in defense of Black rights. Such a statement would have had to oppose lynching. Smith later regretted that he had not followed this course and believed that he would have won the election in 1928 had he taken White's advice.[16]

In the campaign of 1928, Congressman Dyer spoke of the need to enforce the Fourteenth and Fifteenth amendments as well as the Eighteenth. According to press releases, Dyer expected enough anti-Roman Catholic and pro-prohibition votes from the South to elect an administration which would bring this about and pass his anti-lynching proposal. Southern Democrats responded by saying that a vote for Hoover was a vote for the hated Dyer bill. Congressman Dyer was playing his role of mobilizer of Black support for the Republicans. Hoover had no intention of supporting the Dyer bill, much less acting against the disfranchisement of Blacks in the South. Dyer knew this, but he also knew his press releases would tend to keep the Northern Blacks voting Republican. The fact that the Southern Democrats evidenced apprehension over the Dyer bill was seen by the NAACP as reason to keep the issue alive on the grounds that the South would continue to reduce the number of lynchings in order to insure that federal intervention would never come about.[17]

Representative Dyer thought his efforts in behalf of Blacks were poorly repaid. He complained to Walter White in 1930 that "colored people as a whole do not always appreciate loyal service to their cause." He was referring to the Blacks in St. Louis who contested with him for the Republican nomination in the primaries and said that this "has somewhat embarrassed me in my work in Congress in trying to be especially helpful to the colored people."[18]

President Hoover inherited what remained of the association between the White House and Tuskegee which had been built by Booker T. Washington. Hoover also fell heir to the loyalty that most Blacks still had for the Republican party. This loyalty had been much declining since Harding took office and the Republican failure to support the Dyer bill in the Senate accelerated the rate of Black disillusionment. Hoover did much to increase and little to arrest this trend. He did not thing lynching was an important problem. He may have regretted that lynchings occurred, but he did not give the matter much thought because he believed that there was nothing he could do about it. Race relations were far less important to Hoover than enforcing prohibition.[19]

The inauguration of a new president was always a time of hope among Blacks. This had been true from the time of Grant, and was particularly true when the president was Republican. Responding to this hope, a group of St. Louis Blacks predicted that Hoover would be the country's greatest president since Lincoln, because as Lincoln had ended slavery, Hoover would end lynching. The militant Black novelist, Sutton Griggs, was more realistic. He thought that if Coolidge could not stop lynching, Hoover certainly could not. Griggs believed that Hoover would ignore lynching and he concluded that it was up to the Blacks in the South to unite and protest. Grigg's conclusion was that if the federal government would do nothing, perhaps the states might do something.[20]

Some Blacks followed Grigg's advice, but many others continued the old tactic of trying to influence the president and the national parties. The Black and the interracial organizations which had supported earlier efforts in behalf of the Dyer bill continued to bombard Hoover and Congress with demands for the passage of federal legislation. Hoover listened with more patience during the election campaigns than he did at other times. The initial high hopes which Blacks had at his inauguration were rather slow to die considering the actions of the President. Frequently called to the President's attention by Blacks were those actions relating to the segregation of the Gold Star Mothers, the toleration of peonage in the South, the appointment of federal judges who were thought to be antagonistic to Black aspirations, discrimination in federal employment which cut deeper as the depression intensified, and his support of lily-white policies within the Republican party. If this roster of grievances was not enough to alienate many Blacks, the continued apathy of the Hoover administration toward the lynching problem was sufficient to do so.

Hoover called a governor's conference for the fall of 1930 to consider agricultural problems. When the NAACP learned of this, Walter White wrote the President in October regarding the possibility of calling a conference of the Southern governors to consider the lynching problem. White furnished Hoover with the details on the twenty-three lynchings which had already occurred in 1930 and pointed out that this was eleven more than occured in all of 1929. Hoover did not respond to White's request or permit White to visit the White House to discuss any matters of concern to Blacks. White labeled Hoover "The Man in the lily-White House," and charged that the President "bluntly refused to receive Negro citizens who wished to lay before him the facts of their steadily worsening plight."[21]

President Hoover showed more consideration for Monroe Trotter. As nominal head of the National Equal Rights League, Trotter had written Hoover several times in 1930 asking that November 22 to 28 be designated "Anti-lynching Week." Although the President did not accede to this request, he did grant an audience on November 25 to a delegation form the Twenty-third Annual Convention of the NERL. Trotter was spokesman for the delegation which confined its message to protesting the increasing trend in lynchings. Hoover did not issue the requested proclamation, perhaps because it would have confused the country by coming right on the heels of the annual Thanksgiving Day Proclamation. The NERL Convention was held the last week of November to permit the delegates also to attend the Non-Partisan Convention called for December 1-2 by Oscar DePriest, Black congressman from Illinois. DePriest's People's Movement had been cooperating with the NERL in anti-lynching programs for some time. Ida B. Well-Barnett was one of the connecting links between the two organizations. Failing to obtain the proclamation, the Trotter delegation asked Hoover for at least a statement against lynching. Two months later, after three more lynchings, the President had not responded.[22]

Hoover received another delegation from the National Equal Rights League on December 1, 1931. Trotter again attempted to prevail upon the President to issue a positive statement against lynching, but again failed. The following month he wrote Hoover a bitter letter charging that Rear Admiral William V. Pratt defended the navy men who lynched Joseph Kahahawai in Hawaii. Trotter asked Hoover for "your official disavowal and repudiation of lynch-law as a policy in the U. S. Navy." Hoover did not respond.[23]

President Hoover had no intention of using his office to attack lynching. He never supported the Dyer bill and when Black pressures on the Republicans increased as the 1932 election approached, Hoover was informed by William D. Mitchell, the Attorney General, that the Dyer bill "seems utterly impracticable" and that it would do more harm than good because federal interference would "develop angry passions which would stimulate lynchings." The leaders of the anti-lynching reform did not know that Hoover would not support them, so increasing pressures were applied. Black Republicans desperately wanted an anti-lynching statement to use in the 1932 campaign. H. A. Clark, a Black attorney in Washington, wrote Hoover that if he would bring an anti-lynching measure to a vote in 1932 before the election, Democrats would go on record against it and this would result in the defeat of enough Northern Democrats to insure Republican control of Congress.[24]

Along with the political groups and the other civil rights organizations, the NAACP also tried to get Hoover to issue an anti-lynching statement. Such statements were almost routine, and the tradition went back to Benjamin Harrison. Harding had declared against lynching when he accepted the nomination. In his 1921 message to Congress he asked for an end to lynching but did not mention the Dyer bill. Calvin Coolidge spoke against lynching when he accepted the vice-presidential nomination in 1920. As President, Coolidge repeated his opposition to lynching in his messages to Congress in 1923 and again in 1924, but he did not recommend the Dyer bill. In an attempt to get the traditional presidential anti-lynching statement from Hoover, James Weldon Johnson wrote him in May 1929 asking for a statement to be read at the Association's Twelfth Annual Meeting. A month later Johnson sent a telegram repeating the request. The White House staff marked it, "File--no answer." In May, 1930 Walter White made a similar request to the President and in this election year received an answer. Hoover replied, "Every decent citizen must condemn the lynching evil as an undermining of the very essence of both justice and democracy." For the annual meeting of the Association in 1931, a similar expression of good will was sent to Joel Spingarn, President of the NAACP, but Hoover declined to address the convention.[25]

What White really wanted was a public statement to the nation, not just a telegram to be read to the Association delegates, and he continued to press for this. White sent Hoover a copy of Wilson's statement of July 26, 1918, which White said was "very salutary." Many had thought Wilson's statement was weak at the time it was issued, but it was apparently too outspoken for Hoover who continued to remain silent. Hoover believed that he had spoken sufficiently on the subject and that his position was clear.[26]

In September, 1932 the NAACP requested Herbert Hoover to respond to a list of eleven questions in an effort to elicit some campaign promises. As an indication of the re-ordering of priorities then underway in the NAACP and the Black world, the question, "Will you favor enactment of a federal anti-lynching law?" was seventh on the list. The first question dealt with the lily-white policy of the Republican party, and five of the eleven queries were on employment. Jobs were becoming even a more serious problem for Blacks in the 1930s than the increase in lynching. Hoover's attitude on creating jobs could be inferred in a reply to a statement the National Urban League sent him to sign which began, "The right to work is a fundamental right of the American citizen." With his won hand, Hoover penciled in "corrections" so that it read, "Equality of opportunity is a fundamental American ideal."[27]

Of all the pressures on President Hoover to take a more determined stand against lynching, the most gentle came from the Commission on Interracial Cooperation. The CIC would have liked more anti-lynching rhetoric emanating from the White House about the need for more brotherhood, but it did not see the presidential role as consisting of anything more than appeals to the public conscience. The Commission's attitude also included the belief that the South should redeem itself without Northern help. The general Democratic orientation of most of those who worked with the Commission also meant that the CIC would not try to cast the Republican Hoover in the role of militant savior of Blacks. Hoover had a higher regard for the CIC than he had for the NAACP. While Secretary of Commerce in 1925, Hoover had publicly praised the work of the CIC. When Robert Moton was appointed chairman of CIC's fund-raising drive in 1929, he reminded Hoover of his previous remarks and asked for an endorsement of the CIC's work. Hoover responded positively and said that the work of the CIC was "sane, simple and sensible."[28]

Exacerbating the lynching problem during Hoover's term as president was his support of the lily-white faction of the Republican party in the South which sought to force Blacks out of appointive and elective offices. This policy was nowhere more clearly seen than in the prosecution of Perry Howard by the Justice Department. Perry Howard, a Black lawyer, was a Republican Committeeman for Mississippi who was charged with irregularities in the dispensing of patronage and the sale of offices but was acquitted by an all-white jury. The Justice Department than assigned a special agent, Mrs. Mable Walker Willebrandt, to continue the prosecution. Many whites, clearly guilty of this practice had long been tolerated by both parties with no official hand raised against them. The action taken by the Justice Department was therefore viewed by liberals and Blacks as discriminatory.[29]

In at least one instance, efforts to eliminate Blacks from the Republican party in the South resulted in a lynching. S. S. Mincey, a seventy-year old Black leader of Montgomery County, Georgia, was taken from his home late in the night of July 29, 1930, by a hooded mob which beat him into unconsciousness and left his with injuries which proved fatal the following day. Mincey had long been active in politics, he had been a delegate to the Republican National Convention four times and had recently been re-elected over white opposition for the post of county chairman which carried control of some patronage. Although the Grand Jury investigating this lynching was unable to return any indictments, the investigation by the CIC, white Democratic press, and Georgia Blacks, confirmed Mincey's dying statement. Mincey charged that the mob instructed him to resign as chairman of the County Republican Committee so that a white could have the job. This lynching aroused more indignation among whites than most lynchings did, in part because Black Republicans were not the threat to white Democrats that white Republicans were. Southern Democrats believed that a predominantly Black Republican party would never be influential in local matters because the Democrats knew that they were reasonable free to use terror against Blacks. A white Republican party, on the other hand could not be so freely intimidated and might become a real threat to the entrenched and politically corrupt Democratec courthouse rings. Benjamin J. Davis, Sr., Black secretary of the Republican State Central Committee of Georgia, declared that the lynching was a direct result of the demand from Washington for a completely white Republican organization in Georgia. Davis shared the CIC conclusion that the Georgia Democrats would not tolerate the growth of the Republican party among whites.[30]

Hoover was sharply attacked by the anti-lynching reformers for his efforts to enforce the Eighteenth Amendment, not because they opposed prohibition, but because this activity proved that the Chief Executive could make an effort to enforce the Constitutional Amendments and chose to enforce the Eighteenth but not the Fourteenth and Fifteenth. One of Hoover's first presidential acts was the appointment of the National Commission of Law Observance and Enforcement. This body was only interested in enforcing prohibition. In April 1929, C. H. Huston, one of Hoover's political advisers, suggested that Hoover read Robert Moton's latest book and prepare to say something about the other Amendments. Hoover disregarded this advice and concentrated his public interest in law and order on the enforcement of prohibition much to the dismay of many Blacks. The Reverend Thomas S. Harten, president of the National Afro-Protective League, vice-president of the National Baptist Convention, and pastor of the Holy Trinity Baptist Church of Brooklyn, New York, wrote Hoover that the great violation of law and order was the mob spirit which was then increasing. Harten charged that Hoover spent $50 million annually to enforce the Eighteenth Amendment but "uttered not one word against lynching."[31]

A few days after their 1932 defeat, the Republicans reviewed their policies with respect to Black voters and immediately began to look ahead to the 1934 election. Francis E. Rivers, son of the last Black member of the post-Civil War Tennessee Legislature and member of the New York Assembly 1929-1930, prepared a memorandum for Hoover at the request of the Republican National Committee, which outlined the policies the party could adopt to obtain solid Black support for the 1934 election. Rivers recommended that Hoover immediately take steps to provide relief and jobs, and government discrimination, end the policy of requiring photographs for federal applications, and support federal anti-lynching measures. Hoover accepted none of these recommendations, and the popularity of the Republican party among Black voters continued to decline.[32]

As the anti-lynching reform developed, women played an increasingly vital role. In the late 1920s a new organization, the Women's Stop Lynching League, was organized. It held a mass meeting early in June, 1929 in Washington, and its president, Elnora Johnson, requested President Hoover to receive a delegation at that time. The White House did not acknowledge the request.[33] In 1932 the Women's Stop Lynching League served as the coordinator of a nation-wide petition drive in support of the Dyer bill which had been reintroduced in Congress. President Johnson of the League again wrote Hoover on March 5, 1932, requesting that he receive a delegation which would represent the Elks, the Foresters, the Good Samaritans, the Federation of Colored Women's Clubs, the Eastern Star, as well as the Women's Stop Lynching League. Mrs. Johnson also pointed out that the Inter-denominational Preachers Union of Greater New York was backing their upcoming convention. The president's secretary advised that since the president's views on lynching were so well known, the secretary would not suggest that Hoover waste his time considering the problem further. Mrs. Johnson then appealed to Vice-president Curtis to intercede. Curtis referred the matter to the same presidential secretary, and it died there. Mrs. Johnson's next letter to Hoover was totally ignored.[34]

By 1929, the number of lynchings had dropped to a new low of ten, one less then in 1928. This decline had removed the sense of urgency that had characterized the anti-lynching reform just as similar declines in the frequency of lynching had done in the past. The complacency regarding lynchings was only temporary, as the number more than doubled in 1930 to twenty-one. This increase was due in part to the rise of several nativist, white supremacist organizations that came into being early in the depression to oust Blacks from jobs in order to provide more employment for whites. Lynching was one of their tools.

The American Civil Liberties Union (ACLU), along with several other organizations, opposed the nativist "Black Shirts." The ACLU, formed in 1920, had always opposed lynching. It was an interracial coalition which by 1930 included a broad spectrum of liberals and radicals from James Harvey Dillard, liberal Southerner, to William Z. Foster, Chairman of the Communist Party of the United States. The members of the National Committee of the ACLU had membership in other organizations which multiplied its influence. James Weldon Johnson and William Pickens, field secretary for the NAACP, were among the Blacks on the National Committee.

From its beginning the ACLU had included lynching statistics in its annual reports. Through the early 19a0s it emphasized that many of the victims of the Ku Klux Klan were white. The _Messenger_ applauded the ACLU for this tactic on the grounds that no one noticed violence that was only against Blacks. The ACLU and the NAACP worked closely together and each responded positively to suggestions from the other. In 1926 James Weldon Johnson complied with an ACLU request to telegraph President Coolidge to release Sacco and Vanzetti. The ACLU also cooperated with the other organizations opposing lynchings, including the Commission on Interracial Cooperation and the Southern Commission on the Study of Lynching headed by George Fort Milton.[35]

In 1930 the ACLU tried to transfer its sense of urgency to Milton regarding the situation in Atlanta, where the semi-fascist "Black Shirts" were particularly active, by urging his organization to set aside its slow and deliberate investigative process in favor of issuing an immediate statement against the "Black Shirts." The ACLU was only one of several organizations that utilized the fear of fascism to reinforce the anti-lynching reform. Later the ACLU became deeply committed to the drive of the mid-1930s to pass federal anti-lynching legislation.[36]

Lynching was always more than just a domestic matter for concern only within the United States. It affected the credibility of missionaries from the time lynching was first recognized as a problem. It strained foreign relations when foreign nationals were lynched in the United States. Other countries wishing to criticize and weaken the international influence of the United States would point to lynching as proof of hypocrisy on the part of the United States. Opponents of the United States would state that lynching proved that the glorification of the Constitution was a sham; therefore, the United States should not be used as a model. That some of this foreign criticism was self-serving goes without saying. When Germany propagandized among Blacks in World War I concerning the brutal treatment of Africans in the Belgian Congo and compared it to the brutal treatment of Blacks in the South, it was not motivated by any love for the darker races.

The anti-lynching reform had always looked abroad for reinforcements. Several Blacks traveled in England and Europe when the reform was just getting underway in the 1890s and the support they received was helpful. Bishop Henry McNeal Turner, W. E. B. Du Bois, Marcus Garvey, and William Monroe Trotter had all looked abroad for support to improve the status of Blacks within the United States.

As Hitler rose to power in Germany, those with anti-fascist sympathies in the United States became more active, and many became allied with the anti-lynching forces. There was enough in common between the Brown Shirts' treatment of Jews in Germany and the lynch mobs' treatment of Blacks in the United States to join the opponents of each in common cause. As the recognition grew that these geographically separate phenomena were aspects of a common world-wide problem, so did support for the anti-lynching reform. Intellectuals who were primarily motivated by a need to oppose Hitler's anti-semitism had little difficulty in expanding their concern to oppose all racism. Many accepted the belief that an attack on racism anywhere was an attack on it everywhere.

The Scottsboro case which began in 1931 was used by the anti-fascist Left to give world publicity to lynching in the United States. Much of the Communist support for the "Scottsboro Boys" was motivated by a desire to increase Communist strength in order to oppose fascism more effectively. Their publicity contributed to making this case the most widely discussed example of white injustice to Blacks in the history of the nation up to that time. Hoover received pleas for executive clemency for the "Scottsboro Boys" from such diverse people as Subbhas Bose, president of the All-India Trade Union Congress on one side of the world and from Albert Einstein and Thomas Mann from the other side.[37]

After the election of Franklin D. Roosevelt in 1932, the character of the anti-lynching reform changed sufficiently to make the period ushered in by the New Deal a new era in the struggle against lynching which is worthy of a separate study. The changes involved the relative decline in the role of Blacks and the increasing role of whites in the anti-lynching coalition, the subordination of the fight against lynching into a broader campaign for all civil rights, and the selection of the Democratic party by reformers as the primary vehicle for social change.

For fifty years Blacks had led the reform movement. In this task they had been assisted by an increasing number of white liberals, but with the advent of the New Deal, the ability of Blacks and whites to unite on issues that affected them similarly was stimulated by the economic crisis and the new political directions. This increased ability to work together for a common cause was one reason Blacks did not have to carry as large a share of the burden of the anti-lynching reform after 1932. This development of coalition politics continued after World War II and was illustrated in 1966 when Roy Wilkins testified in the Senate Civil Rights Hearings, not as the executive secretary of the NAACP, but as chairman of the Leadership Conference on Civil Rights, an ad hoc group representing more than 100 organizations which had a far greater white than Black membership.[38]

There were other reasons for the decline in the relative importance of the Black leadership in the anti-lynching reform movement. The degree of success that the reform had achieved in its first fifty years was significant. In the half-century, from its inception to the election of 1932, lynchings had declined from an average of over 150 a year in the late nineteenth century to under twenty a year in the ten-year period from the 1922 effort to pass the Dyer bill to the election of Franklin Roosevelt. This decline contributed to the belief of Blacks that lynching was no longer their number one problem.

The depression affected the Black communities of the nation earlier and more severely than it affected other groups. The economic crisis greatly reduced the flow of resources coming in to the Black leaders who had been directing the anti-lynching campaign. The depression particularly influenced the financial support the Black rank and file could give the Black leaders and tended to place these leaders in a position of greater relative dependence on white support. All businesses and organizations that depended on income from Blacks were especially hurt. The NAACP was no exception. Unemployment struck both races, but it struck Blacks more brutally, and the flow of dues and donations to the NAACP was reduced to a trickle. Although Walter White considered renewing the drive for federal anti-lynching legislation in 1930, the NAACP was too burdened with economic problems to make an actual start until 1934. As an indication of the severity of the economic problems, and of the reordering of Black priorities, when lynchings fell to a new annual low of eight in 1932, the NAACP transferred to other uses of the remaining money in the fund accumulated in 1922 by Mary Talbert and the Anti-lynching Crusaders.[39]

The depression forced a change in the Direction of Black protest. The anti-lynching reform movement, in addition to its humanitarian aspects, had been a part of a general struggle to get ahead, to improve the status of Blacks by eliminating a major obstacle to advance on all fronts. With the advent of the economic crisis during Hoover's presidency, the struggle had to turn from strategies aimed at advancement to strategies of maintenance of past advances or even to those of bare survival. This meant that economic issues had to be paramount. The anti-lynching reform continued because lynchings continued, but it was not the common denominator serving as a rallying point for Black protest after the advent of the New Deal that it had been for the preceding fifty years.

Another change in the direction and nature of the anti-lynching movement stems from the election of 1932, and the development of the New Deal coalition which Blacks began to join in 1932. Black support for the Democratic party increased in 1936 and an even larger percentage of the Black voters joined the Democratic camp in 1940. Before 1932 the anti-lynching reformers had placed more hope on the Republican party than on the Democratic party. After 1932 the reverse was true. But no matter how large the reform movement became, or which party it supported, no federal anti-lynching legislation was ever passed.[40]

FOOTNOTES--CHAPTER VIII

[1] Letter L. C. Dyer to John R. Shillady, May 3, 1918, Library of Congress, NAACP papers, Admin. File, C-206; Anti-lynching Crusaders, Minutes of third meeting, n.d., Admin. file, C-205.

[2] Crusaders, Minutes, C-206.

[3] Ibid.

[4] Letter, Mary B. Talbert to Crusaders, September, 1922, NAACP papers, Admin. file, C-206; letter, James Weldon Johnson to Mary B. Talbert, October 2, 1922, C-206.

[5] W. E. B. Du Bois, The Autobiography of W. E. B. Du Bois: A Soliloquy on Viewing My Life from the Last Decade of Its First Century (New York: International Publishers, 1968), p. 275; Letter, Talbert to Anti-lynching Crusader Executive Board Members and State Directors, December 5, 1922, NAACP papers, admin. file C-206. For list of women's periodicals see file C-207.

[6] Letter, Irene Goins, President, Illinois Federation of Colored Women's Clubs to Senator A. B. Cummins, February 11, 1926, National Archives, Record Group 46, 69th Cong., S.121; Letter, Minnie Cravath Simpson, chairman, suppression of lynching department, Northeastern Federations of Women's Clubs, to Herbert Hoover, July 30, 1930, Hoover Presidential papers, Colored Question.

[7] Robert Lewis Zangrando, "The Efforts of the National Association for the Advancement of Colored People to Secure the Passage of a Federal Anti-lynching Law, 1920-1940" (unpublished Ph.D. dissertation, University of Pennsylvania, 1963), p. 148.

[8] Zangrando, "Efforts," p. 148; James Weldon Johnson, Along This Way (New York: Viking Press, 1933), p. 319; Ernest Kirschten, Catfish and Crystal (Garden City: Doubleday & Co., 1960).

[9] This criticism appears in the Black newspapers, particularly in the St. Louis Argus for weeks before and after primary and general elections from 1920.

[10] Harold Cruse, The Crisis of the Negro Intellectual (New York: William Morrow & Co., 1967), pp. 25, 35, 38. For the positive results of the struggle for the Dyer bill see Zangrando, "Efforts," p. xlii.

[11] St. Louis Argus, January 30, 1920.

[12] Ibid., January 20; April 30; March 2; July 1, 23; August 6; October 10, 29; November 5, 1920; January 14, 1921.

[13] Johnson, Along This Way, pp. 313, 358, 361.

[14] Walter White, "I Investigate Lynchings," American Mercury, 16 (January, 1929), 77-84; Fire in the Flint (New York: A. A. Knopf, 1926). Johnson, Along This Way, pp. 317, 334, 376. Rope and Faggot (New York: Alfred A. Knopf, 1929).

[15] "The Sweet Trial," Crisis, 31 (January, 1926), 125-29; David E. Lilienthal, "Has the Negro the Right to Self Defense" Nation, December 23, 1925, pp. 724-25; Walter White, "The Negro and the Supreme Court," Harpers (January, 1931), 238-46; Walter White, A Man Called White: The Autobiography of Walter White (New York: Viking Press, 1948), p. 115. Arthur B. Spingarn, said the Parker case made White. See Zangrando, "Efforts," p. 281.

[16] White, Man, pp. 80, 99-101; "The Negro and the Flood," Nation, June 22, 1927, pp. 688-89.

[17] Atlanta Journal, October 16, 1928; Union Star (Brookneal, Va.), October 5, 1928; NAACP press release, October 12, 1928, NAACP papers, admin. file C-333.

[18] Letter, L. C. Dyer to Walter White, January 23, 1930, NAACP papers, admin. file, C-333.

[19] Richard B. Sherman, "The Harding Administration and the Negro: An Opportunity Lost," Journal of Negro History, 49 (July, 1964), 151-68; for a similar discussion of the Coolidge years see John L. Blair, "A Time for Parting: The Negro During the Coolidge Years," Journal of American Studies, 3 (December, 1969), 177-200. For Black discontent with the Hoover administration see Elbert Lee Tatum, The Changed Political Thought of the Negro: 1915-1940 (New York: Exposition Press, 1951), pp. 114-137.

[20] Letter, Reverend H. H. Jackson to Hoover, March 4, 1929, Hoover Presidential Papers, Colored Question; Sutton Griggs, The Basis of Hope for the Negroes in the South (Memphis: National Public Welfare League, 1929), located in Hoover papers, Colored Question.

[21] Letter, White to Hoover, October 3, November 13, 1930, Hoover Presidential papers, Colored Question; White, Man, p. 104.

[22] Letter, Trotter to Hoover, March 7, 1929; July 1, 1929; November 4, 1930; November 25, 1930; November 30, 1930; February 7, 1931, Hoover Presidential papers, Colored Question. Continuing the NAACP position of minimizing the role of Monroe Trotter and the Equal Rights League, Walter White does not mention him in his autobiography.

[23] Letter, Trotter to Hoover, December 7, 1931; January 16, 1932, Hoover presidential papers, Colored Question.

[24] William D. Mitchell, "Memorandum for the President on the Dyer anti-lynching bill," January 6, 1932; Letter, A. H. Clarke to Herbert Hoover, January, 1932. Typical of the requests Black Republicans made Hoover during the 1932 campaign was one

from the president of the Connecticut Colored Republican State Association regretting "you have never mentioned in any of your speeches any wish that lynchings be stopped in the South," see letter, R. R. Burt to Hoover, August 5, 1932, Hoover presidential papers, Colored Question.

[25] Sherman, "Harding Administration"; Blair, "Time for Parting"; Letter, J. W. Johnson to Herbert Hoover, May 4, 1929; Telegram, Johnson to Hoover, June 19, 1929; letter, White to Hoover, May 19, 1930; letter, Hoover to White, August 20, 1930; Hoover to J. E. Spingarn, June 23, 1931; Hoover presidential papers, Colored Question.

[26] Letter, Walter White to Herbert Hoover, August 19, 1930, Hoover presidential papers, Colored Question.

[27] Letter, Walter White to Herbert Hoover, September 14, 1932, Hoover presidential papers, Colored Question; Hoover to National Urban League, February 25, 1931, Hoover presidential library, Commerce papers, pers., Negro matters.

[28] Letter, R. R. Moton to W. H. Newton, secretary to the president, November 27, 1929; Letter, Hoover to Moton, December 3, 1929, Hoover presidential papers, pers., Comm. on Interracial Cooperation.

[29] "Mrs. Willebrandt Should Quit," New York (New York) News, n.d.; New York World, April 22, 1929, Hoover presidential papers, clipping files; Letter, Charles O'Neal Kansas City American to Herbert Hoover, April 17, 1929, Hoover presidential papers, Colored Question.

[30] Arthur F. Raper, The Tragedy of Lynching (Chapel Hill: The University of North Carolina Press, 1933), pp. 172-202. Letter, B. J. Davis to Walter Newton, secretary to the president, August 4, 1930; Savannah Morning News, July 30, 1930; Greensboro (Georgia) Herald-Journal, n.d.; Hoover presidential papers, Colored Question.

[31] C. H. Huston, "Memorandum for the President," April 25, 1929; Letter, Thomas S. Harten to Herbert Hoover, November 24, 1931, Hoover presidential papers, Colored Question. Robert Moton, What the Negro Thinks (Garden City: Doubleday, Doran & Co., 1929).

[32] Letter, Francis E. Rivers to Herbert Hoover, November 10, 1932, Hoover presidential papers, Colored Question.

[33] Letter, Elnora Johnson to Herbert Hoover, May 10, 1929, Hoover presidential papers, Colored Question.

[34] Letter, E. Johnson to Herbert Hoover, March 5, 1932; Letter, T. G. Joslin, Secretary to the President, to E. Johnson, March 8, 1932; letter E. Johnson to C. Curtis, March 15, 1932; letter, E. Johnson to Herbert Hoover, March 21, 1932, Hoover presidential papers, Colored Question.

[35] Messenger, 5 (January, 1923), 563; Telegram, Baldwin to Johnson, August 12,

1926, NAACP papers, admin. file C-193.

[36] Letter, Forrest Bailey, director ACLU to Milton, October 4, 1930, NAACP papers, admin. file C-193.

[37] Radiogram, Subhas Bose to Hoover, July 7, 1931; Albert Einstein, Thomas Mann, Lion Feuchtwanger, et al., to Hoover, July 4, 1931, Hoover Presidential papers, Secretary's file-Negro. See also Dan. T. Carter, Scottsboro: A Tragedy of the American South (Baton Rouge: Louisiana State University Press, 1969); Haywood Patterson and Earl Conrad, Scottsboro Boy (Garden City: Doubleday & Co., 1930).

[38] U. S., Congress, Senate, Committee on the Judiciary, Civil Rights Hearings before the subcommittee on constitutional rights of the Committee on the Judiciary, Senate, on S. 3296, amendment 561 to S. 3296, S. 1479, S. 1654, S. 2849, S. 2924, and S. 3170, 89th Cong., 2d sess., 1966, pt. 1:540-42.

[39] Donnie D. Bellamy, Glory Road: The Visible Black Man (Middletown, Conn.: Xerox Corp., 1971), p. 4; Zangrando, "Efforts," pp. 243-45; Raymond Wolters, Negroes and the Great Depression: The Problem of Economic Recovery (Westport Conn.: Greenwood, 1970), p. 266.

[40] Over 200 anti-lynching bills have been introduced since 1900, see U. S., Congress, Senate, Congressional Record, 86th Cong., 1st sess., 1959, 105 pt. 6:7124. The most recent anti-lynching legislation is H. R. 9553 (Adam Clayton Powell, Jr.) and H. R. 11730 (William F. Ryan) introduced in the 89th Cong., 1st sess., 1965; H. R. 1217 (William R. Ryan), introduced in the 90th Cong., 1st sess., 1967; and H. R. 623 (William F. Ryan), introduced in the 91st Cong., 1st sess., 1969. All of these bills died in committee and the issue appears to have faded away for the present as no bills were introduced in the 92d Congress.

CONCLUSIONS

By 1883 a new pattern of race relations was clearly emerging in the South. The gains made by Blacks during Reconstruction had been severely limited and in some cases wrested away by superior force by 1883 when the United States Supreme Court overturned the Civil Rights Act of 1875. This decision was immediately perceived by Blacks to be a final reversal of the trend toward equality which had characterized much of the preceding two decades. This action of the Supreme Court absolved the federal government from responsibility for prevention of the further development of a caste system and indicated to the white supremacists that there would be no effective federal interference in the patterns of exploitation of Blacks. The decision, in effect, left Blacks at the mercy of their former masters and insured that any Black who contested the exploitation could be subject to a variety of possible punishments of which torture followed by burning alive at the stake was the ultimate.

The Supreme Court's decision in 1883 also did much to develop an awareness among Blacks that they had few white allies and that they needed to organize more effectively in their own behalf. Because the overwhelming preponderance of power lay in white hands, the earliest reform efforts could do little to combat lynching directly. Blacks, therefore, turned to the indirect methods of acquisition of education, property, and middle-class virtues on the theory that these would lead to a diminution of the proscriptions and an end to lynching.

Those who benefitted from racism were consciously and unconsciously impelled to rationalize lynching by developing false historical concepts and a mythology that placed them in the role of saviors of civilization rather than its subverters. The seeds of this mythology were cultivated by the organizers of the "New South" and they bore bitter fruit in the racist soil of the entire nation.

The first direct attacks on lynching were efforts to undermine the myths with which the white supremacists had enveloped the subject. This was done in the 1880s by militant church leaders such as Bishop Henry McNeal Turner and efitors such as T. Thomas Fortune. With time, more Blacks and a few whites joined in the effort to swing public opinion against lynching by showing that its function was not the prevention of rape as the myth-makers constantly insisted.

The anti-lynching reform always operated on a number of fronts simultaneously. One of these was the political front where many efforts were made to influence local and county officials, state legislators and governors, and members of congress and the president. No president in the entire fifty-year period used his office effectively to promote the anti-lynching reform. The state anti-lynching legislation which did pass was largely unenforced. Nevertheless, the political arena was one of the first areas in which Blacks and whites worked together to oppose lynching. This was true to the extent that Blacks voted; therefore, interraccial cooperation increased as more Blacks migrated to the North where they could enjoy the franchise far more freely than in the South.

Appeal to the democratic and religious conscience of the nation was one tactic all components of the anti-lynching reform used. The originally small, but constantly growing, group of white, middle-class leaders joined Blacks in stating that our concepts of constitutionalism militated against the absolute denial of due process that lynching represented. They bolstered their argument with the theory that the lynching of Blacks could lead to the denial of constitutional guarantees to all and that a dictator might arise to re-establish law and order if the society became too chaotic. Proponents of the anti-lynching reform all joined in giving it religious and moral implications by stating that lynching was a refutation of the Christian doctrine that all mankind should be as borthers, and that each soul was equally valuable in the sight of God. These appeals fell on largely deaf ears before World War I. The white church and the white legal profession which might have been expected to take the lead in the protection of moral values and constitutional liberties, became instead, leading bulwarks of the caste society which required lynching for its maintenance.

Meanwhile, the anti-lynching cause was gradually strengthened by developments which improved the status of Blacks. The Black press grew in readership and influence. Schools produced ever increasing numbers of Black graduates who rebelled against rigid caste barriers and menial employment. The urban Black church, like its white counterpart, began to promote the Social Gospel. As these developments occurred, the level of the protest against lynching rose, and more whites became aware of their responsibility and enlisted in the reform.

White awareness that lynching was a problem which also concerned them grew most rapidly in the periods when it appeared that lynching was increasing. In addition to the growing acceptance of the humanitarian, moral, religious, and legal reasons for opposing lynching, some whites joined the anti-lynching reform because they feared lynching would lead to social disruption. Other whites joined the reform because they feared that lynching, if unabated, might produce an anti-lynching reform movement of sufficient strength to obtain more far-reaching reforms in racial relations than just a reduction in the number of lynchings.

After the Great Migration of Southern Black peasants started in 1915, primarily to Northern urban centers, there was an acceleration in the rate of change of both white and Black attitudes towards lynching. Growing political power in the North meant growing white support of Black demands. The labor shortage in the South led to a rapid growth in the belief that lynching was counterproductive to the best interests of the South. As this happened, anti-lynching work became more respectable and could be promoted to a limited extent without fear of reprisal. The Great Migration also had a profound impact on the world view of Blacks. The holder of these broader views was the "New Negro" who was less inclined to accept the insult and attack that had always characterized so much of almost every Black's experience in the United States.

White-initiated violence aimed at restoring Blacks to their pre-World War I position produced the "Red Summer" of 1919. This was a traumatic experience for the nation. Not only was the level of racial violence the highest for a generation, but the increasing determination of Blacks not to die "like hogs" contributed to the growing realization that the entire society could be endangered if the overt and violent white racism that fueled the 1919 violence was not reined in. This realization led to a large increase in the activities of the anti-lynching reformers. The Southern reform movement grew rapidly, and enough support was generated in the North to obtain the passage of the Dyer anti-lynching bill by the House of Representatives. The Dyer bill did not get past the Senate filibuster, however, despite the great lobbying effort led by the NAACP. This failure indicated to many that the Republican party's custom of paying little but lip service to Black voters' demands had not changed. The disaffection of Blacks with the Republican party grew steadily from this point on through World War II.

Among the forces that contributed to the decline in lynching were the developments in education and the attendant increase in the circulation of popular journals and both Black and white newspapers. Economic developments related to the growth of capitalism and urbanization and the decline in the relative importance of the agricultural sector played a part in the decline of lynching. This decline was encouraged and promoted by the growing importance of Black organizations and leaders who became more effective as the Black masses struggled out of their feudal relationship to Southern Agriculture. All increases in participative democracy reinforced the anti-lynching reform; the more active participation of women in the governance of the nation was a positive factor. Although the federal government played a small role at best, the fear of greater federal interference was a spur to the South to get its house in order with respect to lynching.

A study of the anti-lynching reform shows that the contemporary protest movement has deeper roots than many of the present generation realize. Many of the techniques and much of the ideology of the movements of the late 1950s and early 1960s have rather direct parallels in the earlier anti-lynching movements. The militant calls for self-defense and retaliatory violence that were heard in the mid-1960s were not new, as examination of the anti-lynching editorials in the Black press eighty years earlier will show. Calls for reordering the nation's priorities and returning to what was perceived as the earlier task of making the United States a democratic model for the entire world were as much a part of the anti-lynching reform movement from its inception as such calls are a part of today's reform movements. The post-World War II protest movements owe much to the limited success of the earlier anti-lynching reform. Earlier, the fear of lynching was a pall which had to be removed before there could be the mass grass roots involvement that characterized later protest movements.

BIBLIOGRAPHY

A. MANUSCRIPTS

<u>Department of Justice Records,</u> National Archives Record Group 60, Washington, D.C.

<u>Herbert Hoover Papers,</u> Herbert Hoover Presidential Library, West Branch, Iowa.

<u>Arthur M. Hyde Papers,</u> Western Historical Manuscripts Collection, University of Missouri, Columbia, Missouri.

<u>George Fort Milton Papers,</u> Manuscript Division, Library of Congress, Washington, D.C.

<u>National Association for the Advancement of Colored People papers,</u> Manuscript Division, Library of Congress, Washington, D.C..

<u>Senate Committee on the Judiciary Records,</u> National Archives Record Group 46, Washington, D.C.

<u>Mary Church Terrell Papers</u>, Manuscript Division, Library of Congress, Washington, D.C.

<u>Robert H. Terrell Papers,</u> Manuscript Division, Library of Congress, Washington, D.C.

B. GOVERNMENT PUBLICATIONS

Jamison, Stuart M. <u>Labor Unionism in American Agriculture</u>. Bureau of Labor Statistics Bulletin No. 836. Washington, D.C.: United States Government Printing Office.

United States Department of Commerce, Bureau of the Census. <u>Negroes in the United States: 1920-32.</u> Washington, D.C.: United States Government Printing Office, 1935.

United States Congress. <u>Congressional Record,</u> 48th Cong., 1st sess., 1884.

_____. <u>Congressional Record,</u> 51st Cong., 1st sess., 1890.

_____. <u>Congressional Record,</u> 51st Cong., 2d sess., 1891.

_____. <u>Congressional Record,</u> 53d Cong., 2d sess., 1894.

_____. <u>Congressional Record,</u> 54th Cong., 1st sess., 1895.

United States Congress. Congressional Record, 55th Cong., 1st sess., 1897.

_____. Congressional Record, 55th Cong., 3d sess., 1899.

_____. Congressional Record, 56th Cong., 1st sess. 1900.

_____. Congressional Record, 56th Cong., 2d sess., 1901.

_____. Congressional Record, 57th Cong., 1st sess., 1902.

_____. Congressional Record, 65th Cong., 2d sess., 1918.

_____. Congressional Record, 86th Cong., 1st sess., 1959.

_____. Congressional Record, 89th Cong., 1st sess., 1965.

_____. Congressional Record, 90th Cong., 1st sess., 1967.

_____. Congressional Record, 91st Cong., 1st sess., 1969.

_____. Congressional Record, 92d Cong., 1st sess., 1971.

_____. House. Indemnity for Chinese Killed at Rock Springs, Wyoming. H. Rept. 2044. 49th Cong., 1st sess., 1886.

_____. House. Message of the President Reference Failure of Mexican Colonization. H.R. Doc. 169, 54th Cong., 1st sess., 1895.

_____. House. Lynching of Luis Moreno, Mexican Claim for Indemnity. H. R. Doc. 237, 55th Cong., 2d sess., 1898.

_____. House. Commission to Enquire into the Condition of the Colored People. H. Rept. 2194, 57th Cong., 1st sess., 1902.

_____. House. The East St. Louis Riots. H.R. Doc. 1231, 65th Cong., 2d sess., 1918.

_____. House. Committee on the Judiciary, Antilynching Hearings on H.R. 259, 4123, and 11873, 66th Cong., 1st sess., 1920.

_____. Senate. The Removal of the Negroes from the Southern States to the Northern States. S. Rep. 693, 46th Cong., 2d sess., 1880.

_____. Senate. Lynching of two Seminoles. S. Doc. 99, 55th Cong., 2d sess., 1898.

_____. Senate. Statement of the President of the United States Denouncing Mob Violence and Appealing to his Fellow Countrymen to keep the Nation's Fame Untarnished. S. Doc. 272, 65th Cong., 2d sess., 1918.

_____. Senate. Committee on the Judiciary. <u>Punishment for the Crime of Lynching,</u> <u>Hearings</u> on S. 1978, 73d Cong., 2d sess., 1934.

_____. Senate. Committee on the Judiciary. <u>Civil Rights,</u> Hearings on S. 3296, S. 1497, S. 1654, S. 2845, S. 2846, S. 2923, and S. 3170, 89th Cong., 2d sess., 1966.

Williams, W. T. B. "The Negro Exodus from the South." <u>Negro Migration in 1916-17.</u> Comp. by United States Department of Labor, Division of Negro Economics, Washington, D.C. United States Government Printing Office, 1919.

C. NEWSPAPERS

New York <u>Age,</u> 1887-1904.

St. Louis <u>Argus,</u> 1915-1926.

Washington <u>Bee,</u> 1901.

Chicago <u>Broad Ax,</u> 1897-1925.

<u>Christian Advocate,</u> 1880-1927.

Chicago <u>Defender,</u> 1908-1928.

Indianapolis <u>Freeman,</u> 1886-1898, 1923-1924.

New York <u>Freeman,</u> 1884-1887.

New York <u>Globe,</u> 1884-1887.

Chicago <u>Inter Ocean,</u> 1880-1892.

Norfolk <u>Journal and Guide,</u> 1917-1931.

<u>Vardaman's Weekly,</u> 1908-1923.

D. UNPUBLISHED STUDIES

Carter, Proctor N. "Lynch Law and the Press of Missouri." Unpublished Master's thesis, University of Missouri-Columbia, 1933.

Fry, Gladys-Marie. "The Night Riders: A Study in the Social Control of the Negro." Unpublished Ph.D. dissertation, University of Indiana, 1967.

Grothaus, Larry H. "The Negro in Missouri Politics: 1890-1941." Unpublished Ph.D. dissertation, University of Missouri-Columbia, 1970.

Mitchell, Franklin Dean. "Embattled Democracy: Missouri Democratic Politics, 1918-1932." Unpublished Ph.D. dissertation, University of Missouri-Columbia, 1964.

Milton, George Fort. "Reflections on the Vanishing Mob." Library of Congress, Manuscripts Division, George Fort Milton Papers.

Ogilvie, Leon Parker. "The Development of the Southeast Missouri Lowlands." Unpublished Ph.D. dissertation, University of Missouri-Columbia, 1967.

Terrell, Mary Church. "The Progress of Colored Women." An Address delivered before the National American Women's Suffrage Association, Washington, D.C., February 18, 1898. Library of Congress, Manuscripts Division, Mary Church Terrell Papers.

Worner, Lloyd E., Jr. "Missouri and the National Election of 1920." Unpublished Ph.D. dissertation, University of Missouri-Columbia, 1943.

Zangrando, Robert Lewis. "The Efforts of the National Association for the Advancement of Colored People to Secure the Passage of a Federal Anti-lynching Law, 1920-1940." Unpublished Ph.D. dissertation, University of Pennsylvania, 1963.

E. BOOKS

Afro-American Council. "An Appeal to Set Aside a Day of Fasting as a Protest Against Lynching." *Chronicles of Negro Protest*. Edited by Bradford Chambers. New York: Parent's Magazine Press, 1968.

Afro-American National League. "Constitution and Address to the Nation." *The Negro American: A Documentary History*. Edited by Leslie H. Fishel, Jr. and Benjamin Quarles. Glenview, Ill.: Scott, Foresman, 1967.

Alexander, William T. *The History of the Colored Race in America*. New York: Negro Universities Press, 1968.

Ames, Jessie Daniel. *The Association of Southern Women for the Prevention of Lynching: Beginning of the Movement*. Atlanta: Commission on Interracial Cooperation, n.d.

_____. *The Changing Character of Lynching*. Atlanta: Commission on Interracial Cooperation, 1942.

Aptheker, Herbert. *To be Free: Studies in American Negro History*. New York: International Publishers, 1948.

_____. *Annotated Bibliography of the Published Writings of W.E.B. DuBois*. Millwood, N.Y.: Kraus-Thomson, 1973.

Association of Southern Women for the Prevention of Lynching. *Lynching is Wholesale Murder*. n.p.: By the Association, 1937.

Bailey, Kenneth K. *Southern White Protestantism in the Twentieth Century*. New York: Harper & Row, 1964.

Baker, Ray Stannard. *Woodrow Wilson: Life and Letters*. 6 vol., Garden City, N.Y.: Doubleday, Doran, 1931.

Bancroft, Hubert Howe, *Popular Tribunals*, vols. 36 and 37 of *The Works of Hubert Howe*

     <u>Bancroft.</u> 39 vols. San Francisco: History Company, 1888.

Bellamy, Donnie D. <u>Glory Road: The Visible Black Man.</u> Middletown, Conn.: Xerox Corp.,
  1971.

Bennett, Lerone. <u>Confrontation: Black and White.</u> Chicago: Johnson Publishing Co., 1965.

Bergman, Peter M. <u>The Chronological History of the Negro in America.</u> New York: Harper
  & Row, 1969.

Berry, Mary Frances. <u>Black Resistance/White Law.</u> New York: Meredith Corp., 1971.

Bishop, Joseph Bucklin, ed. <u>Theodore Roosevelt and His Time: Shown in His Own Letters.</u>
  2 vol. New York: Charles Scribner's Sons, 1919-1920.

Bowers, Claude G. <u>The Tragic Era: The Revolution After Lincoln.</u> Cambridge: Houghton
  Mifflin Co., 1929.

Brisbane, Robert H. <u>The Black Vanguard: Origins of the Negro Social Revolution, 1900-1960.</u>
  Valley Forge, Pa.: Judson Press, 1970.

Broderick, Francis L. <u>W.E.B. DuBois: Negro Leader in a Time of Crisis.</u> Stanford: Stanford University Press, 1959.

Bullock, Henry Allen. <u>A History of Negro Education in the South: From 1619 to the Present.</u>
  New York: Praeger Publishers, 1970.

Carter, Dan T. <u>Scottsboro: A Tragedy of the American South.</u> Baton Rouge: Louisiana State
  University Press, 1969.

Carver, Charles. <u>Brann and the Iconoclast.</u> Austin: University of Texas Press, 1957.

Cash, W. J. <u>The Mind of the South.</u> Vintage Books. New York: Random House, 1941.

Cayton, Horace R. <u>Long Old Road.</u> New York: Trident Press, 1965.

Chesnutt, Charles W. "The Disfranchisement of the Negro." <u>The Negro Problem.</u> New
  York: James Pott, 1903.

Chicago Commission on Race Relations. <u>The Negro in Chicago: A Study of Race Relations
  and a Race Riot.</u> Chicago: University of Chicago Press, 1922.

Christopher, Maurine. <u>America's Black Congressmen.</u> New York: Thomas Y. Crowell, 1971.

Clarke, John Henry, et al. <u>Black Titan: W.E.B. DuBois.</u> Boston: Beacon Press, 1970.

Cleage, Albert. <u>The Black Messiah.</u> New York: Sheed and Ward, 1968.

Clowes, W. Laird. Black America: A Study of the Ex-slave and His Late Master. London: Cassell & Co., 1891.

Collins, Winfield H. The Truth About Lynching and the Negro in the South. New York: Neale Publishing Co., 1918.

Cone, James H. Black Theology and Black Power. New York: Seabury Press, 1969.

Conrad, David Eugene. The Forgotten Farmers: The Story of Sharecroppers in the New Deal. Urbana: University of Illinois Press, 1965.

Conrad, Earl. The Invention of the Negro. New York: Paul Erickson, 1966.

Coppin, Bishop L. J. Unwritten History. New York: Negro Universities Press, 1968.

Cox, Oliver Cromwell, Caste, Class and Race. Garden City, New York: Doubleday & Co., 1948.

Cromwell, John W. The Negro in American History: Men and Women Eminent in the Evolution of the American of African Descent. Washington: American Negro Academy, 1914.

Cronon, Edmund David. Black Moses: The Story of Marcus Garvey and the Universal Negro Improvement Association. Madison: University of Wisconsin Press, 1935.

Cruse, Harold. The Crisis of the Negro Intellectual. New York: William Morrow, 1967.

Cunard, Nancy, ed. Negro Anthology. New York: Negro Universities Press, 1969.

Davis, Allen F. Spearheads for Reform: The Social Settlements and the Progressive Movement, 1890-1914. New York: Oxford University Press, 1967.

Davis, Allison; Gardner, Burleigh B; and Gardner, Mary B. Deep South: A Social Anthropological Study of Caste and Class. Chicago: University of Chicago Press, 1941.

Dann, Martin E. The Black Press 1827-1890: The Quest for National Identity. New York: G. P. Putnam's Sons, 1971.

Degler, Carn N. Neither White Nor Black: Slavery and Race Relations in Brazil and the United States. New York: Macmillan, 1971.

_____. Out of Our Past: The Forces that Shaped Modern America. Harper Colophon Books. New York: Harper & Row, 1970.

Detweiler, Frederick G. The Negro Press in the United States. Chicago: University of Chicago Press, 1922.

Dimsdale, Thomas J. The Vigilantes of Montana: Or Popular Justice in the Rocky Mountains. 3d ed. Helena, Mont.: State Publishing Co., 1915.

Dinnerstein, Leonard. The Leo Frank Case. New York: Columbia University Press, 1968.

Dollard, John. Caste-and Class in a Southern Town. New Haven: Yale University Press, 1937.

Douglass, Frederick. Life and Times of Frederick Douglass. New York: Collier Books, 1962.

Drake, St. Clair and Cayton, Horace R. Black Metropolis: A study of Negro Life in a Northern City. New York: Harcourt, Brace, 1945.

Du Bois, Shirley Graham. His Day is Marching On -- A Memoir of W. E. B. Du Bois. Philadelphia: J. B. Lippincott, 1971.

Du Bois, W. E. B. The Autobiography of W. E. B. Du Bois: A Soliloquy on Viewing My Life from the Last Decade of its First Century. New York: International Publishers, 1968.

_____. Black Folk Then and Now: An Essay in the History and Sociology of the Negro Race. New York: Henry Holt, 1939.

_____. Black Reconstruction. New York: Harcourt, Brace, 1935.

_____. "A Mild Suggestion." The Seventh Son: The Thought and Writings of W. E. B. DuBois. Edited by Julius Lester. 2 vols. Vintage Books. New York: Random House, 1971. vol. 1.

_____. The Negro Artisan. Atlanta University Publications, 7. Atlanta: Atlanta University Press, 1902.

_____. The Philadelphia Negro: A Social Study. Philadelphia: Published for the University of Pennsylvania, 1899.

_____. The Quest of the Silver Fleece. Chicago: A. C. McClurg, 1911.

_____. Some Notes on Negro Crime, Particularly in Georgia. Atlanta University Publications, 9. Atlanta: Atlanta University Press, 1904.

_____. "The Tallented Tenth." Negro Problem. New York: James Pott, 1903.

Dumond, Dwight Lowell. Antislavery Origins of the Civil War in the United States. An Arbor Paperbacks. Ann Arbor: University of Michigan Press, 1959.

Duster, Alfreda M., ed. Crusade for Justice: The Autobiography of Ida B. Wells. Chicago: University of Chicago Press, 1970.

Dykeman, Wilma and James Stokely. Seeds of Southern Change: The Life of Will Alexander. Chicago: University of Chicago Press, 1962.

Edmonds, Helen G. The Negro and Fusion Politics in North Carolina. Chapel Hill: University of North Carolina Press, 1951.

Factor, Robert L. *The Black Response to America: Men, Ideals, and Organizations from Frederick Douglass to the NAACP.* Reading, Mass: Addison-Wesley, 1970.

Ferris, William H. *The African Abroad: Or His Evolution in Western Civilization.* New Haven, Conn.: Tuttle, Morehouse, and Taylor Press, 1913.

Filler, Louis. *The Crusade Against Slavery.* Harper Torchbooks. New York: Harper & Row, 1960.

Floyd, Silas Xavier. *Life of Charles T. Walker.* Nashville: National Baptist Publishing Board, 1902.

Foner, Philip S. *History of the Labor Movement in the United States.* Vol. 1: *From Colonial Times to the Founding of the American Federation of Labor.* New York: International Publishers, 1947.

Fortune, T. Thomas. *Black and White: Land, Labor and Politics in the South.* New York: Fords, Howard, and Hulbert, 1884.

_____. *The Negro in Politics.* New York: Ogilvie and Rowntree, 1885.

Fox, Stephen R. *The Guardian of Boston: William Monroe Trotter.* New York: Atheneum, 1970.

Franklin, John Hope, ed. *Reminiscences of an Active Life: The Autobiography of John Roy Lynch.* Chicago: University of Chicago Press, 1970.

_____. *From Slavery to Freedom: A History of Negro Americans.* New York: Alfred A. Knopf, 1967.

_____. *Reconstruction After the Civil War.* Chicago: University of Chicago Press, 1961.

Frazier, E. Franklin. *Black Bourgeoisie.* Glencoe, Ill.: Free Press, 1957.

_____. *The Negro Church in America.* New York: Schocken Books, 1963.

Fullinwider, S. P. *The Mind and Mood of Black America.* Hometown, Ill.: Dorsey Press, 1969.

Gaston, Paul. M. "The 'New South'." *Writing Southern History.* Edited by Arthur S. Link and Rembert W. Patrick. Baton Rouge: Louisiana State University Press, 1965.

_____. *The New South Creed: A Study in Southern Mythmaking.* New York: Alfred A. Knopf, 1970.

Gibbs, Mifflin Wistar. *Shadow and Light: An Autobiography.* Washington, D.C.: Published by the author, 1902.

Gibson, J. W. and W. H. Crogman. *Progress of a Race.* Atlanta: J. F. Nichols, 1902.

Gilbert, Peter, ed. The Selected Writings of John Edward Bruce: Militant Black Journalist. New York: Arno Press and the New York Times, 1971.

Ginzberg, Ralph. 100 Years of Lynching. New York: Lancer Books, 1962.

Gorham, Charles T. Robert G. Ingersoll. London: Watts, 1921.

Gratham, Dewey W., Jr. "The South and the Politics of Sectionalism." The South and the Sectional Image. Edited by Dewey W. Grantham, Jr. New York: Harper & Row, 1967.

Green, Constance McLaughlin. The Secret City: A History of Race Relations in the Nation's Capital. Princeton: Princeton University Press, 1967.

Green, Fletcher Melvin. "Some Aspects of the Convict Lease System in the Southern States." Essays in Southern History. Edited by Fletcher Melvin Green. Chapel Hill: University of North Carolina Press, 1949.

Griggs, Sutton. Basis of Hope for the Negro in the South. Memphis: National Public Welfare League, 1929.

Grimke, Archibald H. "The Ballotless Victim of One-Party Government." No. 16 in The American Negro Academy Occasional Papers: 1-22. New York: Arno Press and the New York Times, 1969.

_____. "The Ultimate Criminal." No. 17 in The American Negro Academy Occasional Papers: 1-22. New York: Arno Press and the New York Times, 1969.

Grimke, Francis J. "The Negro and His Citizenship." No. 11 in The American Negro Academy Occasional Papers: 1-22. New York: Arno Press and the New York Times, 1969.

Gross, Theodore L. Albion W. Rourgee. New York: Twayne Publishers, 1963.

Guzman, Jessie Parkhurst. "Lynching." Racial Violence in the United States. Edited by Allen D. Grimshaw. Chicago: Aldine Publishing Co., 1969.

Hammond, Lily B. In Black and White: An Interpretation of Southern Life. New York: Fleming H. Revel, 1914.

Handy, Robert T. A Christian America: Protestant Hopes and Historical Realities. New York; Oxford University Press, 1971.

Hare, Maud Cuney. Norris Wright Cuney. New York: Crisis Publishing Co., 1913.

Hirshon, Stanley. Farewell to the Bloody Shirt: Northern Republicans and the Southern Negro, 1877-1893. Bloomington: Indiana University Press, 1962.

Hixon, William B., Jr. Moorfield Storey and the Abolitionist Tradition. New York: Oxford University Press, 1972.

Hobsbawm, E. J. The Age of Revolution: 1789-1848. Cleveland: World Publishing Co., 1962.

Hofstadter, Richard. The Age of Reform. Vintage Books, New York: Random House, 1955.

_____ and Michael Wallace, eds. American Violence: A Documentary History. New York/ Random House, 1971.

Holt, Rackham. George Washington Carver: An American Biography. Garden City, New York: Doubleday, Doran, 1943.

_____. Mary McLeod Bethune: A Biography. Garden City, New York: Doubleday, 1964.

Holtzclaw, William H. The Black Man's Burden. New York: Neale Publishing Co., 1915.

Hornsby, Alton, Jr. In the Cage: Eyewitness Accounts of the Freed Negro in Southern Society, 1877-1929. Chicago: Quadrangle Books, 1971.

Ingersoll, Robert. Greatest Lectures. New York: Freethought Press, 1944.

Jackson, Luther Porter. Negro Office-Holders in Virginia: 1865-1895. Norfolk, VA.: Guide Quality Press, 1945.

Jacques-Garvey, Amy, ed. Philosophy and Opinions of Marcus Garvey. 2 vols. New York: Arno Press and the New York Times, 1968.

Johnson, Charles S. Growing Up in the Black Belt: Negro Youth in the Rural South. Washington: American Council on Education, 1941.

_____. Shadow of the Plantation. Chicago: University of Chicago Press, 1934.

Johnson, Charles S.; Edwin R. Embree, and W. W. Alexander. The Collapse of Cotton Tenancy. Chapel Hill: University of North Carolina Press, 1935.

Johnson, E. A. Light Ahead for the Negro. New York: Grafton Press, 1904.

Johnson, James Weldon. Along This Way. New York: Viking Press, 1933.

Jones, Major J. Black Awareness: A Theology of Hope. Nashville: Abington Press, 1971.

Kellogg, Charles Flint. NAACP: A History of the National Association for the Advancement of Colored People. vol. 1 1909-1920. Baltimore: Johns Hopkins Press, 1967.

Kelly, Alfred H. and Winfred A. Harbinson. The American Constitution: Its Origins and Development. New York: W. W. Norton, 1963.

Kirschten, Ernest. Catfish and Crystal. Garden City, N.Y.: Doubleday, 1960.

LaFarge, John. The Race Question and the Negro: A Study of the Catholic Doctrine on Interracial Justice. New York: Longmans, Green, 1944.

Lawson, Jesse, ed. How to Solve the Race Problem. Washington: Sociological Conference on the Race Problem, 1904.

Lester, Julius, ed. The Seventh Son: The Thought and Writings of W.E.B. Du Bois. 2 vols. Vintage Books, New York: Random House, 1971.

Lewis, David E. King: A Critical Biography. Baltimore: Penguin Books, 1970.

Lewis, Hylan. Blackways of Kent. Chapel Hill: Univ. of North Carolina Press, 1955.

Loescher, Frank S. The Protestant Church and the Negro. N.Y.: Association Press, 1948.

Logan, Frenise A. The Negro in North Carolina: 1876-1894. Chapel Hill: Univ. of North Carolina Press, 1964.

Logan, Rayford W. The Negro in American Life and Thought: The Nadir 1877-1901. N.Y.: Dial Press, 1954.

Love, John L. "The Disfranchisement of the Negro." No. 6 in The American Negro Academy Occasional Papers: 1-22. New York: Arno Press and the New York Times, 1969.

Lumpkin, Katherine. The South in Progress. New York: International Publishers, 1940.

McKay, Claude. Harlem: Negro Metropolis. New York: E. P. Dutton, 1940.

May, Henry F. Protestant Churches and Industrial America. N.Y.: Harper & Bros., 1949.

Mays, Benjamin. Born to Rebel. N.Y.: Charles Scribner's Sons, 1971.

_____ Elijah and Joseph William. The Negro's Church. N.Y.: Negro Universities Press, 1969.

Meier, August. Negro Thought in America: 1880-1915. Ann Arbor Paperbacks, Ann Arbor: Univ. of Michigan Press, 1963.

_____ and Elliott Rudwick. The Making of Black America. Vol. 2: The Black Community in Modern America. N.Y.: Atheneum, 1969.

Miller, Kelly. "The Negro Sanhedrin: A Call to Conference." Black Nationalism in America. Edited by John H. Bracy, Jr., August Meier, and Elliott Rudwick. Indianapolis: Bobbs-Merrill, 1970.

_____. Race Adjustment: Essays on the Negro in America. N.Y. Neale Publishing Co., 1908.

Miller, Loren. The Petitioners: The Story of the Supreme Court of the United States and the Negro. N.Y.: Random House, 1966.

Miller, Robert Moats. *American Protestantism and Social Issues: 1919-1939.* Chapel Hill: Univ. of North Carolina Press, 1958.

_____. *How Shall They Hear Without a Preacher: Life of Ernest Fremont Tittle.* Chapel Hill: Univ. of North Carolina Press, 1971.

Mississippi Black Paper. New York: Random House, 1965.

Moon, Henry Lee. *The Balance of Power: The Negro Vote.* Garden City, N.Y.: Doubleday, 1948.

Morton, James F., Jr. *The Curse of Race Prejudice.* N.Y.: by the Author, n.d.

Morton, Robert Russa. *What the Negro Thinks.* Garden City, N.Y.: Doubleday, Doran, 1929.

Murray, Andrew E. *Presbyterians and the Negro---A History.* Philadelphia: Presbyterian Historical Society, 1966.

Myers, Gustavus. *History of Bigotry in the United States.* New York: Capricorn Books, 1960.

Myrdal, Gunnar. *An American Dilemma.* Twentieth Anniversary Edition. N.Y.: Harper & Row, 1962.

National Association for the Advancement of Colored People. *Thirty Years of Lynching in the United States: 1889-1918.* N.Y.: Arno Press and the New York Times, 1969.

National Negro Congress, 1909. *Proceedings.* N.Y.: Arno Press and the New York Times, 1969.

Negro Problem. New York: James Pott, 1903.

Negro Year Book. 11 vols. Tuskegee: Tuskegee Institute, 1912-1952.

Newby, I. A. *Jim Crow's Defense: Anti-Negro Thought in America, 1900-1930.* Baton Rouge: Louisiana State Univ. Press, 1965.

Niagara Movement. "Declaration of Principles." *Negro Protest Thought in the Twentieth Century.* Edited by Francis L. Broderick and August Meier. Ind.: Bobbs-Merrill, 1965.

Nixon, Raymond B. *Henry W. Grady: Spokesman of the New South.* New York: Alfred A. Knopf, 1943.

Nye, Russel B. *Fettered Freedom: Civil Liberties and the Slavery Controversy, 1830-1860.* East Lansing: Michigan State College Press, 1949.

Odum, Howard W. *Race and Rumors of Race.* Chapel Hill: Univ. of North Carolina Press, 1943.

Osofsky, Gilbert. *Harlem: The Making of a Ghetto, Negro New York 1890-1930.* N.Y.: Harper & Row, 1963.

Ottley, Roi. The Lonely Warrior: The Life and Times of Robert S. Abott. Chicago: Henry Regnery, 1955.

Ovington, Mary White: The Walls Came Tumbling Down. N.Y.: Arno Press and New York Times, 1969.

Patterson, Haywood, and Earl Conrad. Scottsboro Boy. Garden City, N.Y.: Doubleday, 1950.

Patterson, Raymond. The Negro and His Needs. N.Y.: Fleming H. Revell, 1911.

Patterson, William L. The Man Who Cried Genocide: An Autobiography. N.Y.: International Publishers, 1971.

Peeks, Edward. The Long Struggle for Black Power. N.Y.: Charles Scribner's Sons, 1971.

Penn, I. Garland. The Afro-American Press and its Editors. Springfield, Mass: Wiley, 1891.

Phillips, Ulrich Bonnell. American Negro Slavery. N.Y.: Peter Smith, 1952.

Pickens, William. "Christianity as a Basis of Common Citizenship." The New Voice in Race Adjustment. Edited by A.M. Trawick. N.Y.: Student Volunteer Movement, 1914.

Pickett, William P. The Negro Problem: Abraham Lincoln's Solution. N.Y.: G.P. Putnam's Sons, 1909.

Porter, Kirk H. A History of Suffrage in the United States. Chic.: Univ. of Chicago Press, 1918.

Powdermaker, Hortense. After Freedom: A Cultural Study in the Deep South. N.Y.: Atheneum, 1968.

Pringle, Henry F. Theodore Roosevelt: A Biography. Harvest Book. N.Y.: Harcourt, Brace, and World, 1956.

Quarles, Benjamin. The Negro in the Making of America. London: Collier-Macmillan, 1964.

Ransom, Reverdy C. The Pilgrimage of Harriet Ransom's Son. Nashville: A.M.E. Sunday School Union, 1950.

_____. The Spirit of Freedom and Justice: Orations and Speeches. Nashville: A.M.E. Sunday School Union, 1926.

Raper, Arthur F. The Tragedy of Lynching. Chapell Hill: Univ. of North Carolina Press, 1933.

Record, Wilson. Race and Radicalism: The NAACP and the Communist Party in Conflict. Ithaca: Cornell University Press, 1964.

Redding, Jay Saunders. The Lonesom Road: The Story of the Negro's Part in America. Garden

City, N.Y.: Doubleday, 1958.

Redkey, Edwin S., ed. Respect Black: The Writings and Speeches of Henry McNeal Turner. N.Y.: Arno Press and the New York Times, 1971.

Reimers, David M. White Protestantism and the Negro. N.Y.: Oxford Univ. Press, 1965.

Rice, Lawrence D. The Negro in Texas: 1874-1900. Baton Rouge: Louisiana State Univ. Press, 1971.

Richards, Leonard L. Gentlemen of Property and Standing: Anti-Abolition Mobs in Jacksonian America. N.Y.: Oxford Univ. Press, 1970.

Richardson, James D., ed. Compilation of the Messages and Papers of the Presidents. vol. 15, n.p.: Bureau of National Literature, n.d.

Riley, B.F. The White Man's Burden. Birmingham, Ala.: by the author, 1910.

Roosevelt, Theodore. The Works of Theodore Roosevelt. Vol. 14. Presidential Addresses and State Papers. Part 2. N.Y.: P.F. Collier and Son, n.d.

Royce, Josiah. Race Questions, Provincialism, and Other American Problems. N.Y. Macmillan, 1908.

Rudwick, Elliott. RaceRiot at East St. Louis, July 2, 1917. Carbondale, Ill.: Southern Ill. Univ. Press, 1964.

Salley, Columbus and Behm, Ronald. Your God is Too White. Downers Grove, Ill.: Intervarsity Press, 1970.

Saloutos, Theodore. Farmer Movements in the South: 1865-1933. Berkeley: Univ. of California Press, 1960.

Scott, Emmett J. Negro Migration During the War. N.Y.: Oxford Univ. Press, 1920.

Seligmann, Herbert J. The Negro Faces America. N.Y.: Harper & Bros., 1920.

Shapiro, Herbert. "The Populists and the Negro: A Reconsideration." The Making of Black America. Edited by August Meier and Elliott Rudwick. Vol. 2. N.Y.: Atheneum, 1969.

Sinkler, George. Racial Attitudes of the American Presidents: From Abraham Lincoln to Theodore Roosevelt. Garden City, N.Y.: Doubleday, 1971.

Skaggs, William Henry. The Southern Oligarchy: An Appeal in Behalf of the Silent Masses of Our Country Against the Despotic Rule of the Few. N.Y.: Devin-Adair, 1924.

Smith, Charles Spencer. A History of the African Metholdist Episcopal Church. N.Y.: Johnson Reprint Corp., 1968.

Smith, Samuel Denny. The Negro in Congress: 1870-1901. Chapel Hill: Univ. of North Carolina Press, 1940.

Smith, Wilfred. "The Negro and the Law." The Negro Problem. N.Y.: James Pott, 1903.

Smith, William B. The Color Line: A Brief in Behalf of the Unborn. N.Y.: McClure, Philips, 1905.

Sochen, June, ed. The Black Man and the American Dream. Chicago: Quadrangle Books, 1971.

Southern Commission on the Study of Lynching. Lynchings and What They Mean. n.p.: by the Commission, 1931.

Southern Society for the Promotion of the Study of Race Problems in the South. Race Problems of the South. N.Y.: Negro Universities Press, 1969.

Spear, Allan H. Black Chicago: The Making of a Negro Ghetto: 1890-1920. Chicago: Univ. of Chicago Press, 1967.

Southern Sociological Society. The Challenge of Social Service. Atlanta: by the Society, 1913.

Stampp, Kenneth M. The Era of Reconstruction. Vintage Books, N.Y.: Random House, 1967.

_____. The Peculiar Institution: Slavery in the Ante-Bellum South. Vintage Books. N.Y.: Random House, 1956.

Stone, Alfred Holt. Studies in the American Race Problem. N.Y.: Doubleday, Page, 1908.

Straker, D. Augustus. The New South Investigated. Detroit: Ferguson Printing Co., 1888.

Tannenbaum, Frank. Darker Phases of the South. N.Y.: G. P. Putnam's Sons, 1924.

Tatum, Elbert Lee. The Changed Political Thought of the Negro: 1915-1940. N.Y.: Exposition Press, 1951.

Tatus, Georgia Lee. Disloyalty in the Confederacy. Chapel Hill: Univ. of North Carolina Press, 1934.

Terrell, Mary Church. A Colored Woman in a White World. Washington: Ramsdell Publishers, 1940.

Thornbrough, Emma Lou, ed. Booker T. Washington. Englewood Cliffs, N.J.: Prentice Hall, 1969.

Tindall, George B. The Emergence of the New South: 1913-1945. Baton Rouge: Louisiana State Univ. Press., 1967.

_____. South Carolina Negroes: 1877-1900. Columbia: Univ. of South Carolina Press, 1952.

_____. "Southern Mythology." The South and the Sectional Image. Edited by Dewey W. Grantham, Jr. N.Y.: Harper & Row, 1967.

Torrence, Ridgely. The Story of John Hope. N.Y.: Macmillan, 1948.

Tourgee, Albion W. A Fool's Errand. Harper Torchbooks. N.Y.: Harper & Row, 1966.

Turner, Arlin, Ed. The Negro Question: A Selection of Writings on Civil Rights in the South by George W. Cable. Garden City, N.Y.: Doubleday, 1958.

Tuttle, William M., Jr. RaceRiot: Chicago in the Red Summer of 1919. N.Y.: Atheneum, 1970.

University Commission on Southern Race Questions. Minutes: 1912-1917. n.p.: by the Commission, n.d.

Vincent, Theodore G. Black Power and the Garvey Movement. Berkeley, Calif.: Ramparts Press, 1971.

Voegeli, V. Jacque. Free but not Equal: The Midwest and the Negro During the Civil War. Chicago: Univ. of Chicago Press, 1967.

Wagenknecht, Edward. The Seven Worlds of Theodore Roosevelt. N.Y.: Longmans, Green, 1958.

Wakefield, Eva Ingersoll, ed. The Letters of Robert G. Ingersoll. N.Y.: Philosophical Library, 1951.

Walton, Hanes, Jr. The Negro in Third Party Politics. Phila.: Dorrance & Co., 1969.

Warner, Charles Dudley. On Horseback: A Tour of Virginia, North Carolina and Tennessee. Boston: Houghton Mifflin, 1888.

Washington, Booker T. My Larger Education. Garden City, N.Y.: Doubleday, Page, 1911.

_____. The Story of the Negro: The Rise of the Race from Slavery. 2 vols. Garden City, N.Y.: Doubleday, Page, 1909.

_____. Up From Slavery. Garden City, N.Y.: Doubleday, 1902.

_____, N. B. Wood, and Fannie Barrier Williams. A New Negro for a New Century. N.Y.: Arno Press and the New York Times, 1969.

_____ and W.E.B. DuBois. The Negro in the South. Phila.: George W. Jacobs, 1907.

Washington, E. Davidson, ed. Selected Speeches of Booker T. Washington. Garden City, N.Y.: Doubleday, Doran, 1932.

Washington, Joseph R., Jr. Black Religion: The Negro and Christianity in the United States.

Boston: Beacon Press, 1964.

Waskow, Arthur I. From Race Riot to Sit-In, 1919 and the 1960's: A Study in the Connections Between Conflict and Violence. Garden City, N.Y.: Doubleday, 1966.

Weatherfor, Willis Duke. Negro Life in the South: Present Conditions and Needs. Miami: Mnemosyn Publishers, 1969.

_____ and Charles S. Johnson. Race Relations: Adjustment of Whites and Negroes in the United States. Boston: D. C. Heath, 1934.

Wells-Barnett, Ida B. On Lynchings: Southern Horrors, A red Record, and Mob Rule in New Orleans. N.Y.: Arno Press and the New York Times, 1969.

Wells, H. G. The Future in America: A Search After Realities. N.Y.: Harper & Bros., 1906.

Wesley, Charles H. Negro Labor in the United States: 1850-1925. N.Y.: Vanguard Press, 1927.

Weston, Rubin Francis. Racism in United States Imperialism: The Influence of Racial Assumptions on American Foreign Policy, 1893-1946. Columbia: Univ. of South Carolina Press, 1972.

Weyle, Nathaniel and Marina, William. American Statesmen on Slavery and the Negro. New Rochelle, N.Y.: Arlington House, 1971.

Wharton, Vernon Lane. The Negro in Mississippi, 1865-1890. Chapel Hill: Univ. of North Carolina Press, 1947.

White, Walter. Fire in the Flint. New York: Alfred A. Knopf, 1924.

_____. A Man Called White: The Autobiography of Walter White. N.Y.: Viking Press, 1948.

_____. Rope and Faggot: A Biography of Judge Lynch. N.Y.: Alfred A. Knopf, 1929.

Williams, Alexander T. History of the Colored Race in America. N.Y.: Negro Universities Press, 1968.

Williams, Daniel T., comp. "The Lynching Records at Tuskegee Institute." Eight Negro Bibliographies. Compiled by Daniel T. Williams. N.Y.: Kraus Reprint Co., 1970.

Williams, George W. History of the Negro Race in America: From 1619 to 1880. N.Y. G. P. Putnam's Sons, 1882.

Wolters, Raymond. Negroes and the Great Depression: The Problem of Economic Recovery. Westport, Conn.: Greenwood, 1970.

Wood, Forrest G. Black Scare: The Racist Response to Emancipation and Reconstruction. Berkeley: Univ. of California Press, 1968.

Wood, Norman B. *The White Side of a Black Subject.* N.Y.: Negro Universities Press, 1969.

Woodson, Carter G. *A Century of Negro Migration.* Washington: Association for the Study of Negro Life and History, 1918.

_____, ed. *The Works of Francis James Grimke.* 4 vols. Washington: Associated Publishers, 1942.

Woodward, C. Vann. *Origins of the New South: 1877-1913.* Baton Rouge: Louisiana State University Press, 1951.

_____. *The Strange Career of Jim Crow.* 2d rev. ed. N.Y.: Oxford Univ. Press, 1966.

_____. *Tom Watson: Agrarian Rebel.* N.Y.: Macmillan, 1938.

F. ARTICLES

Adams, James Truslow. "Our Lawless Heritage." *Atlantic Monthly,* 142 (Dec., 1928), 732-40.

Alexander, Will W. "The Negro in the New South." American Academy of Political and Social Science *Annals,* 90 (Nov., 1928), 145-52.

"Anarchy in Delaware." *Outlook,* July 4, 1903, pp. 543-46.

Bacote, Clarence A. "Negro Proscriptions, Protests, and Proposed Solutions in Georgia: 1880-1908." *Journal of Southern History,* 25 (Nov., 1959), 471-498.

_____. "Some Aspects of Negro Life in Georgia: 1880-1908." *Journal of Negro History,* 43 (July, 1958), 186-213.

Bassett, John Spencer. "String Up Race Antipathy." *South Atlantic Quarterly,* 2 (Oct., 1903), 297-305.

Beck, Earl R. "German Views of Negro Life in the United States, 1919-1933." *Journal of Negro History,* 48 (Jan., 1963), 22-32.

Berthoff, Rowland T. "Southern Attitudes Toward Immigration, 1865-1914." *Journal of Southern History,* 17 (Aug., 1951) 328-360.

Blair, John L. "The Negro During the Coolidge Years." *Journal of American Studies,* 3 (Dec., 1969), 177-200.

Blumenthal, Henry. "Woodrow Wilson and the Race Question." *Journal of Negro History,* 48. (Jan., 1963), 1-21.

Bode, Frederick A. "Religion and Class Hegemony: A Populist Critique in North Carolina."

Journal of Southern History, 37 (Aug., 1971), 417-38.

Chafe, William H. "The Negro and Populism: A Kansas Case Study." *Journal of Southern History,* 34 (Aug., 1968), 402-419.

"Civilization at Evansville." *Independent,* July 16, 1903, pp. 1694-95.

Clark, Walter. "The True Remedy for Lynch Law." *American Law Review,* 28 (Nov.-Dec., 1894), 801-07.

"Conference at Tuskegee." *Competitor,* 1 (April, 1920), 29.

Cranfill, J. B. "Story of a Mob." *Independent,* Jan. 24, 1901, pp. 213-14.

Crofts, Daniel W. "The Black Response to the Blair Education Bill." *Journal of Southern History,* 37 (Feb., 1971), 41-65.

Crouthamel, James L. "The Springfield Race Riot of 1908." *Journal of Negro History,* 45 (July, 1960), 164-81.

Crowe, Charles. "Tom Watson, Populism, and Blacks Reconsidered." *Journal of Negro History,* 55 (April, 1970), 99-116.

Curtis, George Ticknor. "Law and the Lynchers." *North American Review,* 152 (June, 1891), 691-95.

Daniel, Pete. "The Case of the Tuskegee Veterans Hospital." *Journal of Southern History,* 36 (Aug., 1970), 368-88.

_____. "Up From Slavery and Down to Peonage: The Alonzo Bailey Peonage Case." *Journal of American History,* 57 (Dec., 1970), 654-70.

De Santis, Vincent P. "Negro Dissatisfaction with the Republican Party in the South, 1882-1884." *Journal of Negro History,* 36 (April, 1951), 148-159.

_____. "The Republican Party and the Southern Negro, 1877-1897." *Journal of Negro History,* 45 (April, 1960), 71-87.

Drake, Donald E., II. "Militancy in Fortune's New York *Age.*" *Journal of Negro History,* 55 (October, 1970), 307-322.

Douglass, Frederick. "Jubilee Day." Indianapolis *Freeman,* Sept. 9, 1893, p. 1.

_____. "The Lessons of the Hour." Indianapolis *Freeman,* Feb. 17, 1894, p. 4.

_____. "The Negro Exodus from the Gulf States." *American Journal of Social Science,* 11 (May, 1880), 1-21.

Du Bois, W.E.B. "Close Ranks." *Crisis*, 16 (July, 1918), 111.

_____. "Of the Training of Black Men." *Atlantic Monthly*, 90 (Sept., 1902), 289-97.

_____. "The Freedom to Learn." *Midwest Quarterly*, 2 (Winter, 1949), 9-11.

Eleazer, R. B. "Interracial Committee Methods." Chicago *Broad Ax*, March 1, 1924, p. 2.

_____. "Origin of the Interracial Committee." Chicago *Broad Ax*, Feb. 23, 1924, p. 2.

Flynt, Wayne, "Dissent in Zion: Alabama Baptists and Social Issues, 1900-1914." *Journal of Southern History*, 35 (Nov. 1969), 523-542.

Fortune, T. Thomas. "A Proposed Afro-American National League." New York *Freeman*, May 28, 1887, p. 1.

_____. "The Voteless Citizen." *Voice of the Negro*, 1 (Sept., 1904), 397-402.

Franklin, John Hope. "The Great Confrontation: The South and the Problem of Change." *Journal of Southern History*, 38 (Feb., 1972), 3-20.

Frazier, E. Franklin. "Georgia: Or the Struggle Against Inpudent Inferiority." *Messenger*, 6 (June, 1924), 173-77.

Gibbons, John Cardinal. "Lynch-Law: Its Cause and Remedy." *North American Review*, 181 (Oct., 1905), 502-09.

Goodnow, Marc N. "Turpentine: Impressions of the Convict Camps in Florida." *Survey*, May 1, 1915, pp. 103-08.

Grantham, Dewey W., Jr. "The Progressive Movement and the Negro." *South Atlantic Quarterly*, 54 (Oct. 1955), 461-77.

Greener, Richard T. "The Emigration of Colored Citizens From the Southern States." *American Journal of Social Science*, 11 (May, 1880), 22-35.

Grimshaw, Allen D. "Lawlessness and Violence in America and Their Special Manifestations in Changing Negro-White Relationships." *Journal of Negro History*, 44 (January, 1959), 52-72.

Guzman, Jessie P. "Monroe Work and His Contribution." *Journal of Negro History*, 34 (Jan., 1949), 428-61.

Halliburton, R., Jr. "The Tulsa Race War of 1921." *Journal of Black Studies*, 2 (March, 1972), 333-58.

Harlan, Lewis. "The Southern Education Board and the Race Issue in Public Education." *Journal of Southern History*, 23 (May, 1957), 189-202.

Harrison, Shelby M. "A Cash-Nexus for Crime." Survey, Jan. 6, 1915, pp. 1541-56.

Holmes, William F. "Whitecapping: Agrarian Violence in Mississippi, 1902-1906." Journal of Southern History, 35 (May, 1969), 165-85.

Hood, J. W. "The Enfranchisement of the Negro No Blunder." Independent, Aug. 27, 1903, pp. 2021-24.

"Hopeful Signs in Mississippi." Voice of the Negro, 1 (April, 1904), 173.

Hoss, E. E. "Lynching, Its Cause and Cure." Independent, Feb. 1, 1894, p. 128.

Hutson, A. C., Jr. "The Coal Miners' Insurrection of 1891 in Anderson County." East Tennessee Historical Society's Publications, 7 (1935), 103-15.

"Inability of the Governor of Kentucky to Bring Lynchers to Justice." American Law Review, 34 (March-April, 1900), 238-39.

Jefferson, Wilson. "The Church and the South." Voice of the Negro, 3 (Sept., 1906), 651-52.

Johnson, Charles S. "How Much is the Migration a Flight From Persecution." Opportunity, 1 (Sept., 1923), 272-74.

Johnson, Guion Griffis. "Southern Paternalism Toward Negroes After Emancipation." Journal of Southern History, 23 (Nov., 1957), 483-509.

Kerlin, Robert T. "Open Letter to the Governor of Arkansas." Nation, June 15, 1921, p. 847.

Lasch, Christopher. "The Anti-Imperialists, the Philippines, and the Inequality of Man." Journal of Southern History, 24 (Aug., 1958), 319-31.

Lee, George B. "Tennessee." Messenger, 7 (July, 1925), 252-53.

Lilienthal, David E. "Has the Negro the Right to Self-Defense?" Nation, Dec. 23, 1925, pp. 724-25.

Link, Arthur S. "The Negro as a Factor in the Campaign of 1912." Journal of Negro History, 32 (Jan., 1947), 81-99.

Link, Eugene P. "The Civil Rights Activities of Three Great Negro Physicians, 1840-1940." Journal of Negro History, 32 (July, 1947), 169-84.

Lodge, Henry Cabot. "Lynch Law and Unrestricted Immigration." North American Review, 152 (May, 1891), 602-12.

Logan, Rayford W. "Review of The Tragedy of Lynching by Arthur F. Raper." Journal of Negro History, 18 (Jan., 1933), 486.

"Lynching: How Far the Courts are Responsible for its Prevalence." *American Law Review*, 33 (July-August, 1899), 596-98.

McAllister, Henry. "What Can Be Done to Stop Lynching." *American Law Review*, 39 (Jan.-Feb., 1905), 101-03.

McKelvey, Blake. "Penal Slavery and Southern Reconstruction." *Journal of Negro History*, 20 (Jan., 1935), 153-179.

McTeer, Will A. "The Mountaineers of East Tennessee and Kentucky." *American Law Review*, 26 (May-June, 1892), 469-70.

Mandel, Bernard. "Samuel Gompers and the Negro Workers, 1886-1914." *Journal of Negro History*, 40 (Jan., 1955), 34-60.

Meier, August. "The Negro and the Democratic Party, 1875-1915." *Phylon*, 17 (Summer, 1956), 173-91.

Meier, August and Elliott Rudwick. "Negro Retaliatory Violence in the Twentieth Century." *New Politics*, 5 (Winter 1966), 41-51.

Miller, Robert M. "The Attitudes of American Protestantism Toward the Negro, 1919-1939." *Journal of Negro History*, 41 (July, 1956), 215-40.

_____. "The Protestant Churches and Lynching." *Journal of Negro History*, 42 (April, 1957), 118-131.

Moore, A. M. "Brotherly Love Must Abide Throughout the Land." *Competitor*, 3 (April, 1921), 9.

"More Lynch Law." *American Law Review*, (March-April, 1892), 248-49.

Morton, Robert Russa. "The South and the Lynching Evil." *South Atlantic Quarterly*, 18 (July, 1919), 191-96.

"Moving Against Lynching." *Nation*, August 3, 1916, pp. 101-02.

Muraskin, William. "The Social Foundations of the Black Community, The California Masons as a Test Case." *Midcontinent American Studies Journal*, 11 (Fall 1970), 12-35.

Nash, Royal Freeman. "The Cherokee Fires." *Crisis*, 11 (March, 1916), 265-70.

"North Carolina Uprising." *Nation*, Aug. 23, 1906, pp. 158-59.

"Not by Violence." *Independent*, April 4, 1901, pp. 796-97.

Osofsky, Gilbert. "Progressivism and the Negro: New York 1900-1915." *American Quarterly*, 16 (Summer 1964), 153-68.

Ovington, Mary White. "The National Association for the Advancement of Colored People." *Journal of Negro History,* 9 (April, 1924), 107-16.

Partington, Paul G. "The Moon Illustrated Weekly--The Percursor of the *Crisis*." *Journal of Negro History,* 48 (July, 1963), 206-16.

Phelps, H. A. "The Voice of Black Folk." *Half Century,* 8 (February, 1920), 15.

Poe, Clarence. "Lynching: A Southern View." *Atlantic Monthly,* 93 (Feb., 1904), 155-65.

Powdermaker, Hortense. "The Channeling of Negro Aggression by the Cultural Process." *American Journal of Sociology,* 48 (May, 1943), 750-58.

Preston, Fanny M. "The South Yet in the Saddle." *Independent,* Feb. 1, 1894, p. 130.

"Protest Against Judge Parker." *Nation,* April 23, 1930, p. 477.

"Reaping the Whirlwind." *Nation,* Nov. 5, 1908, pp. 428-29.

"Recollections of a Retired Lawyer." *Southern Literary Messenger,* 5 (March, 1839), 218-22.

Rogers, William B. "The Negro Alliance in Alabama." *Journal of Negro History,* 45 (Jan., 1960), 38-48.

Roosevelt, Theodore. "Lynching and the Miscarriage of Justice." *Outlook,* Nov. 25, 1911, pp. 706-07.

Rudwick, Wlliott M. "The Niagara Movement." *Journal of Negro History,* 42 (July, 1957), 177-200.

_____. "W.E.B. Du Bois: In the Role of *Crisis* Editor." *Journal of Negro History,* 43 (July, 1958), 214-40.

Saunders, Robert. "Southern Populists and the Negro, 1893-1905." *Journal of Negro History,* 54 (July, 1969), 240-261.

Scarborough, William S. "An Inside View of the Convict-Lease System." Indianapolis *Freeman,* Dec. 7, 1891, p. 5.

Schuler, Edgar A. "The Houston Race Riot, 1917." *Journal of Negro History,* 29 (July, 1944), 301-38.

Sherman, Richard B. "The Harding Administration and the Negro: An Opportunity Lost." *Journal of Negro History,* 49 (July, 1964), 151-68.

"Significance of the Niagara Movement." *Voice of the Negro,* 2 (Sept., 1905), 600-04.

Snyder, Howard. "Negro Migration and the Cotton Crop." *North American Review,* 219

(January, 1924), 21-29.

"Soul of a Lyncher." *Competitor*, 2 (Oct.-Nov., 1920), 192.

Strange, Robert. "Some Thoughts on Lynching." *South Atlantic Quarterly*, 5 (Oct., 1905), 349-51.

Straton, John Roach. "Will Education Solve the Race Problem." *North American Review*, 170 (June, 1900), 14-39.

Sullivan, Joseph Mathew. "Lynching Statistics." *Journal of Criminal Law*, 9 (May, 1918), 144-46.

Taylor, George Edwin. "The National Liberty Party." *Voice of the Negro*, 1 (Oct., 1904), 479.

Taylor, Harris. "The True Remedy for Lynch-Law." *American Law Review*, 41 (March-April, 1907), 255-66.

Taylor, Julius. "The Religions or the Teachings of Jesus and Mohomet Compared." Chicago *Broad Ax*, October 24, 1903, p. 1.

Thornbrough, Emma Lou. "The Brownsville Episode and the Negro Vote." *Mississippi Valley Historical Review*, 44 (Dec., 1957), 469-83.

_____. "The National Afro-American League: 1887-1908." *Journal of Southern History*, 27 (Nov., 1961), 494-512.

Tindall, George B. "The Question of Race in the South Carolina Constitutional Convention of 1895." *Journal of Negro History*, 37 (July, 1952), 277-303.

Tinsley, James F. "Roosevelt, Foraker, and the Brownsville Affair." *Journal of Negro History*, 41 (Jan., 1956), 43-65.

Van Deusen, John G. "The Exodus of 1879." *Journal of Negro History*, 21 (Jan., 1936), 111-129.

Villard, Oswald Garrison. "A Race Commission--A Constructive Plan." *Nation*, April 27, 1921, p. 612.

Walling, William English. "The Race War in the North." *Independent*, Sept. 3, 1908, pp. 529-34.

Warnock, Harry V. "Andrew Sledd, Southern Methodists and the Negro." *Journal of Southern History*, 31 (Aug., 1965), 251-71.

Washington, Booker T. "Chapters from my Experience." *World's Work*, 21 (Nov., 1910), 13627-40.

_____. "Is the Negro Having a Fair Chance?" Century, (Nov., 1912), 46-55.

Weaver, Valeria W. "The Failure of Civil Rights, 1875-1883 and its Repercussions." Journal of Negro History, 54 (Oct., 1969), 368-82.

Wells-Barnett, Ida B. "The National Afro-American Council." Howard's American Magazine, 6 (May, 1901), 415-18.

Wesley, Charles H. "The Civil War and the Negro-American." Journal of Negro History, 47 (April, 1962), 77-96.

White, Walter F. "I Investigate Lynchings." American Mercury, 16 (Jan., 1929), 77-84.

_____. "The Negro and the Flood." Nation, June 22, 1927, pp. 688-89.

_____. "The Negro and the Supreme Court." Harper's, 162 (Jan., 1931). 238-46.

Wish, Harvey. "Slave Disloyalty Under the Confederacy." Journal of Negro History, 23 (Oct., 1938), 426-34.

Wolgemuth, Kathleen DeLong. "Woodrow Wilson's Appointment Policy and the Negro." Journal of Southern History, 24 (Nov., 1958), 457-71.

Work, Monroe N. "Negro Criminality in the South." American Academy of Political and Social Science Annals, 49 (Sept., 1913), 74-80.

Wright, R. R., Jr. "Migration of Negroes to the North." American Academy of Political and Social Science Annals, 27 (May, 1906), 559-78.

Wyllie, Irving G. "Race and Class Conflict on Missouri's Cotton Frontier." Journal of Southern History, 20 (May, 1954), 183-96.

Zangrando, Robert Lewis. "The NAACP and a Federal Anti-Lynching Bill, 1934-1940." Journal of Negro History, 50 (April, 1965), 106-117.

Zimmerman, Jane. "The Penal Reform Movement in the South During the Progressive Era." Journal of Southern History, 17 (Nov., 1951), 462-492.

NAME INDEX

Addams, Jane, 131
Allen, R. H., 115
Alexander, Will W., 133, 134, 139, 140
Altgeld, John P., 30
Andrews, Mrs. J. E., 141
Ames, Mrs. Jessie Daniel, 137, 138, 139, 140
Amos, Thomas, 87
Armour, Philip, 5
Arthur, Chester A., 20, 49
Ashurst, Henry F., 138

Bagnall, Robert W., 148
Baldwin, Roger, 138
Baldwin, William H., 5
Barber, J. Max, 35, 40, 77, 108, 118, 149
Barnard, Kate, 131
Beckum, T. Alex, 50
Bell, Thomas, 118
Bennett, Lerone, 84
Bethune, Mary McLeod, 83, 84, 136
Bickett, Thomas A., 70, 71
Blackwell, Rev. E., 134
Blair, Henry W., 65
Blease, Cole, 3, 58, 87, 132
Bloxham, William D., 71
Blyden, Edward Wilmont, 114, 145
Bose, Subbhas, 167
Bradley, Andrew N., 13
Bradley, William O., 70
Brann, W. C., 9
Breckenridge, Clifton R., 33, 34
Brewer, David J., 12
Briggs, Cyril, 142, 143, 146
Brooks, Graham, 5
Brown, Charlotte Hawkins, 136
Brown, William, 122
Bruce, Blanche K., 22, 49
Bruce, John Edward, 33, 91, 94, 106, 113, 121
Bryan, Rev., 115

Bundy, Charles, 27
Bundy, Leroy, 141
Burleson, A. S., 58
Bushnell, Asa S., 70

Cabaniss, George, 69
Cable, George W., 23, 81
Campbell, John T., 55
Capehart, H. J., 71
Carranza, Venustiano, 58
Carver, George Washington, 38
Cato, William, 106
Chase, Calvin, 49
Cheatham, Henry P., 107
Chesnut, Charles, W., 108
Chivers, Walter, 138
Church, Robert R., 29, 68, 110
Clark, George, 69
Clark, H. A., 163
Clark, Justice Walter, 12
Clement, William, 105
Cleveland, Grover, 49, 50, 115
Cone, James H., 90
Cook, Helen, 29
Cook, Joseph, 115
Coolidge, Calvin, 145, 161, 163
Cooper, E. E., 80, 107
Corrothers, James D., 89
Cox (Brothers), 5
Cox, Oliver Cromwell, 88
Crawford, Anthony, 4
Crogman, W. H., 83, 87, 116
Crummel, Alexander, 90
Crumpacker, Edgar D., 54
Cruse, Harold, 158
Cuney, Norris Wright, 49, 69
Curtis, Charles, 104
Czolgosz, Leon, 52

Dalton, Joseph, 107
Dancy, John, 79
Darrow, Clarence, 5
Davis, Benjamin J., Sr., 146, 164
Davis, C. P., 121
Dean, James, 109
Degler, Carl N., 86
DePriest, Oscar, 68, 162
Derrick, William B., 80, 91
Dillard, James H., 131, 132, 166
Dixon, Richard, 120
Dixon, Rev. Thomas, Jr., 9
Dollard, John, 109
Dorsey, Hugh M., 68, 119, 135
Douglass, Frederick, 20, 21, 22, 28, 36, 52, 79, 91, 108, 116, 146
Doyle, H. S., 91
Du Bois, W. E. B., 4, 5, 31, 35, 37, 40, 58, 59, 83, 84, 85, 87, 106, 108, 110, 140, 142, 145, 146, 148, 149, 160, 166
Dudley, Thomas, 68
Duke, Jesse Chisholm, 77
Durbin, Winfield, 54
Dyer, Leonidas C., 143, 156, 158, 159, 161

Easton, Lewis D., 90
Eberhardt, Lee, 119
Edgar, Richard, 70
Einstein, Albert, 105
Eleazer, Robert B., Jr., 134
Embree, Edwin, 140
Embry, James C., 78
English, James, 35

Fair, Will, 72
Felton, Mrs. W. H., 31,
Ferris, William, 33, 37, 79, 86, 104
Forbes, George W., 37
Foraker, J. B., 51
Fortune, Emmanuel, Jr., 25
Fortune, T. T., 6, 7, 21, 22, 26, 31, 65, 76, 104, 112, 114, 147
Foster, William Z., 166
Fox, Stephen R., 144
Frank, Leo, 92
Franklin, John Hope, 53, 91
Franklin, Pink, 57
Frazier, E. Franklin, 80

Fullinwider, S. P., 89

Gale, Zona, 96
Gallinger, Jacob H., 67
Gardiner, C. A., 115
Garfield, James A., 49
Garrison, William Lloyd, Jr., 39
Garvey, Marcus, 141, 142, 143, 166
Gibbons, John Cardinal, 92
Gladden, Washington, 92
Glann, Joe, 36
Gompers, Samuel, 56
Gould, Theodore, 114
Grady, Henry, 54, 55, 141
Graham, Shirley, 85
Grantham, Dewey, 53
Graves, John Temple, 35, 36, 54
Green, Edward, 70
Green, John P., 22
Greener, Richard T., 22, 106
Griggs, Sutton, 89, 161
Grimke, Archiblad, 78, 85, 143
Grimke, Francis, 48, 85, 89

Hammond, Mrs. John D., 131, 132, 133
Hammond, Nathaniel Job, 11
Hanna, Mark, 51, 53
Harding, Warren G., 142, 145, 163
Hardwick, Thomas W., 68, 119
Harrison, Benjamin, 49, 56, 163
Harten, Thomas S., 165
Hawkins, John P., 87
Haynes, George E., 134
Henderson, W. E., 31
Higginson, Thomas Wentworth, 9, 54
Hitler, Adolph, 167
Hoar, George F., 67, 115
Hogg, James S., 69
Hood, J. W., 78
Hooper, Ben W., 131
Hoover, Herbert C., 140, 160, 161, 162, 163, 164, 165, 167
Hope, John, 35, 92, 131
Hopkins, Charles T., 36
Hose, Sam, 52
Hoss, E. E., 10
Howard, Perry, 164
Howell, Clark, 35, 38, 132

Hubert, John W., 108
Huston, C. H., 165

Ingalls, John J., 1-
Ingersoll, Robert, 21, 81
Ireland, John, 59

Jacks, John W., 29
Jefferson, Thomas, 33
Johnson, A. N., 25
Johnson, Charles S., 117
Johnson, E. A., 109
Johnson, Elnora, 165
Johnson, James Weldon, 120, 122, 146, 148, 157, 160, 163, 166
Johnson, Joseph F., 83
Johnson, Mrs. Luke G., 136
Jones, Daniel W., 107
Jones, J. A., 109
Jones, Major, 94
Jones, Nelson, 64
Jones, Robert E., 133
Jones, Samuel L., 121
Jones, Thomas, 54

Kahahawai, Joseph, 162
Kellogg, Charles F., 93, 148
Kelly, Florence, 159
Knox, George L., 27, 48, 77, 80, 107

La Follette, Robert, 143
Langston, John Mercer, 22, 24
Lanham, Samuel, 69
Lee, J. R. E., 87
Leo XIII, 91
Linney, Romulus Z., 48
Logan, John A., 65
Logan, Rayford, 53
Lore, Charles P., 23
Love, John L., 33
Lovejoy, Elijah, 23
Lynch, John R., 6
Lyons, Maritcha, 29

McCoy, Celeste H., 115
McElwee, 68, 85
McEnery, Samuel D., 104
McKinley, William, 32, 51, 52

Majors, M. A., 110
Manley, Alec, 30, 31
Mann, Thomas, 166
Matthews, Victoria Earle, 29
Mays, Benjamin E., 8, 78, 90, 95, 138, 139
Meier, August, 89
Menard, J. William, 25
Meredith, (Deputy Sheriff), 72
Middlebrooks, A. M., 108
Milholland, John, 34, 54
Miller, Kelly, 55, 146
Miller, Thomas E., 65
Milton, George Fort, 138, 139, 165
Mims, Edwin, 131
Mincey, S. S., 164
Mitchell, Arthur, 39
Mitchell, Clark, 70
Mitchell, William D., 163
Mooney, C. P. J., 132
Moore, A. M., 137
Moore, J. J., 89
Moppin, T. J., 146
Morris, E. H., 145
Morris, R. C., 91
Morrow, Edwin P., 70, 71
Moton, Robert Russa, 117, 133, 157, 164
Murray, Daniel, 108, 113

Neibuhr, Reinhold, 87
Northern, William J., 36, 68

Oates, William C., 48
Odum, Howard, 90
O'Neal, Emmett, 10
Ovington, Mary White 132
Owen, Robert N., 161
Owens, Chandler, 143

Page, A. N., 108
Parker, H. H., 36
Parker, James, 52
Parker, John J., 160
Patterson, Raymond, 108
Payne, Daniel A., 116
Pearsall, Z. T., 24
Penn, I. Garland, 51, 80, 81
Penrose, Boise, 143
Petty, Sam, 106

...ips, Wendell, 23
...kens, William, 95, 142, 166
...lsbury, Albert, 54
...inchback, P. B. S., 52, 78
Platt, Thomas, 54
Pledger, William A., 66, 105, 114
Plessy, Homer A., 33
Poe, Clarence, 131
Pope, Alexander, 79
Powdermaker, Hortense, 120
Powell, Adam Clayton, Sr., 55, 89
Pratt, William V., 162
Preston, Fanny M., 12, 13
Pritchett, Henry, 54

Quarles, Benjamin, 3

Randolph, Asa Philip, 143
Randolph, Oliver, 71
Ransom, Reverdy C., 52, 89
Raper, Arthur, 138
Rauchenbusch, Walter, 92, 131
Reed, Isaiah, 69
Reed, James, 159
Reed, Paul, 106
Rhodes, James Ford, 54
Rice, Lawrence D., 69
Riley, Benjamin F., 11
Rivers, Francis E., 165
Roberts, Albert H., 71
Roosevelt, Franklin D., 138, 167
Roosevelt, Theodore, 12, 39, 53, 56, 71
Ruffin, Josephine St. Pierre, 29
Russell, Daniel L., 4, 30

Sacco, Nicola, 166
Sanford, Frank, 54
Scarborough, William S., 3, 59
Schomburg, Arthur, 33
Schuyler, George, 146
Scoby, Mr., 83
Scott, Emmett J., 32, 117, 121
Scottsboro (case) 105
Seligmann, Herbert J., 78, 118
Sengstack, John H., 89
Shaw, M. A. N., 146
Sherrill, William, 141
Shillady, John R., 160

Shorter, James Alexander, 22
Silverman, Joseph, 93
Sinclair, William A., 34, 148
Singleton, Benjamin "Pap," 110
Skaggs, William, 80
Slaughter, H. P., 145
Smith, Alfred E., 160, 161
Smith, C. S., 22
Smith, Charles A., 87
Smith, Harry C., 51, 70
Smith, Hoke, 35
Smith, R. J., 85
Smith, Sewell, 7
Smith, William B., 115
Snyder, Howard, 116
Spingarn, Joel, 162
Stead, W. T., 30
Stemons, James S., 59
Stewart, T. McCants, 50, 114
Stone, William J., 29
Story, Morefield, 54, 146
Straker, Augustus, 6, 51, 83, 94
Strange, Howard, 12
Strong, Josiah, 91
Swayze, George, 49
Sweeney, W. Allison, 89

Taft, William Howard, 12, 56, 108, 145
Talbert, Mary B., 156, 157
Tannenbaum, Frank, 108
Tanner, B. T., 89
Taylor, C. H. J., 53, 57
Taylor, Caesar, 112
Taylor, George E., 53
Taylor, Julius, 36, 52, 96
Taylor, N. S., 144
Terrell, James L., 35
Terrell, Mary Church, 29, 30, 78, 109, 110.
Terrell, Robert H., 121
Thomas, Nevel, 143
Tillman, Benjamin, 11, 31, 35, 54,
Tindall, George, 8
Tinsley, (Masonic Grand Master), 145
Tourgee, Albion B., 33, 49, 54, 80, 107, 108
Trotter, William Monroe, 32, 37, 40, 79, 142, 144, 145, 146, 166
Tucker, J. W., 118
Turner, Henry McNeal, 10, 21, 26, 49, 53, 68, 81, 84, 89, 107, 114, 115, 147, 166

Vance, Baird Z., 9
Vanzetti, Bartolomeo, 166
Vardaman, James K., 10, 49, 87, 119, 132
Vaughn, George L., 159
Villard, Oswald Garrison, 56, 58, 149
Vincent, Theodore G., 143

Waldron, A. T., 89
Walker, Charles T., 33, 34, 35, 89
Walker, Dick, 77
Walling, William English, 57, 132, 148, 158
Walters, Alexander, 58, 89, 93, 111
Warner, A. J., 27
Washington, Booker T., 3, 5, 10, 33-40, 66,
   77, 86, 89, 91, 104, 53, 108, 111, 132, 133,
   134, 144, 145, 161
Washington, Mrs. Booker T., 29, 136
Washington, Joseph R., 90
Watson, Thomas E., 6
Watterson, Marse Henry, 132
Weatherford, Willis Duke, 5, 131, 134, 140
Wells, Ida B., 23, 28, 29, 30, 32, 33, 77, 107,
   144, 145, 158, 162
Wells, H. G., 8
White, George, 120
White, George H., 30, 66, 67, 159
White, W. J., 72, 113
White, Walter, 160, 161, 162, 163
White William Jefferson, 35, 91
Whitfield, Henry L., 136
Wilkens, Roy, 167
Willebrandt, Mable Walker, 164
Williams, Fannie Barrier, 29
Williams, S. Laing, 33
Wilson, Woodrow, 56, 57, 58, 59, 70, 93, 145
Woodson, Carter G., 143
Woodward, C. Vann, 6
Work, Monroe, 39
Wright, R. R., Jr., 89
Wright, R. R., Sr., 116

Zangrando, Robert, 158

HV6459
.G7

Grant

The anti-lynching movement: 1883-1932